CW01065201

H.E. PANTELEIMON LAMPADARIOS,
METROPOLITAN OF ANTINOES
(Retired Metropolitan of the Greek Orthodox Patriarchate
of Alexandria and All Africa)

THE HOLY SACRAMENTS OF THE EASTERN ORTHODOX CHURCH

LONDON 2022

H.E. PANTELEIMON LAMPADARIOS, METROPOLITAN OF ANTINOES
(Retired Metropolitan of the Greek Orthodox Patriarchate
of Alexandria and All Africa)

THE HOLY SACRAMENTS OF THE EASTERN ORTHODOX CHURCH

ISBN (UK): 978-1-915848-07-9
© 2022-2023 PANTELEIMON LAMPADARIOS

EDITING: MARGUERITE PAIZIS

His Eminence PANTELEIMON LAMPADARIOS,
METROPOLITAN OF ANTINOES
Mobile: +30-684-415-3114 (Metropolitan Panteleimon)
Email: metropolitanantinoes@gmail.com

Printed by European Printers Ltd
Published by AKAKIA Publications

December 2022

46 Warberry Road, N22 7TQ, London, UK
T. 0044 208 2457 849

publications@akakia.net
www.akakia.net

NOTE BY THE AUTHOR

The *"The Holy Sacraments of the Orthodox Church"* is the continuation of my humble book entitled "The Orthodox Teachings".

The purpose of this book is to enlighten all English speaking Orthodox Christians, Greeks, Arabs and Africans as well as those who desire knowledge of the Truth, so that they may be informed about the teachings of our Holy Orthodox Church concerning the Holy Sacraments (Holy Sacraments) that were delivered to us from our Lord and Saviour Jesus Christ and His holy Apostles. For this reason *"The Holy Sacraments of the Orthodox Church"* is based upon the two Sources of Divine Revelation: Holy Scripture (Old and New Testament) and Apostolic Tradition.

Following the Teachings of the Holy Apostles and the Fathers of the Orthodox Church, this book presents to the reader the clear Teachings of Orthodoxy concerning the Holy Sacraments. This book has been enriched with many biblical references and opinions of the great and Holy Fathers, Ecclesiastic Writers and Scholars of the One, Holy, Catholic and Apostolic Eastern Orthodox Church.

I wish to express me heartfelt gratitude to my beloved friends in Port Elizabeth – South Africa, **Mr** and **Mrs DIMITRI and MARGUERITE PAIZIS** for all their hard work, help and assistance in correcting the final text. Thank you, Marguerite and Dimitri, for sacrificing your time for God's work. The whole Orthodox Church is grateful for your devotion in the Lord's Vineyard. May the Lord our God grant you all that is necessary for your good health, both of body and spirit, and lead you to the Salvation in Christ.

I pray that this humble effort will bring forth its fruits for the glory of our God, the Father and the Son and the Holy Spirit and the benefit of His people

+PANTELEIMON P. LAMPADARIOS
Metropolitan of Antinoes

Kalymnos-Greece

NOTE BY THE EDITOR

Throughout the years I have been constantly blessed by the Grace of God to know many special people who have contributed to my spiritual growth and progress along the path of life. However, I have been especially blessed with the love, support, encouragement, guidance and teaching of His Eminence PANTELEIMON, Archbishop of Pelusium (today Metropolitan of Antinoes).

After devoting three long years to his latest book on Orthodoxy, he honoured me with the task of editing it. A year later, with many distractions along the way, I planned to join him in Port Said, Egypt, to complete the last of the editing. However, ill health prevented me from travelling, so His Eminence, with his usual sincere humility and despite his own personal health problems, made the long journey to Port Elizabeth, South Africa.

The three weeks we spent together working on this wonderful book of precious Orthodox Treasure, has been a very special time, truly blessed by the Grace of God. I am sure that many Orthodox Christians as well as all others who seek God's Divine Truth will find this labour of love to be most enlightening.

Many years ago, when I converted to Orthodox Christianity, there were very few English publications available to laymen that explained Orthodoxy in terms we could understand. Now we have access to far more writings of the Church Fathers and ecclesiastic writers that have been translated into English. However, there is still a great need for books written particularly for the layman such as this one.

As a convert who had no guidance or teaching to begin with and being dependent on my beloved husband, Dimitri's limited knowledge until my Calling in Jerusalem in 1980 when God granted me the Gift of Teaching, I was determined that no other Orthodox Christians would ever be made to feel like an outsider due to the lack of understanding of the exquisite Divine Services throughout the year and Orthodoxy in general.

Over the years, by the Grace of God, I have taught many willing souls and have compiled Sacred Lessons for Sundays and Feastdays of each month as well as various translations of the exquisite Divine Services of our beloved Church, (which have now been corrected by His Eminence, to the infinite gratitude of all who will be making use of these!)

For this reason, I am overjoyed with this important and most necessary book, which is the fruit of His Eminence's dedicated mission to enlighten and educate everyone in the Perfect Truth of God.

Throughout the years, far and wide in the world, he has taught, guided and encouraged so many people, both young and old, who will never forget him because of the priceless Treasure he has bestowed upon them. His simplicity of language and humility of demeanour endears him to all who are fortunate enough to spend any amount of time in his blessed company.

I pray that this heartfelt effort will bear abundant good fruit throughout the world and that many who are now stumbling along in spiritual darkness and ignorance, will discover God's Perfect Truth and, being more knowledgeable, will be compelled to become willing and eager disciples of Christ. I pray, too, that God in His Infinite Wisdom and Mercy grants our beloved Spiritual Father many years of good health so that he is able to continue his labours of love that benefit so many of us who hunger and thirst for enlightenment and guidance.

May God Bless His Eminence Panteleimon Archbishop of Pelusium and all those who peruse these pages.

With Love in Christ,

Marguerite Paizis
Port Elizabeth,
Republic of South Africa
December 2005

THE HOLY SACRAMENTS
AS WAYS OF DIVINE GRACE, WHICH INCORPORATE US IN
GOD'S KINGDOM

CHAPTER ONE
THE HOLY SACRAMENTS AS THE MEANS OF GRACE

The work of Grace is accomplished in all sinners who do not oppose its action, through certain ways, which were instituted by our Lord and Saviour Jesus Christ, the Son of God, and His Holy Disciples and Apostles. These ways comprise the channels through which the Holy Spirit transmits the necessary supernatural support and strength to create the Regeneration and the new Creation within those who receive them, and which enables them to progress even more in the newness of Life in Christ.

Without disregarding the power and necessity of prayer, as well as the preaching of the Divine Word, we do not include them in the special ways by means of which Divine Grace is transmitted and which are the only God-instituted Sacraments.[1] Prayer and the hearing of the Divine Word are part of the preparation Grace and the future growth of the newness of Life in Christ, but the transmission of this life and the creation of the new Creation in Christ takes place through the Holy Sacraments.

These Holy Sacraments draw their saving Power from the death on the Cross of our Lord and Saviour Jesus Christ, the Son of God. They are not as common as prayer and the knowledge of the Divine Will, but are the actions of the Holy Trinity within the Holy Orthodox Church. And in the Old Testament the Holy Sacraments were prefigured but lacked Grace or any other Supernatural substance. On the contrary the Holy Sacraments of the Divine *Economia* in Christ are performed within the Holy Orthodox Church as the main, common and necessary channels of Divine Grace, which have within them the Power that makes them active and effective even in situations when those partaking of them, do not resist them. Even more so, without the participation in these Holy Sacraments, the work of prayer and Divine Word remains incomplete because only through the Holy

---

[1] Cf. Damalas, *Catechesis,* pp. 78-82. Mitsopoulos, *Themata,* pp. 88-89.

Sacraments is one incorporated into the Mystical Body of Christ and becomes a partaker of the Redemption in Christ.

1. The Ways of Divine Grace are God-instituted Rites

The term *"ways of Grace"* is not found in Holy Scripture but generally prevails in Christian Theological literature signifying the God-instituted Rites, which as Divine Gifts lead towards piety and the newness of Life in Christ. Through these Rites Divine Grace is transmitted to the faithful, which regenerates them and makes them grow *"to the measure of the stature of the fullness of Christ."*[2] These Sacraments are characterized as being God-instituted because they were instituted by our Lord and Saviour Jesus Christ, the Son of God, Who is the Leader of the Orthodox Church. From Him and His Sacrifice on the Holy Cross, they received Supernatural and Sanctifying attributes.

And it is true that only two of the Holy Sacraments, that of Holy Baptism and Holy Eucharist, were instituted directly by our Lord and Master. However, taking into consideration that the rest of the Holy Sacraments were passed down to the Church by the Holy Apostles, once again their institution is attributed indirectly to the same Lord, since His Disciples, in organizing the Church, always had as their guideline the inseparable Teachings of Christ, to Whom they always wanted to prove themselves as faithful co-workers, stewards and guardians.

Besides, in the words and actions of our Lord, we find the central core around which all Holy Sacraments were formed through the Enlightenment of the Holy Spirit Who guided the Holy Apostles to complete understanding of the Teachings of the departed Master. Thus, in the words of Christ concerning the insoluble marriage,[3] the Authority of the keys of Heaven[4] with which He vested His Apostles and the practice of the *"anointing with oil* (of the sick) *in the Name of the Lord,"*[5] we find the Divine foothold and the Holy Sacraments of Marriage, Confession and Repentance, Priesthood, Chrismation and Unction.

---

[2] Ephes. 4:13.
[3] Matth. 19:6.
[4] Matth. 16:19; 18:18. John 20:22-23.
[5] James 5:14.

When we assign the Institution of the Holy Sacraments to the Lord, we must keep in mind that this Institution comes down to the determination of the details of the order of the Mystical Rites. Nonetheless, if we then accept that the Lord promised the Apostles the Grace of the Holy Spirit through a certain relationship, leaving the Guidance of the Helper Who alone would remind and teach them *'all'* the saving Truth in order to organize the visible part of certain Sacraments, once again the Divine Institution of the Holy Sacraments remains unassailable.[6]

According to the above, since the Holy Sacraments were instituted by our Lord and Saviour Jesus Christ, the Son of God, and were determined by Him as ways of granting and transmitting Divine Grace, it is obvious that the use of these Sacraments is necessary and absolutely essential.

And assuredly, we cannot say that the Holy Spirit is limited by these Sacraments to the extent that in extraordinary situations He cannot grant His Gifts and Graces without them. On the contrary, it is accepted that the Holy Spirit is the Ruler of all and even without these Sacraments He can act. This is manifested when the Holy Apostles were Regenerated and finally Ordained by the descent of the Holy Spirit upon them on the Day of Pentecost, thus proving that *"the Saviour baptized the Apostles in the Holy Spirit and fire,[7] when 'suddenly there came a sound from Heaven, as of a rushing mighty wind.[8]"*[9] This is also manifested in the case of Cornelius the centurion[10] and all those in his house: *"while Peter was still speaking these words, the Holy Spirit fell upon all those who heard the Word."*[11] Even in the Tradition of the Orthodox Church, at the time of Martyrdom when a Catechumen was not yet received in the Church through the Holy Mystery of Baptism, by the calling upon the Name of the Holy Trinity as their blood was flowing, they were Baptized with their own blood. This type of Baptism is called the '*Baptism of Martyrdom*' and is considered as the most perfect and honorable way of Baptism, as imitating the Baptism of Christ on the Cross.[12] There

---

[6] Androutsos, *Dogmatique,* p. 296.
[7] Matth. 3:11.
[8] Acts 2:2.
[9] St Cyril of Jerusalem, *Catechesis,* III, § 9, in Migne, *P.G.,* 33, 440.
[10] Acts 10:1-48.
[11] Acts 10:44.
[12] Matth. 20:22-23.

is also a "*Baptism in the air*" which is still in use within the Orthodox Church, according to which new born babes who are in danger of dying are Baptised if no Priest is available. The Orthodox parents or doctor or nurse or any layman regardless of age or sex, may Baptise the new born by raising it up and down three times in the air, calling upon the Name of the Father and of the Son and of the Holy Spirit. These extraordinary ways of Baptism reveal that the Holy Spirit is not restricted by any typical orders.

Nevertheless, the Holy Spirit uses these Sacraments according to the Divine definition and institution, as ways to transmit Divine Grace, which regenerates and creates the new Creation. Thus they are essential and necessary for the incorporation of all men into the spiritual Body of Christ, in order to progress and grow in the newness of the Life in Christ and to be Sanctified within the Church. Thus, the Holy Sacraments are the main channels and means of Divine Grace.

2.   Prayer and the Preaching of the Word as Secondary Ways

Concerning prayer, we shall note that no one is allowed to ignore its importance and power since our Lord and Saviour Jesus Christ, the Son of God, urges us to: "*Ask, and it will be given to you; seek, and you will find; knock, and it will be opened to you. For everyone who asks receives, and he who seeks finds, and to him who knocks it will be opened*"[13] and "*how much more will your Father Who is in Heaven give good things to those who ask Him?*"[14] Even the major part of the Holy Sacraments consists of prayer but it is obvious, as in the case of the centurion Cornelius, that prayer prepares the soul at first to receive the work of Divine Grace, guiding it to the Faith, the Saviour and the Baptism. When the faithful through Baptism and the Sacraments of Holy Chrismation and Eucharist are incorporated into the spiritual Body of Christ, they receive through it the special Power, of which our Lord assured us, that "*in that day*"[15] when the Holy Spirit, through His descent will inaugurate the New Age of Grace by which we will participate through the Holy Sacraments, "*you will ask in My Name*"[16] and "*the Father Himself Who loves you*"[17] "*will give you in My Name,*

---

[13] Matth. 7:7-8.
[14] Matth. 7:11.
[15] John 16:23.
[16] John 16:26.
[17] John 16:27.

because you have loved Me, and have believed"[18] in Me. As the prayers and alms of Cornelius could not assure him Salvation in Christ without receiving Baptism, likewise for every man prayer prepares him to receive Divine Grace, which transmits Adoption and Regeneration to him by receiving the Holy Sacraments.

The same can be applied to the preaching of the Divine Word. No one can deny that the Grace of the Holy Spirit influences the hearing of Divine preaching, stimulating their interest and enlightening them with the understanding of the Teachings, as in the case of St. Lydia, the *"seller of purple from the city of Thyatira"* when *"the Lord opened her heart to heed the things spoken by Paul."*[19] St. Paul declared that *"faith comes by hearing, and hearing by the Word of God."*[20] Hence the questions: *"How then shall they call on Him in Whom they have not believed? And how shall they believe in Him of Whom they have not heard? And how shall they hear without a preacher? And how shall they preach unless they are sent?"*[21] St. Peter also assured us that the Orthodox Christians *"having been born again, not of corruptible seed but incorruptible, through the Word of God which lives and abides forever.*[22] St. James, the Brother of God, urged us: *"Therefore lay aside all filthiness and overflow of wickedness, and receive with meekness the implanted Word, which is able to save your souls."*[23] The Epistle to the Hebrews presents *"the Word of God"* to be *"living and powerful, and sharper than any two-edged sword, piercing even to the division of soul and spirit, and of joints and marrow, and is a discerner of the thoughts and intents of the heart."*[24]

The Word of God spread through preaching into the hearts of those who listen, remains fruitless if the action of Divine Grace of the Holy Sacraments is not added to the advice given by the preaching. For without participation in them, no matter how much man is moved by the hearing of the Divine Word, he will remain alien to Christ and the Salvation through His Blood.[25] The preaching of St. Peter on the

---

[18] John 16:23.
[19] Acts 16:14.
[20] Rom. 10:17.
[21] Rom. 10:14-15.
[22] 1 Peter 1:23.
[23] James 1:21.
[24] Heb. 4:12.
[25] Androutsos, *Symbolique,* p. 282. Leeming, *Principles,* p. 5.

Day of Pentecost clearly informs us of this. Those who *"were cut to the heart"* were urged by St. Peter and the rest of the Holy Apostles, to *"repent, and let every one of you be Baptized in the Name of Jesus Christ for the remission of sins; and you shall receive the Gift of the Holy Spirit."*[26] After Baptism they received forgiveness of their sins and the Gift of the Holy Spirit. It is obvious then, that, if they had not been Baptised, the hearing of the Divine Word of God would not have had any effect upon them.

No one should misuse the case of Cornelius, according to which as St. Peter spoke, the Holy Spirit fell upon all those who were listening to the Word of God, because this case is particularly extraordinary. It is very important to realise that even after the descent and the outpouring of the Gift of the Holy Spirit, St. Peter did not consider it unnecessary to Baptise them all as he *"commanded them to be Baptised in the Name of the Lord."*[27]

On the one hand the hearing or reading of the Divine Word of God influences mankind according to the skills of those who preach or the writers who interpret the Word; whereas, on the other hand, it influences them according to their capability of receiving, hearing or reading the Word of God and their willingness to accept and practice it. The preachers are not always the leaders of the Apostles, nor is it the work of all to become preachers. Nevertheless, Divine Grace, which is granted through the Holy Sacraments, is not influenced by moral status or worthiness of the officiator because at that moment God Himself is the One Who is celebrating the *"Mystagogia."* In addition, the effectiveness of the Sacraments is manifested not only to those intellectuals who participate in them, but to infants as well, and generally speaking, to all those who do not oppose the Grace of God. This, however, does not apply to the hearing of the Word because only those who are in a position to follow it, can benefit from it.

3. The Holy Sacraments as Gifts

According to the above, the Word of God can be considered only as secondary and to be numbered generally among the ways of Divine Grace. The Divine Sacraments instituted by Christ Himself and His

---

[26] Acts 2:37, 38.
[27] Acts 10:48. Cf. St John Chrysostom, *To Acts,* in Migne, *P.G.,* 60, 183 and 184.

Holy Apostles, are the only methods of Sanctification within the Church.

Truly, prayer and preaching of the Word of God are found in the Old Economia. Prayer was exercised not only in the public worship of the Synagogue, but also in private and was addressed by all the God-lovers and all levels of the faithful. The Book of Psalms is a book of prayers. The Word of God appears to be preached by God-called and God-inspired men, Patriarchs and Prophets - all those who appeared from the time of Noah and Moses until Malachi - and was read in the Temple of the Lord and in the Synagogues.

The Divine Sacraments are the exclusive inheritance of the New Economia of the Divine Grace, according to which, after the Death, Resurrection and Ascension into Heaven of our Lord and Saviour Jesus Christ, the Son of God, the Holy Spirit was sent into the world.

The Sacraments in the Old Testament are mentioned as such: the Circumcision, the Paschal Lamb, the Bread of Prothesis, the Rites of Cleanliness and Purification and the Sacrifices of Atonement. All these can be characterized only as types and shadowy prefigurations of the Holy Sacraments of the New Testament, which have real and Divine effectiveness and which are more elevated than the prototypes.[28]

Thus, the Jewish Rites of Purification through the washing with water could not free any one from sin, but only from the stains of the body and for the cleanliness of the flesh,[29] not Sanctifying spiritually. On the contrary, our Baptism is much greater, filled with Divine Grace, for it frees one from sin and cleanses the soul through the Gift of the Holy Spirit. Circumcision prefigures the *"Circumcision made without hands, by putting off the body of the sins of the flesh, by the Circumcision of Christ, buried with Him in Baptism."*[30] The Circumcision of the Old Testament worked towards the putting aside of the flesh, whereas Baptism is the putting aside of sins, while the anointing through Holy Chrismation that Orthodox Christians receive, is the symbol according to which, in the Holy Scriptures, kings and Prophets were anointed. Although for them it worked typically, for

---

[28] St Augustine, *In Psalm LXXIII*, 2, in migne, *P.L.*, 36, 931. Bartmann, *Theologue Dogmatique*, v. II, p. 267.

[29] St John Chrysostom, *To the holy and saving Baptism of our Saviour Jesus Christ*, in Migne, *P.G.*, 49, 366.

[30] Col. 2:11-12. Cf. Rom. 2:25-29; 3:1, 30; 4:9-12; 15:8. 1 Corinth. 7:19. Gal. 2:7-9, 12; 5:6, 11; 6:15. Ephes. 2:11. Phil. 3:3-5. Col. 3:11.

Orthodox Christians it works truly because we are actually anointed by the Holy Spirit. In the Old Testament there was also the Bread of Preparation or Prothesis, but it came to an end, whereas according to the New Testament the Heavenly Bread and the Saving Cup Sanctify the soul and body. The basin that was in the Temple also symbolised Baptism. So how can they be compared to our Divine Sacraments? Consider the differences that separate the Passover of the Old Testament to that of the Lamb of God, Who takes up the sins of the world, and Whose Sacrifice on the Cross was offered once and for all as an Everlasting Sacrifice. Our Passover[31] consists of *"Christ, our Passover (Who) was Sacrificed for us."*[32]

4. The Holy Sacraments Receive their Power from Christ's Sacrifice

It was necessary to present the Sacrifice offered for us by the Lamb of God and then to receive the Gift of the Holy Spirit. Before Christ was Crucified and Ascended into Heaven *"the Holy Spirit was not yet given, because Jesus was not yet glorified."*[33] It was to be poured forth from on High after the Cross because before then, we were enemies,[34] having sinned and consequently, were deprived of the Gift of God. When the Sacrifice was offered for us, not only did we receive the Enlightenment of the Holy Spirit as did the Prophets of the Old Testament, but He now dwells and abides within us causing us to become temples of God contrary to the Prophets, of whom none ever became a temple of God.[35]

Consequently, the Source from which the Divine Sacraments of the New Testament receive their supernatural Power, which is distributed to those who partake of them, is the Sacrifice on the Cross of our Lord and Saviour Jesus Christ, Who reconciled us to God the

---

[31] St Ecumenius, *To Hebrews* 9, 13, in Migne, *P.G.,* 119, 337. Kalogeras, *Maria,* 2, 406. St John Chrysostom, *To the holy and saving Baptism of our Saviour Jesus Christ,* in Migne, *P.G.,* 49, 366. Ibid, *To Genesis,* Homily 39, § 5, in Migne, *P.G.,* 53, 368. St Cyril of Jerusalem, *Catechesis,* XXI, § 6, in Migne, *P.G.,* 33, 1193 and 1100. Ibid, *Catechesis,* III, § 5, in Migne, *P.G.,* 33, 433.
[32] 1 Corinth. 5:7.
[33] John 7:39.
[34] Rom. 5:10.
[35] St John Chrysostom, in Migne, *P.G.,* 59, 284. St Cyril of Alexandria, *To John,* in Migne, *P.G.,* 73, 757.

Father[36] and Who became the reason for sending the Holy Spirit into the world, by Whom we were *"anointed"* and *"sealed"* giving *"us the Spirit in our hearts as a guarantee."*[37]

This Truth was proclaimed by St. Irenaeus who observed that if Christ did not truly suffer, He would have no Grace, due to that lack of suffering.[38]

St. John Chrysostom, interpreting the supernatural Event of the piercing of the Lord's *"side with a spear, and immediately blood and water came out,"*[39] observed that *"not only these fountains accidentally came out, but because from these two the Church was composed, and those who participate in the Mystagogia are healed being Regenerated through water, and being fed through (His) Blood and Flesh. Hence the Sacraments receive their beginning."*[40]

Earlier than this, the great Father of the Orthodox Church, Methodius of Olympus referred to the Church as the Lord's *"Wife."* He presents her as being created from His Side, just as Eve was once created from the side of Adam,[41] and receiving from His Side some kind of Power enabling the growth of all those who are formed in her.[42]

St. Augustine speaking of Baptism, observed that this is the Saving Water because it is Sanctified through the Name of Christ Who shed His Blood for us from this and through His Cross, the Water is Sealed.[43]

St. Cyril of Jerusalem accepts that the outpouring of the Blood and Water from the Side of Christ are symbols of the Saving Baptism and from which the Church was born. *"As Eve was made from the side of Adam, likewise are we from the Side of Christ."*[44]

---

[36] Rom. 5:10. 2 Corinth. 5:18-20.

[37] 2 Corinth. 1:21, 22.

[38] St Irenaeus, *Heresies*, book III, ch. 18, § 6, in Migne, *P.G.,* 7, 936. Cf. Ibid, in Hadjephraimides, p. 242.

[39] John 19:34.

[40] St John Chrysostom, *To John,* Homily 85, in Migne, *P.G.,* 59, 463. Ibid, in Migne, 51, 229.

[41] Gen. 2:21-22.

[42] Methodius, *Symposium,* III, 8, in Migne, *P.G.,* 18, 73.

[43] St Augustine, *Sermo* 352, § 3, in migne, *P.L.,* 39, 1551.

[44] St Cyril of Jerusalem, *Catechesis,* XII, § 11, in Migne, *P.G.,* 33, 788.

CHAPTER TWO
THE MEANING AND NATURE OF THE SACRAMENTS

The word *"Mystery"* (Sacrament) means a hidden and silent Truth, which is revealed through Divine Revelation. This term was introduced into Theological and Liturgical terminology signifying those God-instituted Rites, which comprise the visible aspects of Divine Grace, not merely symbolising it but invisibly and with Supernatural Creative Action transmitting it. Having been instituted by Christ Himself, they have value and Power, being the active means of Divine Grace whereby the old nature corrupted by sin is removed from those who are worthy. They raise the New Creation in Christ by transmitting the Newness of Life in Christ. Thus, the Holy Sacraments have invisible Supernatural Powers that inscribe the inexhaustible Saving results in the inner man, Regenerating and causing all those who faithfully, sincerely and honestly approach and participate in them to progress in the New Life.

1. The Meaning of the Term *"Mystery"*

The first meaning of the term *"Mystery"* is derived from the Greek verb *"μύειν"* (meaning *"...to close the eyes or the mouth as instruments of transmitting or seeing the hidden things..."*) according to which it is *"a hidden and Mystic Thing."* During the Roman period the term signified the Militant Oath that soldiers vowed at their Enlistment in the Roman Army and which was generally referred to as the *"Sacramentum."* In Roman Law the term *"Sacramentum"* means the Covenant that was placed in the temples by those who disputed it.

In Holy Scripture, in both Old and New Testaments, the term is used 45 times. It means the secret Will of God that is related to the Salvation of mankind *"...according to the Revelation of the Mystery kept secret since the world began but now made manifest by the Prophetic Scriptures made known to all nations, according to the Commandment of the Everlasting God."*[45] In other cases it refers to a hidden and symbolic institution, such as that of Marriage symbolising the Union of Christ with the Church[46] or some kind of narration, such

---

[45] Rom. 16:25-26.
[46] Ephes. 5:32.

as in the case of King Nabuchodonosor[47] or a certain symbolic name, such as the Mystery of the Seven Stars mentioned in the Book of Revelation,[48] or even the Mystery of the name of the great city of Babylon.[49] In any case, nowhere in Holy Scripture is the term *"Mystery"* used, meaning a Sacred Rite by means of which Supernatural Divine Grace of the Holy Spirit is transmitted through material symbols.

Even up to 4th century Christian writings, the term preserved its classical meaning, signifying something secret, hidden and Sacred. St. Ignatius of Antioch proclaimed that the Death of our Lord Jesus Christ is *"the Mystery"* of our Salvation because *"through Him and His Death (which some deny), the Mystery through which we came to believe, and because of which we patiently endure, we might be found to be Disciples of Jesus Christ, our only Teacher."*[50] Also in his letter to the Ephesians he wrote: *"now the Virginity of Mary and her giving Birth were hidden from the ruler of this age, as was also the Death of the Lord – three Sacraments to be loudly proclaimed, yet which were accomplished in the Silence of God."*[51]

Tertullian also used the term generally, referring to Christian Teaching as a *"Mystery,"* especially the Teaching concerning the Holy Trinity as well as the whole Christian Faith and the entire Work of Salvation. (*"Sacramentun Oikonomia'"*). Furthermore, he spoke of Holy Baptism and Eucharist as Sacraments,[52] commenting that *"the body is Washed in order to Clean the soul; the body is Anointed in order to Sanctify the soul; the body is Sealed in order to Strengthen the soul; the body is covered by the laying on of the hands in order to Enlighten the soul by the Holy Spirit; the body eats the Flesh and Blood of Christ, in order that the soul would be fed by God."*[53]

---

[47] Daniel 2:18, 27 and 30.

[48] Rev. 1:20.

[49] Rev. 17:5.

[50] St Ignatius, *To Magnesians,* 9, 1, in Lightfoot, *Apostolic Fathers,* p. 95.

[51] St Ignatius, *To Ephesians,* 19, 1, in Lightfoot, *Apostolic Fathers,* p. 92.

[52] Tertullian, *De praescriptione haereticorum,* XX, in migne, *P.L.,* 2, 20. Ibid, *Adversus Praxeam,* II and XXX, in migne, *P.L.,* 2, 180 and 220. Ibid, *De Baptismo,* 13, in migne, *P.L.,* 1, 323. Ibid, *Adversus Marcianem,* IV and XXXIV, in migne, *P.L.,* 2, 442. Ibid, *De resurrectuion carne,* C, IX, in migne, *P.L.,* 1, 806. Ibid, *De coron. militiae,* III, in migne, *P.L.,* 2, 79.

[53] Ibid, *De resurrectuion carne,* VIII, in migne, *P.L.,* 2, 852.

St. Cyprian used the term *"Mystery" ("Sacramentum")* in a general meaning, to manifest the different institutions of Christianity, especially those of Baptism, Chrismation, Divine Eucharist, Repentance-Confession and Ordination.[54]

2. The External and Internal Aspect of Sacraments

Although the Mystery has an external and perceptible aspect, simultaneously it includes an internal and Supernatural Reality, which is not conceivable or understandable to our physical senses as only through Faith is it accepted. The Mystery is the visible Sign of the invisible Grace of God, which is outpoured upon the Faithful having been instituted by our Lord Jesus Christ whereby each Faithful receives Divine Grace.[55] It consists of the natural and the Supernatural.[56] It is the material symbol that upholds the immaterial Grace of God, which works towards the Salvation of man.[57] Holy Mystery is not restricted to special Ceremonies alone but extends to all Divine Truths of Christian Faith.

St. John Chrysostom explained that Divine Mystery is those things that are normally unseen but which, through Faith *"we see differently and we believe differently. This is our Faith about the Sacraments."* Concerning the Truths of Faith, he observed, *"I hear that Christ was Crucified and I admire the Philanthropy; the unbeliever hears and he thinks about the weakness. I hear that He became a servant and I admire the Dominion. He (the unfaithful) hears and thinks about the dishonour. I hear that He died and I am astonished, that He came under Death and was not held but dissolved Death; he (the unfaithful) hears and suspects weakness. Differently am I and the unbeliever disposed about these."* Particularly with regard to Sacred Rites that are the ways of the Grace, St. John Chrysostom noted that *"the unbeliever hears of the Bath (Baptism) and he thinks simply of water; I do not see only what is seen but the Cleanliness of the soul through the Holy Spirit. He (the unbeliever)*

---

[54] St Cyprian, Epistola70 *Ad Januarium*, § 3, in migne, *P.L.,* 3, 1082. Ibid, *Epist 73 Ad Jubaien*, § 20 and 21, in migne, *P.L.,* 3, (?). Ibid, *De unitate Ecclesiam,* in migne, *P.L.,* 4, 528. Ibid, *de lapsis*, c. 25, in migne, *P.L.,* 4, 500. Ibid, *Epist.* LXIII, § 14, in migne, *P.L.,* 3, (?).

[55] Mogilas, A, 99, in Karmeris, *The dogmatics,* p. 635.

[56] Dositheus of Jerusalem, *Confession,* ch 15, p. 39.

[57] St Athanasius of Paros, *Epitome*, p. 344, in Jugie, *Theologia,* v. II, p. 14.

thinks only of the bath of the body; I believe that the soul becomes Clean and Holy   For I do not judge the events only by their appearance but through the eyes of the mind."[58]

St. Augustine in a similar manner expressed his opinion by referring to the Sacraments as "*Sacramentalia.*"[59] He distinguished the internal aspect of the Sacraments from their external aspect, observing that the Mystery itself is different to that of the Power of the Mystery.[60] Thus the Bread and the Cup of Divine Eucharist are called Sacraments because in them we see other aspects that are contemplated at the time, the Fruit of which is spiritual.[61] Similarly concerning the Water of Baptism, which is visible. It Washes away the contamination of sin from the body and this Bath signifies whatever is acting within the soul.[62] Consequently, the external event is different to that of the context of the Sacraments. Some aspects are seen while others are thought. Whatever is seen has a physical aspect whereas whatever is thought bears special Fruit.[63]

This combination of sensual and material with invisible and spiritual aspects within the Sacraments correspond completely to the fact that man consists of both matter and spirit. And as he consists of two elements, body and soul, he receives double Purification: the spiritual through the invisible aspects and the physical through the body.[64] God wanted to grant His Grace not only invisibly - although this was not impossible for Him to do because for anything He Wills He does – but through some visible Signs as well, thereby assuring His Promises to His Elect. Because mankind consists of two elements, God granted two methods of transmitting His Divine Grace - through matter and through the Holy Spirit.[65]

St. Gregory of Nyssa observed that in Baptism "*sensible Water is offered to the body*" whereas "*upon the soul the invisible Spirit is called to descend in an indescribable manner*" "*and the Water cleans the body, whereas the Spirit Seals the soul in order that, through the sprinkling of the heart and the Bathing of the body, we approach*

---

[58] St John Chrysostom, *To 1 Corinthians*, Homily 7, § 1, in Migne, *P.G.*, 61, 55-56.

[59] St Augustine, *De catech. Rudibus*, § 50, in migne, *P.L.*, 40, 344-345. Ibid, *Sermo 227*, in migne, *P.L.*, 38, 1099-1100. Ibid, *Sermo, 228*, § 3, in migne, *P.L.*, 38, 1102.

[60] Ibid, *In Johannis evangelium. Tractatus XXVI*, § 11, in migne, *P.L.*, 35, 1011.

[61] Ibid, *Sermo 272*, in migne, *P.L.*, 38, 1246.

[62] St Augustine, *In EpistolaJoannis ad Parthos. Tractatus VI*, § 11, in migne, *P.L.*, 35, 2026.

[63] Ibid, *Sermo 272*, in migne, *P.L.*, 38, 1247.

[64] St Cyril of Jerusalem, *Catechesis*, III, § 4, in Migne, *P.G.*, 33, 429.

[65] Kritopoulos, in Karmeris, *The dogmatics*, v. II, p. 524.

God." Similarly at the Anointing "*the visible myrrh Anoints the body, whereas the Holy and Life-giving Spirit Sanctifies the soul.*"[66]

3. Holy Sacraments as Symbols & Bestowers of Divine Grace

Thus, the Sacraments are Signs and Ways, Symbols and Bestowers of Divine Grace. In these spiritual and Supernatural nature rule over the perceptible and material. The Sacraments are perceptible Signs that symbolise the invisible Divine Grace, which is transmitted to the Faithful and which stimulate their Faith assuring the Truthfulness of Divine Promises. Hence the "*Bath through Water*" can be characterised as being symbolic "*of the Washing of the soul, which cleans every stain of evil.*" Furthermore, in Baptism we symbolically "*insinuate the three-day Burial of Christ*" and being Baptised "*we do not die in reality, nor we are buried, nor we are really raised having been crucified, but the imitation is in image.*" It can be said of the transmission of the Body and Blood of our Lord in the Divine Eucharist that "*in the type of the bread the Body is offered to you and in the type of the wine is the Blood of Christ is given to you*" "*in order that in the different elements you partake of the Body and Blood of Christ, becoming of the same Body and the same Blood with Him.*"[67]

Considering that the elements that are used in the Holy Sacraments remain unchanged in their nature, even after the Blessing and Perfection of Divine Mystery, we must not be surprised when the bread used in the Divine Eucharist is referred to, especially before its Consecration, as the "*Image of the Body of the Only Begotten*" and be assured that indeed "*this Bread is the Image of the Holy Body*"[68] or that the elements used for the Consecration are called "*antitypes of the Body and Blood of Christ.*"[69] However, even after the Consecration we hear some Holy Fathers stating that "*we are Commanded to eat not bread and wine but the antitype of the Body and Blood of Christ*"[70]

---

[66] St Gregory of Nyssa, *To the day of the Lights,* in Migne, *P.G.,* 46, 581. St Cyril of Jerusalem, *Catechesis,* XXI, § 3, in Migne, *P.G.,* 33, 1092.

[67] Origen, *To John* VI, § 17, in Migne, *P.G.,* 14, 257. St Cyril of Jerusalem, *Catechesis Mystagogia,* II, §§ 4 and 5, in Migne, *P.G.,* 33, 1081. Ibid, *Catechesis Mystagogia,* IV, § 3, in Migne, *P.G.,* 33, 1100.

[68] Report of Serapion, in Rauschen, *Fiorilegium,* p. 29.

[69] In the Divine Liturgy of St Basil, the Great, before the consecration.

[70] St Cyril of Jerusalem, *Catechesis Mystagogia,* V, § 20, in Migne, *P.G.,* 33, 1124.

and they generally speak of *"antitypes of the precious Body and Blood."*[71]

The Sacraments are real ways, active bestowers and channels of Divine Grace, through which and by which it is transmitted to those who partake of it. They are the Mysterious Energies[72] and Actions of God within the Church for the Salvation of the world.

St. John Chrysostom proclaimed that *"Christ did not deliver us anything material but through material things, He gave us the spiritual."* Referring specifically to Holy Baptism he observed that *"through perceptible thing the Gift is offered, but the content is spiritual, the Birth and the Rebirth, in other words the Regeneration."* Emphasising the necessity by which the spiritual was combined with the perceptible, he added *"if you were bodiless, they would have been delivered to you naked; but, because the soul is engaged with the body, the spiritual are delivered to you through perceptible things."*[73]

The previously mentioned Holy Fathers used the terms *"type"* and *"antitype"* to clarify their opinions and exalt, especially the internal aspect and Supernatural Attributes of the Holy Sacraments. Thus, St. Cyril of Jerusalem, concerning the bread and wine used in Divine Eucharist, stressed that it is prohibited for anyone to comment on the flavour or quality of the bread and wine because they *"are the Body and Blood of Christ according to the Despotic Decision"* by which we become of *"the same Body and the same Blood"* of Christ. We should never judge by *"the taste"* but the Faith must inform us *"without any hesitation"* that we are deeply honoured to received *"the Body and Blood of Christ."* In addition, he literally and clearly proclaimed that the Water of Holy Baptism, *"the simple water, receives the Power of Sanctification by the Invocation of the Holy Spirit and Christ."* Therefore, he urged all who would be Baptised to be careful *"when they descend into the Water"* not to pay attention *"to the simple water but to the Action of the Holy Spirit"* from which they receive their Salvation, *"for without both it is impossible to be Perfected."* With regard to the Anointing of Holy Chrismation, he observed that *"as the Bread of Eucharist after the Invocation of the*

---

[71] St Gregory of Nazianzus, *Homily 8, To his sister Gorgonia,* § 18, in Migne, *P.G.,* 35, 809. *Apostolic Diatagae,* V, 14, 7, in **B**, v. 2, p. 85; VI, 30, 2, **B**, v. 2, p. 116; VII, 25, 4, **B**, v. 2, p. 125.

[72] St Irenaeus, *Heresies,* book II, ch. 30, § 7, in Migne, *P.G.,* 7, 820. Cf. Ibid, in Hadjephraimides, pp. 177-178.

[73] St John Chrysostom, *To Matthew,* Homily 82, § 4, in Migne, *P.G.,* 58, 743.

Holy Spirit is no longer simply bread but the Body of Christ" "*likewise the Holy Myrrh is not simply myrrh, neither should anyone consider it as something common with invocation, but a Charisma of Christ*" that through the Presence "*of the Holy Spirit becomes energetic.*"[74]

St. Serapion speaking of the "*likeness of the Body of the only Begotten*" during the consecration at the time of the invocation, requested "*the bread to become the Body of the Word*" and "*the cup the Blood of the Truth*", so that "*all those who have communion to receive the medicine of life.*"[75]

St. Gregory of Nyssa concerning the changes that take place in the Holy Sacraments and the rest of the ecclesiastic ceremonies through the Action of the Holy Spirit observed that in Baptism "*the water does not grant the benefit, but the command of God and the invocation of the Spirit.*" "*For this reason, do not disregard the Divine bath, neither consider it as something common because of the use of the water.*" Referring to the rest of the Holy Sacraments he stressed that "*the Bread*" of the Eucharist before it is Sanctified "*is previously common bread, but when he celebrates this Mystery, it is said to have become the Body of Christ.*" The same refers for the "*Mystical Oil*" and for "*the wine.*" "*Being small in value before the blessing, after the sanctification by the Spirit each one acts invisibly.*" He emphasized the same regarding Ordination. The "*one who was yesterday alone becomes leader of many, president, teacher of piety, celebrant of Sacraments*" "*according to the appearance he exists as he was*" but "*through some kind of invisible power and Grace his soul is transfigured to the better.*"[76]

4. The Internal Aspect of the Holy Sacraments.

The Roman Catholics distinguished the external aspect of the Sacraments into two parts, that of "*matter*" and "*form*".[77] These terms were unknown in the ancient and united Orthodox Church. The Orthodox Church regards these scholastic terms as unnecessary and prefers to uphold the terms "*visible*" or "*external*" or "*natural*". The

---

[74] St Cyril of Jerusalem, *Catechesis Mystagogia,* III, § 2; and XXI, § 3, in Migne, *P.G.,* 33, 429 and 1092.
[75] Report of Serapion, in Rauschen, *Fiorilegium,* p. 30.
[76] St Gregory of Nyssa, *To the day of the Lights,* in Migne, *P.G.,* 46, 581.
[77] Cf. Ott, "Précis", pp. 458-459. Jugie, v. III, pp. 16 and 33.

Sacraments include spiritual acts and conditions, as well as essential words of consecration that instituted the Sacraments[78].

Concerning the internal and invisible aspect of the Mystery it must be noted, that all the Holy Sacraments offer to those who partake of them the sanctifying Grace of the Holy Spirit, which either regenerates them and strengthens them in the new life in Christ (Baptism, Chrismation), either nourishes and gives life to them through their union with Christ (Divine Eucharist), either offers to them the healing of the wounds of their souls and bodies (Repentance, Unction), either making them capable and strengthening them to serve in the various diakonia of the Church (Priesthood), or exalting and sanctifying their union in life (Marriage).[79]

According to Androutsos, the Sacraments *"are not of the same value, neither of equal necessity."* Thus *"the Eucharist surpasses all the rest and in value and according to its benefits, and together with Baptism is the main of the Sacraments."*[80]

Mogilas spoke of the Eucharist that *"this Mystery surpasses all the others and benefits more than the others to our salvation."*[81]

Kritopoulos characterized the three Sacraments, Baptism, Eucharist and Repentance that they are *"in type of the Holy Trinity."* He distinguished these from the other four which are *"mystical ceremonies, which are called by the Church Sacraments, because they incorporate some kind of mystical and spiritual Grace."*[82]

The Holy Sacraments have their Supernatural Attributes not because of the worthiness of those who officiate them or of those who partake of them. Their holiness and truth derive from Christ Who instituted them.[83] Receiving their Supernatural Attribute from our Lord and Saviour Jesus Christ, the Son of God, they have the Divine Grace that characterises or symbolises each one separately and transmits Divine Grace to those who do not resist or oppose to them.

When we say, that the Holy Sacraments contain Divine Grace, we do not mean that this Divine Grace is contained within them as the water in a container but rather that they are contained within them in power as the result of their cause. Except the Holy Mystery of the

---

[78] Androutsos, *Dogmatique,* p. 297. Ibid, *Symbolique,* p. 289.
[79] Cf. Scheeben, *Les Mystères,* p. 576.
[80] Androutsos, *Symbolique,* p. 298.
[81] Mogilas, A, 106, in Karmeris, *The dogmatics,* v. II, p. 638.
[82] Kritopoulos, in Karmeris, *The dogmatics,* v. II, p. 525.
[83] St Augustine, in migne, *P.L.,* 43, 559.

Divine Eucharist, in which the change of the used elements – bread and wine- takes place in reality. The Sacraments are instruments which transmit the Divine Grace of God to those who partake of them, as this is manifested by Holy Scriptures by the use of the terms *"of"* and *"through"*. Our Lord and Saviour Jesus Christ, the Son of God, taught us saying: *"Most assuredly, I say to you, unless one is born of water and the Spirit, he cannot enter the kingdom of God."*[84] St. Paul emphasized *"not by works of righteousness which we have done, but according to His mercy He saved us, through the washing of regeneration and renewing of the Holy Spirit"*[85] and he added "that *He might sanctify and cleanse her with the washing of water by the word."*[86] Elsewhere it is assured *"that through the laying on of the apostles' hands the Holy Spirit was given"*[87] to those who were Baptised and transmit *"the gift of God"* – the charisma of the *Diakonia* - to St. Timothy *"through the laying on of, the hands"*[88] of St. Paul. The Sacraments are the instruments and channels through which the Divine Grace of God is granted and transmitted to the faithful.

St. John Chrysostom concerning Baptism observed that in Baptism *"the water becomes the childbirth to him who is being born. As the womb is to the embryo, likewise the water to the faithful; for in the water, he is fashioned and formed."*[89]

St. Cyril of Alexandria spoke of the water in Baptism that *"as the water which is poured into the boiler through the flames of the fire reveals its power, likewise through the energy of the Spirit the perceptible water is changed to some kind of Divine and unspeakable power, and sanctifies those who enter in it."*[90]

St. Cyril of Jerusalem assured that the Myrrh of Holy Chrismation *"as the bread of the Eucharist after the invocation of the Holy Spirit, it is not anymore simply bread, but the body of Christ, likewise and this holy myrrh is not anymore simple, neither should anyone say that it is something common with invocation; but that it is*

---

[84] John 3:5.
[85] Tit. 3:5.
[86] Ephes. 5:26.
[87] Acts 8:18.
[88] 2 Tim. 1:6.
[89] St John Chrysostom, *To John,* Homily 26, § 1, in Migne, *P.G.,* 59, 153.
[90] St Cyril of Alexandria, *To John,* book II, 1, in Migne, *P.G.,* 73, 245.

Christ's gift, and the presence of the Holy Spirit, who becomes active."[91]

In relation to the way of the dwelling and transmission of the Divine Grace in the Divine Sacraments one must never forget the image, which our Lord and Saviour Jesus Christ used concerning the action of the Holy Spirit saying: *"The wind blows where it wishes, and you hear the sound of it, but cannot tell where it comes from and where it goes. So is everyone who is born of the Spirit."*[92] In other words *"as the wind cannot be seen, although it gives a sound"* likewise and *"even more the action of the Spirit cannot fall under the laws of nature, nor to the rules of bodily birth, nor to any of such things."*[93]

Consequently, the ways by which the Divine Grace is transmitted within the Divine Sacraments remains inconceivable, unspoken and always a mysterious Mystery to all intellectual.

God Himself Acts in the Holy Sacraments transmitting His Divine Grace bringing an essential change to the receiving soul. The power and result of the Mystery derives not from any human factor but from its Divine Institution and Power. The Holy Sacraments have their perfection not in their use but even before their use. Neither are they perfected because of the faith of the faithful.[94] To receive the Gifts of the Holy Sacraments it is required to have faith as an indispensable pre-requirement but neither the faith, the good will nor the devotion of the partaker is the cause of the Gift and Grace of God within the Mystery. The Mystery has within it and from it the Supernatural Power and Grace to Act either way for the Salvation of those who with faith and piety receive it or for the condemnation of those who with ungodliness approach it.

This validity and effectiveness of the Holy Sacraments is proclaimed by the Orthodox Church, according to the ancient practice of offering these even to infants who enjoy the same Gifts and Charismata regardless of their understanding and faith as they do not resist or oppose the Grace. So, the Grace of God is offered not because of the work of the Celebrant or of the one who partakes of it (*'ex opera operantis'*), but from its own Energy, from the Power

---

[91] St Cyril of Jerusalem, *Catechesis Mystagogia,* III, § 3, in Migne, *P.G.,* 33, 1092.
[92] John 3:8.
[93] St John Chrysostom, *To John,* Homily 26, in Migne, *P.G.,* 59, 155.
[94] Dositheus of Jerusalem, *Confession,* Term XV, in Karmeris, *The dogmatics*, v. II, p. 758.

within it ('*ex opera operato*'), through the exact work of the Mystery itself as the instrument of Divine Grace.[95] It is true that these terms used by the Scholastics remained unknown to the Orthodox Theology of the Eastern Orthodox Church to such extent that some Orthodox Theologians rejected this teaching.[96]

5. The Indelible Character of Divine Grace

With regard to the effectiveness of the Divine Sacraments and their results upon those who partake of them, the belief of the Roman Catholic Church concerning the indelible character of the three main Sacraments of Baptism, Chrismation and Priesthood, is that they cannot be repeated.[97] However, the term "*character indelebilis*" ("*indelible character*") is not found in the writings of the Greek Fathers and is considered to have no foundation in either Holy Scripture or in Holy Tradition and therefore they are considered only as theological terms.[98]

The Greek Fathers do not use the term "*character*" but speak of Baptism as the "*Holy Seal indelible*" and "*Mystical Seal*" through which the one who is Baptised becomes known to the Master and is numbered amongst "*the holy and logic flock of Christ*" and "*is sealed with the Seal made without hands*" and "*Seal unbreakable.*"[99]

Clement the Alexandrian used the example of the image and seal on coins, as well as the seal which is branded upon animals displaying "*the owner*" and from this analogy he declared that "*the faithful soul, which has received the Seal, carries the stigmata of Christ.*"[100]

The *Shepherd of Hermas* mentions "*the Seal*"[101] which when one "*receives*" it, "*he lays aside his deadness and receives life.*"[102] "*It was necessary, he said, for them to come up through water in order to*

[95] Trempelas, *Dogmatique,* v. III, p. 23.

[96] Androutsos, *Dogmatique,* p. 312.

[97] Denzinger 695, in Leeming, *Principles,* pp. 134, 136-139.

[98] Androutsos, *Dogmatique,* p. 314. Ibid, *Symbolique,* p. 297. Dyobouniotes, *The Mysteries,* p. 26. Dositheus of Jerusalem, *Confession,* Term XVI, in Karmeris, *The dogmatics,* v. II, p. 760.

[99] St Cyril of Jerusalem, *Pre-catechesis,* §§ 16 and 17; Ibid, *Catechesis,* I, § 2, in Migne, 33, 360, 365 and 372. St Basil, *To the Holy Baptism,* § 5, in Migne, *P.G.,* 31, 433. *Apostolic Orders,* III, § 6, in Migne, 1, 797. Leeming, *Principles,* p. 155.

[100] Clement the Alexandrian, *Epistles* 86, in Migne, *P.G.,* 9, 697.

[101] *Shepherd of Hermas,* Parable 9, 16, 4, in Lightfoot, *Apostolic Fathers,* p. 276.

[102] Ibid, Parable, 9, 16, 3, in Lightfoot, *Apostolic Fathers,* p. 276.

be made alive, for otherwise they could not enter the Kingdom of God, unless they laid aside the deadness of their former life. So even those who had fallen asleep received the seal of the Son of God and entered the Kingdom of God. For before a man, he said, bears the Name of the Son of God, he is dead, but when he receives the seal, he lays aside his deadness and receives life. The seal, therefore, is the water; so they go down into the water dead and they come up alive. Thus, this seal was proclaimed to them as well, and they made use of it in order that they might enter the Kingdom of God."[103]

In the Apocrypha "*Acts of Paul and Thecla,*" St. Paul speaks to St Thecla about future temptations and she responded by asking to be given "*the Seal*" so that the tempters would not touch her. St. Paul advised her to have patience, assuring her that she would receive "*the water.*"[104]

St. Basil raised the question of how could an Angel claim us and how could he separate us from the enemies "*if he does not recognize the Seal? How can you say that I am of God without bearing the characteristics?*" He responded: "*The unsealed treasure is easy for the thieves; the unsealed sheep without danger can be attacked.*"[105]

St. Gregory the Theologian of Nazianzus observed that "*the sealed sheep is not an easy game, the unsealed is susceptible to thieves.*"[106]

St. John Chrysostom, using the image of the seal of the soldier, observed that "*As the soldiers are sealed, likewise the faithful receive the Spirit; even if he is a deserter, he is made known to all.*" By means of the last sentence he proclaimed the indelible character of the Seal since even after a Christian's desertion he is openly known as a Christian. Elsewhere the same Holy Father observed that the Orthodox Christians received the indelible character of the Seal in Baptism "*as sons in the Spirit.*"[107]

St. Athanasius the Great of Alexandria commented that "*Chrismation is called Seal and is from the Holy Spirit, the Seal imprints the Son on our souls, as though we have the form of Christ,*

---

[103] Ibid, Parable, 9, 16, 2-4, in Lightfoot, *Apostolic Fathers,* p. 276.

[104] *Acts of Paul and Thecla,* in Leeming, *Principles,* p. 162.

[105] St Basil the Great, *To the Holy Baptism,* § 4, in Migne, *P.G.,* 31, 433.

[106] St Gregory of Nazianzus, *Homily* 15, in Migne, *P.G.,* 36, 377.

[107] St John Chrysostom, *To 2 Corinthians,* Homily 3, § 7, in Migne, *P.G.,* 61, 418. Ibid, *To Ephesians,* Homily 2, § 2, in Montfaucon, v. 11, p. 13. Leeming, *Principles,* p. 169.

as the Apostle says; 'My little children for whom I labour in birth again until Christ is formed in you.[108],[109]

St. Paul also proclaimed: *"For as many of you as were Baptised into Christ have put on Christ."*[110] *"For if we have been united together in the likeness of His death, certainly we also shall be in the likeness of His Resurrection, knowing this, that our old man was crucified with Him, that the body of sin might be done away with, that we should no longer be slaves of sin."*[111]

St. Cyril of Jerusalem, referring to the newly Illuminated said that they were *"Baptised into Christ and having vested Christ they became of the same image of the Son of God partaking of Christ we are called Christs."*[112]

The terms *"to seal"* and *"seal"* are used. Even in the Service the celebrant invokes the words: *"Seal of the Gift of the Holy Spirit. Amen."* The use of this invocation is believed to be from the *"Catecheses"* of St. Cyril of Jerusalem who taught that after Baptism *"the Seal was given for the communion of the Holy Spirit"* when *"the Holy Myrrh is anointed upon the forehead and the other parts of the body"* of the newly Illuminated who *"become the anointed ones receiving the antitype of the Holy Spirit, because they are images of Christ."*[113]

Parallel to this, the *"Euchologion"* of St. Serapion refers to the anointing of the newly Illuminated with the Holy Myrrh that is called *"Seal"* which strengthens them to *"remain solid and unmovable, unharmed and spotless"* having the *"Seal of Christ on the forehead."*[114]

The Holy Fathers of the Orthodox Church used of the term *"Seal"* in relation to the Sacraments of Holy Chrismation and Baptism based upon the following New Testament teachings, according to which: *"In Him you also trusted, after you heard the word of truth, the gospel of your salvation; in Whom also, having believed, you were sealed with the Holy Spirit."*[115] *"Now He Who establishes us with you*

---

[108] Gal. 4:19.
[109] St Athanasius the Great, *To Serapion,* Epistle 1, § 23, in Migne, *P.G.,* 26, 584.
[110] Gal. 3:27.
[111] Rom. 6:5-6.
[112] St Cyril of Jerusalem, *Catechesis Mystagogia,* III, § 1, in Migne, *P.G.,* 33, 1091.
[113] Ibid, *Catechesis,* XVIII and XXI, § 1, in Migne, *P.G.,* 33, 1056, 1088.
[114] *Euchologion,* prayer 16, in Trempelas, *Small Euchologion,* v. I, p. 395. Cf. Didymus The Blind, *About the Holy Trinity,* II, 15, in Migne, *P.G.,* 39, 720.
[115] Ephes. 1:13.

in Christ and has anointed us is God, Who also has sealed us and given us the Spirit in our hearts as a guarantee."[116] St. Paul urged the Christians "*not to grieve the Holy Spirit of God, by Whom you were sealed for the Day of Redemption.*"[117]

In the 2nd century written Apocrypha book entitled "*Acta Barnaba,*" one finds the expression "*sealed of the bishop.*"[118] In the *Egyptian Order* (Apostolic Tradition of St Hippolytus) the term "*sealing*" is used on the laying on of hands during the Ordination.[119] The Bishop "*seals the head of the candidate thrice.*" During the preparation part of Ordination of a Bishop the confirmation of the election is called "*small seal*" to differentiate from the "*Great Seal*" which is the Ordination itself.[120] Some Canons of the Ecumenical or Local Councils speak of invalid ordinations,[121] which refer not to the invalidation of the Ordination, but to the invalid installation of the ordained person. The Holy Mystery continues to have its value until the unfrocking of those who performed the illegal ordination. The rights and authorities which derive from Ordination with the jurisdiction and installation to the uncanonical bishopric or parish are the ones which are cancelled and proclaimed invalid.

Generally, it can be said for all the Holy Sacraments that within them the Action of the Divine Grace is purely creative and that the Holy Spirit is He Who acts and recreates through the Holy Sacraments perfecting all those who partake of them without any need of repetition. This refers to all Holy Sacraments in which the Holy Spirit acts with the same Divine Power.

The form of the Seal which is imprinted through the Holy Sacraments, as well as how their prints cannot be removed, especially in the Holy Mystery of Baptism, remain indescribable.[122] Who can possibly understand the Actions of God? Who can understand with his limited mind the movements of the Holy Spirit? Who can comprehend the inexpressible ways of Regeneration and Recreation of the Newness of Life in Christ? Again, one must never forget the

---

[116] 2 Corinth. 1:21-22.
[117] Ephes. 4:30.
[118] *Acta Barnabae,* ch. 20, in Bonnet, *Acta apostolorum apocrypha*, v. III, p. 299.
[119] Publication: Connoly, p. 179.
[120] Georgios Codinos Pseudonicodinus, *About the Officialians,* ch. 20, in Migne, 157, 117.
[121] Canon XVI of the 1st Ecumenical Synod; Canons XIII, XXII and XXIII of the Coucil in Antioch; Canons LXXVI and XV of the Apostles; Canon VI of the 4th Ecumenical Synod.
[122] Dyobouniotes, *The Mysteries,* p. 26. Androutsos, *Dogmatique,* p. 314. Trempelas, *Dogmatique,* v. III, p. 29.

Biblical words: *"For who has known the mind of the Lord? Or who has become His counsellor?"*[123]

6. The Necessity of the Holy Sacraments

From all the above the necessity of the Holy Sacraments is obvious. They were instituted by our Lord and Saviour Jesus Christ, the Son of God, and were assigned as the ways through which the Divine Grace accomplishes the Regeneration and Sanctification of the faithful. It is also evident that the abstention from Holy Communion, Repentance and all Holy Sacraments result in the deprivation of Salvation. The Lord clearly proclaimed that Baptism is the only way for one to become a member of God's Kingdom. He taught that *"unless one is born of water and the Spirit, he cannot enter the Kingdom of God"*[124] and concerning Holy Communion He stated that *"unless you eat the Flesh of the Son of Man and drink His Blood, you have no Life in you."*[125]

The case of the thief on the cross[126] who entered Paradise without partaking of the Holy Sacraments, the Holy Apostles receiving of the Holy Spirit through the breathing upon them by Christ[127] and the descent of the *Paracletus* (Holy Spirit) upon the Disciples on the Day of Pentecost[128] by which they received the Authority of forgiving or not the sins, were exceptional and unique, necessary for their Regeneration and their fulfilment of their mission. These cases are extraordinary events, which were performed by our Lord and Saviour Jesus Christ, the Son of God. The only thing that is clearly revealed is that God can save man in different ways or to strengthen him for a mission to which He calls him. Under no circumstances is it permissible to predetermine where and when and how God should Act.

The differentiation of the Holy Sacraments as *"compulsory"* or *"at will"* (marriage and priesthood) is inaccurate because all the Holy Sacraments are necessary. It is dependent upon the free will of the faithful to choose between marriage or celibacy. In the case where we

---

[123] Rom. 11:34.
[124] John 3:5.
[125] John 6:53.
[126] Luke 23:43.
[127] John 20:22-23.
[128] Acts 2:2-4.

choose Marriage, it is necessary to Sanctify our union through the Holy Mystery of Marriage. The same applies if one wishes to enter the Mystery of Priesthood.[129]

CHAPTER THREE
THE PERFECTION OF THE HOLY SACRAMENTS

In order that a Holy Mystery is perfected and bears the saving fruits of its energy the following are prerequisites: The Mystery, besides the extraordinary cases of Baptism, is not permitted to be celebrated by lay faithful but only by a canonical ordained bishop or priest The validity and authority of the Holy Mystery does not depend on the moral status, way of life, worthiness or unworthiness of the celebrant, because according to the common teachings of the Holy Fathers of the Orthodox Church, Christ is the One Who celebrates all the Holy Sacraments through the celebrant who becomes His instrument. It is required for the celebrant to act willingly in order to perfect the Mystery according to the Rites of the Orthodox Church. The bishop or priest must be canonical and not in heresy or in schism. Sacraments performed outside the Orthodox Church, in communities of heretics or schismatics, are invalid. Such events must be performed canonically.

1. Those Who Have the Special Priesthood Are the Necessary Instruments for the Perfection of the Holy Sacraments

It has been mentioned in previous chapters that all faithful who are canonically baptised are members of the One Body of our Lord and Saviour Jesus Christ, the Son of God, and comprise the Royal Kingdom but not all have the authority to perform the Holy Sacraments. Only those who have the special gift of priesthood with unbroken Apostolic Succession, bishops and priests,[130] are capable of officiating the Holy Sacraments. Just as deacons, although having received the first level of priesthood, cannot celebrate any of the Holy Sacraments, likewise the laity, who, although they comprise the Royal

---

[129] Trempelas, *Dogmatique,* v. III, p. 31.
[130] Jeremias, in Karmeris, *The dogmatics,* p. 406. Mogilas, (A 109, A 107), in Karmeris, *The dogmatics,* pp. 640 and 638.

Kingdom,[131] have neither the authority nor the capability of performing the Holy Sacraments except in extreme necessity. As for example, when death is impending upon an infant, they may perform the Holy Mystery of Baptism as long as they are not in heresy or schism. Bishops and priests, when celebrating the Holy Sacraments are not the main celebrants but only instruments of God through whom the invisible great High Priest, Jesus Christ, Who is inseparable from His Mystical Body, His Church, Sanctifies and Perfects the Holy Sacraments.

Christ Himself is He Who offers the Sacrifice without the shedding of blood, and Who is being offered. The bishop or priest calls upon the Holy Spirit to sanctify the offerings on the Altar and change them into Christ's precious Body and Blood. In addition, during the Consecration and the Transmission of the Mystery, the celebrant gives his place to Christ Who Sanctifies the Sacraments, making the bread and the cup the Body and Blood of Christ. The celebrant avoids referring to himself by saying "*I baptise*" or "*I anoint*" or "*I ordain*" but rather uses the terms "*the servant of God*" is baptised, sealed, crowned, ordained, etc and gives his place to the invisible Lord.

St. Cyril of Jerusalem taught that "*the Grace is not from men, but from God through men.*"[132]

St. John Chrysostom, above all the other Fathers of the Orthodox Church, observed that "*the Father and the Son and the Holy Spirit act altogether while the priest lends his own tongue and gives his own hands*" but "*Grace works everything.*" The celebrant during the Holy Sacraments "*opens only his mouth but God works everything. The celebrant is only present as an instrument of God.*" Elsewhere, he spoke of the Divine Eucharist that "*no man enters into the present things, but everything is the work of God, and He is the One Who leads us to the mystagog.*" Concerning Baptism, he said that it is great "*but great is not he who baptises, but He Who is called to the Baptism*" in other words, the Holy Trinity. Concerning Ordination, he emphasised that "*The hand of man is placed upon the head, in other words that of the bishop's, but everything is worked by God and His Hand touches the head of the one who is being ordained.*" Elsewhere, he invites the faithful to believe that now, when the Divine Liturgy is

---

[131] Rev. 1:6.
[132] St Cyril of Jerusalem, *Catechesis,* XVII, § 15, in Migne, *P.G.,* 33, 1009.

celebrated "*it is truly the Supper at which the Lord sat For no man works this, but He Himself.*" He also advised those who partake of Holy Communion that when they see "*the priest giving*" them the Holy Mystery, they must not think that he is the one who makes this but strongly believe that "*it is the Hand of Christ which is stretched out. For as when someone is baptized*" the priest is not the one who baptises him "*but God is the One Who holds His Hand on the head through His invisible Power, and neither an Angel, nor an Archangel, nor anyone else dares to approach and touch, likewise in the Mystical Supper of the Divine Eucharist.*"[133]

St. Augustine considers Christ to be the true Celebrant of the Holy Sacraments. "*Christ,*" he says, "*baptizes in the Holy Spirit. This is unique in Christ, that although there are many celebrants, either just or sinners, they baptise, but the holiness of Baptism is ascribed to the only Holy One, upon Whom the Holy Spirit descended and about Whom it was said that 'He shall baptise in the Holy Spirit.' Peter baptized, but Christ was baptising. Paul baptised, but Christ was baptising. And Judas could have baptised, but, even then Christ would have been the One Who was baptising.*"[134]

2. The Unworthiness of the Officiator does not Affect the Power of the Mystery

The Orthodox Church supports the opinion that neither the private life nor the unworthiness of the clergymen could affect the Holiness and Power of the Holy Mystery in any way.

St. Cyril of Jerusalem exhorted every catechumen to approach "*Baptism, not as to the person who appears, but calling to mind the Holy Spirit*" Who sanctifies the water of Baptism and acts through it "*for He is ready to seal the soul*" of the one who is being baptised.[135]

Jeremiah observed that "*although the Sacraments are celebrated by some unworthy (clergymen) who are not themselves benefited, being spiritually damaged, those who receive (the Sacraments) are*

---

[133] St John Chrysostom, *To John,* Homily 86, § 4, in Migne, *P.G.,* 59, 472. Ibid, *To 2 Timothy,* Homily 2, § 4, in Migne, *P.G.,* 62, 612. Ibid, *To 1 Corinthians,* Homily 8, § 1; and Homily 3, § 2, in Migne, *P.G.,* 61, 69 and 25. Ibid, *To Acts,* Homily 14, § 3, in Migne, *P.G.,* 60, 116. Ibid, *To Matthew,* Homily 50, § 3, in Migne, *P.G.,* 58, 507.

[134] St Augustine, *In Johannis evangelium. Tractatus,* in migne, *P.L.,* 35, 1024. Cf. Leeming, *Principles,* p. 54.

[135] St Cyril of Jerusalem, *Catechesis,* XVII, § 35, in Migne, *P.G.,* 1009.

sanctified and do benefit. For Divine Grace and through unworthy (clergymen) acts and perfects the Sacraments. We must honour those who serve and must not dishonour the good (clergymen) because of the unworthy ones (as in the case of Judas who was among the Apostles)." He continues asking, *"Does God not ordain all, even the unworthy?"* He answers the question by stating: *"God does not ordain all but He acts through all, even though they are unworthy, in order to save the people."*[136]

St. Gregory the Theologian of Nazianzus prevented a candidate who was preparing himself for Baptism because he said *"Let a Bishop baptise me and he must be a Metropolitan or Jerusalemite"* or *"a presbyter, but from the unmarried who leads an abstemious and angelic life."* St. Gregory continued: *"Do not judge the judges, he who needs the healing, do not love to judge those who are worthy to be unfrocked."* He then uses the imagery of the ring by saying that although the ring which is used to seal official documents is made out of gold or iron, the image will be stamped one and the same.[137]

St. John Chrysostom stressed that, if the divine Grace *"seeks everywhere the worthy ones"*, there will be neither *"Baptism, nor Body of Christ"*. But now *"through the unworthy God acts"* and under no circumstances is the Grace of Baptism damaged because of the unworthy life of the priest. *"God acts through all, even if they are unworthy"* and this is because He seeks the salvation of the people. For, when He sent out the disciples to preach, and *"through Judas* (although unworthy) *He acted."* Also, concerning the false prophets who were prophesying in God's name, *"He says: 'I never knew you; depart from Me, you who practice lawlessness'*[138], *and others had cast out demons."*[139] If God acted through such unworthy persons in order to benefit His people how *"much more will He act through the priests?"* He urged strongly *"that no one should be scandalized by examining the life of the priest"* and reminds the faithful that the Grace *"that God grants should not be dependent on the virtue of the priest"* for *"no man introduces it, but Grace is the work of God and God is He Who leads us to mystagog"*. He concludes that *"if we were to examine*

---

[136] Jeremias, Answer A', in Karmeris, *The dogmatics,* v. I, p. 391.

[137] St Gregory of Nazianzus, *Homily 40 to Holy Baptism,* § 26, in Migne, *P.G.,* 36, 396.

[138] Matth. 7:23

[139] Matth. 7:22.

the life of the rulers, we should then ordain the teachers and the up will be down, and the feet will be up and the head down."[140]

St Isidorus of Pelusium states that "no one is harmed by receiving" the Sacraments through the "unworthy" and under no circumstances "are the precious Sacraments spoiled", even if the officiator "priest is the worst of all sinners." He reminds us about the raven by which the Prophet Elijah was fed.[141] As in the case of that great Prophet, God was feeding him through an unclean instrument, likewise within the Church the unclean priests do not prevent, because of their sins, the Grace of God to regenerate us and to lead us to mystagog.[142]

3. What the Church officiates is necessary for the perfection

If the private life of the priest and his unworthiness under no circumstances prevents the action of the Holy Spirit to perfect the Holy Sacraments, it is necessary and an important term, that the officiator has to have the good will, to perform whatever the Orthodox Church performs in the Holy Sacraments and to invocate and repeat the same words and movements as well as the prayers which the Orthodox Church uses. For the priest sanctifies the Sacraments by the power of the Holy Spirit.[143] To this aim, right from the beginning, it was the practice that the officiator priest after preparation vested himself with special vestments in order to perform any of the Sacraments and in order that through these he will separate himself from the daily and common life and be prepared for the sacred diakonia. It is also worthy to note, that in all the Holy Sacraments there is a preparatory part, prayers and invocations during the service. In order that the Holy Mystery be considered valuable, it must keep the form and the words of invocation and prayers which the Orthodox Church has established, not because they act as some kind of magic instruments, but because they express the faith and the opinion of the Orthodox Church and describe the full character of that which the Church performs and aims to transmit through the performed Mystery the divine Grace of God.

---

[140] St John Chrysostom, *To 1 Corinthians,* Homily 8, § 1, in Migne, *P.G.,* 61, 69. Ibid, *To 2 Timothy,* Homily 2, §§ 3 and 4, in Migne, *P.G.,* 62, 610 and 612.

[141] 1 Samuel (I Kings) 17:6.

[142] St Isidorus of Pelusium, *Epistles,* book III, Epistle 340, in Migne, *P.G.,* 78, 1000.

[143] Mogilas, A' 100, in Karmeris, *The dogmatics,* v. II, p. 635.

Hence, the validity of the Mystery is not affected if the officiator prays carelessly or indifferently and even celebrates the Holy Sacraments without faith. It is enough that he celebrates the divine Sacraments exactly as the holy Orthodox Church received them from her Founder. For his impiety and indifference, the priest is responsible and accountable before God, Who invisibly performs the Holy Sacraments. The unfaithfulness of the priest cannot eliminate the effectiveness and power of the Holy Sacraments. Since he still remains within the Church and is not separated from her Head by renouncing the Orthodox faith, he can perform the Sacraments, although within his soul he remains alien to the Divine Grace.

The keeping of the order within the Holy Sacraments is necessary and indispensable in expressing the Church's opinion and faith.

St. Justin the Philosopher and Martyr, stated that the *"first* (in honour presbyter) *during the Eucharist prays according to his power."*[144] Afterwards, when special liturgical types of celebration were introduced, not all the local churches used the same type. But all the liturgical types were united through the one and same faith, which created a harmonious agreement.

Again, if someone performs exactly the liturgical type of the one holy Orthodox Church, but expresses a different faith, then the Sacraments are invalid, although the external form is correct.

St. Athanasius the Great of Alexandria rejects the baptism of the Arians, although they kept the type which was delivered by Christ, the invocation of the Holy Trinity, because *"although the perfection was given in the name of the Father and of the Son, they (the Arians) do not call upon the Father truthfully, because by renouncing the sameness of the essence they also renounce the true God."* Because they did not accept the Son being of the same Essence of the Father, they did not perform the baptism *"in the Father and the Son but to the Creator* (Father) *and the creature* (the Son), *to the Maker and the thing which was made."* Elsewhere, he also observes that *"many other heresies use only the names* (of the Holy Trinity), *but they do not believe correctly, neither have the healthy faith, thus the water* (of baptism*) which they offered is useless, for the lack of piety; and consequently, he who is sprinkled by them is polluted in irreverence rather than being saved."*[145]

---

[144] St Justin the Philosopher and Martyr, *I Apology,* 67, 5, *B*, v. 3, p. 198.
[145] St Athanasius the Great, *Against Arians,* II, §§ 42-43, in Migne, *P.G.,* 26, 236-237.

St. Basil the Great considers that some heretics should be baptized, because they were *"the branches of Marcion and according to their heresies, marriage was impure and they did not partake of wine and that they said that the creation of God was polluted"*. *"For they should not say that they were baptized in the name of Father and of the Son and of the Holy Spirit, for they supposed God to be the creator of evil, just as Marcion and the rest of the heresies."*[146]

4. The Sacraments of the Heretics.

Now we come to deal with the question: *"What happens with the Sacraments of the heretics or schismatics?"* Concerning this major subject we must emphasise that the One, Holy, Catholic and Apostolic Eastern Orthodox Church deals with this matter on a different basis to that of the Western Roman Catholic Church. Without remaining indifferent towards the canonical performance of the Holy Sacraments, the Orthodox Church takes into consideration the fact that the Sacraments of the heretics were performed outside the One, Holy, Catholic and Apostolic Church and are considered invalid. St. Cyprian, expressed in his writings that *"outside the Church there is no salvation."* This opinion was the general belief and principal of the first Church.

Tertullian considered the baptism of the heretics[147] invalid and his predecessor Agrippinus in the Synod of 198 took similar decisions[148]. Simultaneously this was the opinion of all the Churches of the East. This is manifested in an epistle of Dionysius of Alexandria to Xystus II (257-258), according to which Stephen threatens to cut all communion with the Churches of Cilicia, Cappadocia and Galatia and all the surrounding Churches *"because they rebaptized the heretics."* Dionysius speaks about Synods which took place in Phrygia between the years 230-245, which renounced the baptism of the heretics[149]. In an epistle addressed to Phirmilianus, archbishop of Caesarea, we find literal witness of this practice[150].

---

[146] St Basil the Great, *Epistle* 199, § 47, in Migne, *P.G.*, 32, 732.

[147] Tertullian, *De Baptismo*, § 15, in migne, *P.L.*, 1, 1216.

[148] St Cyprian, Epistola71, § 4, in migne, *P.L.*, 4, 424. Ibid, *Epist.* 73, § 3, in migne, *P.L.*, 3, 1157.

[149] St Dionysius of Alexandria, in Eusebius, *Church History*, VII, 4 and 5, in Migne, *P.G.*, 20, 641 and 644.

[150] St Cyprian, Epistola75, § 7, in migne, *P.L.*, 3, 1208.

Thus, all the Churches of Pontus and Asia Minor appeared to agree on this matter with the Churches of Africa.

The *Apostolic Orders* proclaim that *"those who receive anything from heretics receive infection for they became partakers of their erroneous opinion. For they are not priests then neither those who were baptized by them are initiated but are infected, and have not received the forgiveness of their sins but a bond of impiety."*[151]

St. Cyril of Jerusalem assures us that *"the heretics are rebaptized because they have not received Baptism."*[152]

Thus, the entire ancient Church was against heretical baptism.

On the other hand what was accepted for the validity of the Holy Mystery of Baptism was also accepted for all the Holy Sacraments, and especially for that of Ordination. Thus Innocentius I in his epistle dated 13th December 414 concerning the ordinations of the defrocked bishop of Sardica Bonosus literally stated that when he ordained he could not transmit whatever he did not have but what he had, in other words, his condemnation.[153] When he was asked by Alexandros of Antioch (413-420), if it was possible to recognize the ordinations of the Arians who were returning to the Orthodox Church, he excluded any possibility because, although their baptism was accepted as being performed in the type of the invocation of the Holy Trinity, they do not have the Holy Spirit. By breaking away from the true Faith they alienated themselves from the perfection of the Holy Spirit and consequently could not transmit the fullness of the Holy Spirit.[154]

5. The Sacraments of the Schismatics

It was not only the heretics who departed and separated themselves from the original Body of Christ, but also the schismatics. Consequently, it was natural that the Sacraments which were officiated by them, although they were performed exactly as in the Orthodox Church, and officiated by bishops or priests who were previously ordained canonically but afterwards had split, these Sacraments were considered invalid by the Orthodox Church.

---

[151] *Apostolic Orders,* VI, 15, in ***B***, v. 2, p. 104.

[152] St Cyril of Jerusalem, *Pre-catechesis,* § 7, in Migne, *P.G.,* 33, 445.

[153] Innocent, *Epistola*17, c. 3, in migne, *P.L.,* 20, 530.

[154] Ibid, *Epistola*24, in migne, *P.L.,* 20, 549. Gelasianus, *Sacramentarium,* in migne, *P.L.,* 74, 1145 and 1147. Johannis Papae, *Epistola*267, in migne, *P.L.,* 136, 887. Paschalis Papae, *Epistolato the archbishop of Magentia,* in migne, *P.L.,* 163, 175.

St. Cyprian, when asked by the bishop Magnus, proclaimed the invalidity of the Sacraments of the heretics and schismatics. He emphasised that since they are out of the Church, they are deprived of the only Source of the divine Grace and are abandoned by the Holy Spirit.[155] This was also the practice of the Churches in Pontus and Asia Minor. All those who separate themselves from the Church do not have the Grace of the Holy Spirit.

In order for a Mystery to be valid, it is not enough that it is officiated canonically according to the Rites of the ancient Church or by a clergyman who was canonically ordained, but it is essential that the clergyman has to be in communion of Faith with the Orthodox Church. A bishop or priest who is separated through heresy or schism from the true Church, breaks the line of Apostolic Succession, falls from the Grace of the Priesthood, alienates himself from the perfection of the Holy Spirit and becomes once again a layman who has no authority to baptize. In other words, any mystery which is officiated outside the Orthodox Church can be under no circumstances recognized as valid.

The fact that the canonically ordained bishop or priest remains an instrument of Divine Grace, of which the only source and treasury is the Church. We must never forget that the canonically ordained through Divine Grace which was transmitted to him, makes him for life an instrument for diakonia of the Divine Word and steward of the Divine Sacraments.

The Sacraments which are officiated by heretics or schismatics or by defrocked Orthodox clergymen are not only illegal, but invalid and powerless and consequently must be repeated canonically.

6. The term *"Economia"* (=Economy, dispensation)

"Economia" (dispensation) is the temporary deviation from the accurate practice of the Church in order to achieve a greater benefit[156]. St. Cyril of Alexandria uses the example of sailors who, when they are out at sea and face the winter storms, they empty the ship of its cargo, in order to save the whole ship and the crew; likewise, the Church, when required, uses *"Economia"*, in order not to suffer damage but to

---

[155] St Cyprian, Epistola76, §§ 2 and 7-11, in migne, *P.L.,* 3, 1886 and 1191. Ibid, *Epistola69*, § 1, in migne, *P.L.,* 4, 413. Ibid, *Epistola72*, in migne, *P.L.,* 3, 1084.
[156] St Cyril of Alexandria, *Epistle 46 to Gennadius,* in Migne, *P.G.,* 77, 319.

accomplish greater benefit[157]. *"Economia"* is used not to deviate from the essential correctness of the Church, but in order to achieve greater benefits or to avoid greater damage.

If *'Economia'* is used for extraordinary reasons and deviates from the Church's correctness, it is obvious that this does not create a permanent condition but is an exception to the rule and for a specific case only (*"jus singulare"*). It lasts briefly, in order that those who are outside of the Orthodox Church enter her bosom, as when a door is opened and immediately closed, in order that the Church's accuracy is not disturbed[158].

'Economia' cannot at first and in advance be offered to all the members of the Orthodox Church; neither can it be said that the Orthodox Church is obliged to recognize as valid the Sacraments of those outside the Orthodox Body.

Through *"Economia"* the Orthodox Church completes, gives life and grants the Gift and the Charismata of the Holy Spirit to those who were not previously canonically included within the body of the Church because when *"a heretic returns to Orthodoxy he corrects the previous error and heresy is removed; the Baptism by the anointing with holy Myrrh, the ordination by the laying on of the hands."*[159] *"Economia"* can also be exercised even to members of the Church who require special dispensation for some reason or another. In this case the Canons (Laws) of the Church are set aside but only for that moment.

"Economia" can only be applied to the Canons of the Orthodox Church which have been established by the Fathers under the inspiration of the Holy Spirit and can be regarded as flexible. But under no circumstances can *"Economia"* be applied to the Dogma of the Church which is the Revelation of God to His Church.

---

[157] Ibid, *Epistle 46 to Gennadius*, in Migne, *P.G.*, 77, 320. Ibid, *Epistle* 87, in Migne, *P.G.*, 77, 376.
[158] Trempelas, *Dogmatique,* v. III, p. 49.
[159] St Justin the Philosopher and Martyr, *Answer* 14 *to the Orthodox,* in Migne, *P.G.*, 6, 1282.

CHAPTER FOUR
THE NUMBER OF THE HOLY SACRAMENTS

The number of Holy Sacraments were not determined either by the New Testament or by the Holy Fathers and ecclesiastic writers. Indications are found in Holy Scripture that reveals their Divine institution. The Holy Fathers of the ancient Orthodox Church simply named them while from the 12th century and onwards others raised their number to seven. In different ages the Fathers included the mysterious ceremonies as God-instituted such as the Funeral Service, the Blessings of Water, etc among the Holy Sacraments and their number was increased. Henceforth, after the 13th century the reason for determining the number of Holy Sacraments was raised and all Orthodox Churches, despite their differences, were in agreement on this matter. Many have struggled to find the reason for the Divine Wisdom having had the good will to grant the Holy Sacraments to the Church. The only answer to this question is that God Willed it and had the good pleasure.

1. The Number of the Holy Sacraments According to the New Testament and the Holy Fathers

Each Holy Mystery is witnessed in the New Testament as having its institution either directly from our Lord and Saviour Jesus Christ, the Son of God, the Founder and Head of His Church, or indirectly through His Holy Apostles and Disciples. Each Holy Mystery is a special way and main pipeline by means of which Divine Grace is transmitted to the faithful within the Church. In the New Testament we do not find any specific number[160] concerning the Holy Sacraments.

This is also noticed among the oldest Holy Fathers and ecclesiastic writers of the Orthodox Church. For practical purposes and not for any dogmatic reasons they (the Apostolic Fathers and the Apologists) mention two main Holy Sacraments, which introduce the faithful to the Church and incorporate him within Christ - those of Holy Baptism and Holy Eucharist. St. Justin the Philosopher and Martyr gave us very important and detailed information in his 1st Apology. The Didache, besides other guidelines concerning the way

---

[160] See: Meyendorff, *Theology,* pp. 191-192.

that the Holy Sacraments should be officiated, gives us the ancient types of prayers that were used at the *"tables of love"* (*"agapae"*) and at the Divine Eucharist, which was associated with them. The Apostolic Fathers also mentioned ordinations of bishops and deacons,[161] confession of the sins[162] and the Holy Mystery of Marriage, which was conducted *"with the consent of the bishop"* so *"that the marriage may be in accordance with the Lord and not due to lustful passions."* [163]

For the same practical reasons, in order to initiate the newly illumined and to make them understand their participation in the Divine Sacraments, St. Cyril of Jerusalem, Theodorus of Mopsuestias and St. Ambrosius and the author of the book *"de Sacramentis"* referred in their writings (Catechises) only to Baptism, Chrismation and Holy Eucharist. In the African Church Tertullian does not only mention these three Sacraments but also that of repentance, distinguishing *"the preparation repentance"* for Baptism from that of the exact Baptism. He also refers to Ordination (*"ordinatio"*) as well as Marriage, through which *"the Church united the Divine Eucharist assured and the blessing sealed."*[164] Likewise, St. Cyprian includes Baptism, Chrismation, Holy Eucharist, Repentance and Ordination[165] in the Sacraments. St Augustine, on the other hand, presented in a more advanced manner the teaching concerning the Holy Sacraments. He determined Baptism and Eucharist as Sacraments, characteristically adding *"and whatever else is constituted in the canonical Scriptures."*[166] He referred to Marriage and Ordination as Sacraments that he compared to Baptism. Elsewhere, he also called the Symbol (Creed of Faith) and the Lord's Prayer Sacraments, which,

---

[161] *Didache*, 15, 1, in Lightfoot, *Apostolic Fathers,* p. 157. St Clement of Rome, *1st Corinthians*, 7, 4-8, 1-5; 42, 4-5; 44, 2, in Lightfoot, *Apostolic Fathers,* p. 32-33, 51, 52.

[162] *Didache*, 4, 14 and 14, 1-3, in Lightfoot, *Apostolic Fathers,* pp. 152 and 157. *Barnabas*, 19, 12, in Lightfoot, *Apostolic Fathers,* p. 186. St Clement of Rome, *1st Corinthians*, 51, 3 and 52, 1, in Lightfoot, *Apostolic Fathers,* p. 57.

[163] St Ignatius, *To Polycarp*, 5, 2, in Lightfoot, *Apostolic Fathers,* p. 117.

[164] Tertullian, *De praescriptione haereticorum,* 41 and *Adversus uxorem,* II, 9, in migne, *P.L.,* 1, 68 and 1415.

[165] St Cyprian, EpistolaLXX, 3, in migne, *P.L.,* 3, 1080. Ibid, *Epistola*LXXIII, §§ 20 and 21, in migne, *P.L.,* 3, 1668. Ibid, *Epistola*LXIII, § 14, in migne, *P.L.,* 4, 396-397. Ibid, *De lapsis,* c. XXV, in migne, *P.L.,* 4, 499.

[166] St Augustine, *Epist.* LIV, 1, in migne, *P.L.,* 33, 200.

during the preparation for Holy Baptism, children were taught.[167] St Hippolytus' prayers of Ordination and Blessing of Oil were preserved in the *"Egyptian Order."* Origen spoke of the confession of sin committed against priests, in order to expose the sin and to request the proper medicine to cure it[168]. He also combined repentance as well as the laying on of hands with the use of oil and prayer, according to the teaching of St James.[169] Furthermore in the *"Euchologion"* (Prayer Book) of St. Serapion three prayers for Ordination are found, two prayers *"concerning the offered oil"* of which the one concerns *"the offered oils"* and the second *" the oil of the ill."*[170]

Thus, all those Sacred Ceremonies which were used within the entire Orthodox Church were numbered as Holy Sacraments. St. Augustine assured that *"whatever the universal Church upholds were not laid down by Holy Synod, but were always practised and correctly believed as having been passed down by Apostolic authority."*[171]

2. Later Attempts for Systematic Numbering of the Holy Sacraments

In the East some attempts were made to number the Holy Sacraments. At first in the writings that were believed to be by St Dionysius the Aeropagite, the Holy Sacraments of *"Illumination"* or Baptism, *"the Gathering or Communion,"* *"the Rite of Myrrh"* (Chrismation or Confirmation) and *"the Hierarchal Orders"* (Priesthood) are explained. Also, amongst the Holy Sacraments the *"Mystery for those who have sacredly fallen asleep"* (Funeral Rite) and the tonsuring of Monks are numbered. In this catalogue according to St Dionysius, of the six Sacraments only four are characterised as *"Hierarchal Sacraments,"* *"Divine and Sacred Symbols,"* *"perceptible images of the Heavenly,"* *"Divine and Holy Symbols,"* *"the perceptibly sacred intellectual images"* and especially the Holy Eucharist which is

---

[167] Ibid, *Enarratio in Psalm,* 103(104), § 9, in migne, *P.L.,* 37, 1343. Ibid, *De bono conjugal,* § 32, in migne, *P.L.,* 40, 394. Ibid, *Contra EpistolaParmenia,* II, 28, in migne, *P.L.,* 40, 70. Ibid, *Sermo* 228, § 3, in migne, *P.L.,* 38, 1102.

[168168] Origen, *In Leviticus,* II, 4, in Migne, *P.G.,* 12, 418. Cf. Ibid, *To Psalm* 37(38), homily II, § 6, in Migne, *P.G.,* 12, 1386.

[169] James 5, 14-15.

[170] Serapion, in Trempelas, *Dogmatique,* v. III, p. 60.

[171] St Augustine, *De Baptismo contra Donatus,* IV, 24, § 31, in migne, *P.L.,* 43, 174.

called *"Divine and perfect Mystery"* and *"Ceremony of Ceremonies."*[172]

St. Theodore the Studite numbered the Sacraments up to six although from his biography we learn that at his death he participated in the Mystery of Holy Unction. In another letter he himself bore witness to the custom of the Christians of confessing.[173] Thus during the 9th century neither the term *"Mystery"* ceased to be used in its general meaning nor was the final list of Holy Sacraments completed.

Peter Abelardus (+1142) numbers the Sacraments up to six including Marriage. After him, Peter Lombardus (+1160) presented the final list of seven Sacraments in his work *"Sententiae"* and referred to them as the Sacraments of the New Law listing them as follows: Baptism, Chrismation, Eucharist, Repentance, Unction, Ordination and Marriage. Later different Provincial Synods[174] in agreement proclaimed that the number of Holy Sacraments is seven.

Afterwards in the Synod of Lyon in the year 1274, those who participated from the East, the leader of whom was the Orthodox Emperor Michael Palaeologus, accepted the Confession of Faith of Pope Clement IV without any hesitation, in which the Holy Sacraments are seven. Three years later, in April 1277, the Patriarch of Constantinople, John Bekkos, repeated the list of Holy Sacraments in the same order as that of Lyon. In the second half of the 13th century, a Monk by the name of Job, in his work concerning the Holy Sacraments, added to the list the Tonsuring of Monks and Repentance combined with Holy Unction, although he distinguishes the two Holy Sacraments from one another.[175] In this manner, in his list, the Sacraments remained seven. In the Orthodox Church, in contemporary times, the Theologians express the abovementioned opinion in their writings.[176]

---

[172] St Dionysius, *Ecclesiastic hierarchy,* I, §§ 1 and 5; II, §§ 1 and 2, in Migne, *P.G.,* 3, 372, 376, 392, 397, 424 and 425.

[173] St Theodore the Studite, *Epistle,* book II, 165, in Migne, *P.G.,* 99, 1524. Ibid, *The life of Theodore of Studites,* II, 67, in Migne, *P.G.,* 99, 325. Ibid, *Epistle,* book II, 162, in Migne, *P.G.,* 99, 1845, 1504-1516.

[174] The Provincial Synods of Durham in 1217, of Oxford in 1222, of Ratisbonne in 1235, of Valentia 1255 and of Cemon in 1247.

[175] Codex 61, Supplem. Graeci Paris, fol. 239, in Trempelas, *Dogmatique,* v. III, p. 62.

[176] Cf. Mogilas (A' 98); Kritopoulos (ch. 5); Dositheus of Jerusalem, *Confession,* (Term 15), in Karmeris, *The dogmatics,* pp. 635, 388, 526, 757, 690 and 580.

3. The Mysterious Ceremonies

The term *"Mystery"* has also a wider meaning and includes some other ceremonies in the Sacraments as well. These ceremonies are similar to the Holy Sacraments and transmit Divine Grace invisibly through words and the use of matter as the Holy Sacraments but have not been Divinely instituted by Christ or by His Apostles. They are not essential for man's Salvation such as the Holy Sacraments. They were introduced by the Holy Fathers of the Orthodox Church according to the authority of our Lord and Saviour Jesus Christ, the Son of God, Who assured and promised that *"if two of you agree on earth concerning anything that they ask, it will be done for them by My Father in Heaven. For where two or three are gathered together in My Name, I Am there in the midst of them."*[177] Furthermore, these Ceremonies are similar to the Holy Sacraments and for this reason they are called Mysterious (*"sacramentaux," "sacramentalis," "sacramentalien"*). They were distinguished into *"consecrations"* and *"benedictions,"* both referring to persons or lifeless things and places.

CHAPTER FIVE
THE HOLY MYSTERY OF BAPTISM
I.MEANING, NAME AND DIVINE ESTABLISHMENT

Baptism is the Holy Mystery in which man through three immersions and elevations within and out of water and the invocation of the name of the three Persons of the Holy Trinity is regenerated by the Holy Spirit and becomes the New Creation in Christ[178]. St. Paul refers to it as *"the washing of regeneration and renewing of the Holy Spirit."*[179] Divine Grace descents upon the water giving to Baptism the cleanliness from sins and the power of regeneration. Baptism offers the Newness of Life in Christ, implants them in the Orthodox Church, which is the only Canonical Body of Christ, and offers to them the right to participate in all the Holy Sacraments. This Holy Mystery has been described by many names and each one clarifies it. Thus,

---

[177] Matth. 18:19-20.
[178] Cf. Damalas, *Catechesis,* pp. 82-83. Frangopoulos, *Christian Faith,* pp. 193-196. For the biblical interpretation of the Holy Mystery see: Labadarios, *Explanation,* Johannesburg, 1990. Ibid, *Sermons,* v.1, pp. 99-110. Meyendorff, *Theology,* pp. 192-195. Georgopoulos, *Anthology*, pp. 9-17.
[179] Tit. 3:5. Cf. Evdokimov, *Orthodoxia,* pp. 368-370. Kefalas, *Catechesis,* pp. 180-181.

Baptism was called *"Illumination," "Bath," "Charisma," "Gift," "Vestment of Immortality," "Seal," "Phylacterion," "Vehicle to Heaven,"* etc.

The importance of this Holy Mystery is manifested by Holy Scripture through the prototypes and prefigures of the Old Testament. The baptism of St. John the Forerunner and Baptist prepared the God-given Baptism of the Messiah through repentance. The importance of this Mystery is evident from the fact that it was instituted shortly before His glorious Ascension by the Son of God Who is our Lord, Master and Saviour. He commanded His Holy Apostles and Disciples to evangelise the entire world *"baptising"* those who believe in the Name of the Father and of the Son and of the Holy Spirit.[180] Simultaneously He threatened all those who disbelieve and would not be baptised with condemnation.[181]

1. The New Testament Determination of Baptism

The New Testament characterises the Holy Mystery of Baptism as *"the washing of regeneration and renewing of the Holy Spirit"*[182] as well as *"the washing of water by the word"*[183] which means the complete immersion and washing of the body within water that cleanses the soul from sin. One can understand Baptism to be the *"cleansing of sins and forgiveness of transgressions and the cause of renewal and regeneration"* when it is comprehended that the benefit *"is not granted by the water"* but *"by the descent of the Spirit which comes secretly"* and bestows *"Grace and Power"* resulting in the *"cleansing of sin and complete deliverance from the pollution of evil."* This Grace and Power is given by the Master Himself through the invocation *"in the Name of the Father and of the Son and of the Holy Spirit"*[184] being taught *"in the confession of the Father and of the Son and of the Holy Spirit."*[185]

---

[180] Matth. 28:19.
[181] Mark 16:16.
[182] Tit. 3:5.
[183] Ephes. 5:26.
[184] Matth. 28:19.
[185] St Justin the Philosopher and Martyr, *1 Apology*, 65, in **B**, v. 3, p. 197. St Gregory of Nazianzus, *To holy Baptism*, Homily 40, § 7, in Migne, *P.G.*, 36, 368. St John of Damascus, *Exposition. About faith and Baptism*, IV, 82, 9, in Migne, *P.G.*, 94, 1117.

2. The Entrance in the Church and the Participation in the Holy Sacraments

Baptism offers the newness of Life in Christ and makes one a member of the Orthodox Church. It gives him the right of Communion and participation in all the Holy Sacraments. This is witnessed by the ancient practice and tradition of the Orthodox Church according to which only those who were baptised were considered worthy to be accepted in the Divine Eucharist. *"But let no one eat or drink of your Eucharist except those who have been baptised into the Name of the Lord, for the Lord has also spoken concerning this: 'Do not give what is Holy to dogs.'[186]"*[187] The newly Illuminated were led from the Baptismal Font to the gathering of the faithful in order for them to participate in the celebration of Divine Eucharist and to partake of it. This is witnessed by St. Justin the Philosopher and Martyr[188] as well as by the Egyptian Order and the Canons ascribed to St Hippolytus.[189]

On the contrary, the Catechumens *"who have known the deity of Christ and have confessed already the faith"* had to depart from the *"Sacred Table"* because *"in those who have not yet been baptised the Holy Spirit does not dwell; afterwards they are proved to be partakers of the Holy Spirit"* through Baptism *"then nothing prevents them touching our Saviour Christ."*[190] Without the reception of Baptism no one can partake in the rest of the Holy Sacraments.[191]

3. The Multiplicity of Names of Baptism

The importance and Power of Baptism is such that it is natural to be given many and various names describing the effects on the soul.[192] It was called:

---

[186] Matth. 7:6.

[187] *Didache*, 9, § 5, in Lightfoot, *Apostolic Fathers,* p. 154.

[188] St Justin the Philosopher and Martyr, *1 Apology,* 65, in *B*, v. 3, p. 197.

[189] St Hippolytus, *Egyptian Order*, ch. 46, XXI, 19, § 141-143. Trempelas, *Small Euchologion,* v. 1, pp. 390-391 and 393.

[190] St Cyril of Alexandria, *To John,* book XIII, *to John,* 20, 17, in Migne, *P.G.,* 74, 696.

[191] Bartmann, *Theologie Dogmatique,* v. II, p. 275.

[192] Mitsopoulos, *Themata,* pp. 305-306.

1. *"Illumination"*[193] because before it is given, the Catechumen was taught, prepared and *"enlightened in his mind to learn*[194] *these things"*

2. *"Enlightenment"*[195] because through Baptism *"that sacred and saving Light is seen."*

3. *"Washing"*[196] because through it *"we wash away our sins"* and we partake in *"the clear waters which clean greater than hyssop, or the blood of Law clearer and more sacred than the ashes of a deer which is sprinkled upon those who partake and receive the temporary cleanness, but not the complete refutation of sin"* (Old Testament) whereas the New Testament Baptism accomplishes this.

4. *"Gift of righteousness"*[197] as through it *"the punishment of sin is removed."*

5. *"Gift"*[198] because it is *"the best majestic Gift from God"* given to us.

6. *"Vestment of immortality"* *"as covering the disgrace"*[199] of the nakedness caused by sin

7. *"Anointment, as Holy and Royal"* because the priests and kings *"were anointed"*[200] in the Old Testament.

In the New Testament through Baptism the newly Illuminated are incorporated into the One King and High Priest by their own becoming priests and kings[201] *"to God and Father."* Baptism is referred to as *"Seal"*[202] because, although it is granted by Christ, *"the despotic sign"* *"signing upon them the Light of the face of the Master"* and *"by sealing"*[203] each of them, He proves them to be His sheep that *"the thieves do not dare to steal so easily because they consider them to be insignificant."* By *"bearing the signs"* that are *"requested"* by the Angels it is clear that they belong to God and they are able to

---

[193] Heb. 10:32.

[194] 2 Corinth. 4:4-6.

[195] Heb. 6:4.

[196] Ephes. 5:26. Tit. 3:5.

[197] Rom. 5:17.

[198] Rom. 6:23; 12:6-8. 1 Corinth. 12:13. 1 John 3:24.

[199] 1 Corinth. 15:53.

[200] Lev. 16:32. Ex. 37:29. I Sam. 16:6. 2 Samuel (2 Kings) 19:21; 22:51. 1 Chron. 16:22. Psalm 20:6. Zech. 4:14.

[201] 1 Peter 2:9.

[202] 2 Tim. 2:19.

[203] Rev. 7:4. Ephes. 4:30. 2 Corinth. 1:22.

recognise the Seal and protect these souls from adversity stemming from Satan and his demons.[204] It is called *"Phylactery"* and *"Perfect"* because *"those who are baptised are Illuminated"* and being " *Illuminated they become sons by adoption"* and by " *becoming sons they are perfected and become immortal"*. However, *"the Baptism is a cross. For the old man was crucified together with Christ and was buried with Him through Baptism to death."*[205]

According to the ancient western Holy Fathers and ecclesiastic writers of the One united Orthodox Church, the Mystery of Baptism is called: *"sacramentum aquae," "fons sacer," "unda gentitalis," "aquavitalis," "sacramentum fidei," "sacramentum Trinitatis," "lavacrum regenerationis," "ablution peccatorum"* and *"sigillum."*[206]

St. Basil the Great characterised the Holy Mystery of Baptism as *"the bath of those in slavery, forgiveness of sins, death of sin, Regeneration of the soul, bright vestment, Seal without hands, vessel to Heaven, cause of the Kingdom, Gift of sonship."*[207]

St. Gregory of Nazianzus determined Baptism as *"the brightness of the souls, transmission of Life, help to our weakness, putting down of the flesh, the following of the Spirit, communion of the Word, restoration of the creature, the cataclysm of sin, light transformation, abolition of darkness, vessel to God, passing with Christ, support of faith, perfection of the mind, the keys of the Heavenly Kingdom, reward of life, refuting of slavery, freedom of bonds."*[208]

4. The Prototypes and Pre-figurations of Baptism

The Gifts and Charismata that are granted to man through the Holy Mystery of Baptism are many and are mentioned in Holy Scripture. Even the Prophets foresaw these Gifts and spoke of the

---

[204] Theophylactus of Bulgaria, *To 1 Peter 2:9,* in Migne, *P.G.,* 125, 1212. Aristeides, *Apology,* XX, 2 and 14, in *B,* v. 3, pp. 135 and 147. Rev. 1:6. St John Chrysostom, *To 2 Corinthians,* Homily 18, § 3, in Migne, *P.G.,* 61, 523. St Gregory of Nazianzus, *Homily 40 to HolyBaptism,* in Migne, *P.G.,* 36, 361-364. St Basil the Great, *To holy Baptism,* Homily 13, § 4, in Migne, *P.G.,* 31, 432.

[205] St John of Damascus, *Exposition. About faith and Baptism,* IV, 82, 9, in Migne, 94, 1121. Clement the Alexandrian, *Pedagogus,* I, 6, in *B,* v. 7, p. 92. St John Chrysostom, *To Hebrews,* 9, § 3, in Migne, *P.G.,* 63, 79.

[206] Bartmann, *Theologie Dogmatique,* v. II, p. 275.

[207] St Basil the Great, *To Holy Baptism,* Homily XIII, § 5, in Migne, *P.G.,* 31, 433.

[208] St Gregory of Nazianzus, *To holy Baptism,* Homily XL, § 3, in Migne, *P.G.,* 36, 361.

prototypes in the Old Testament. The Baptismal Rites through sprinkling with water or baths in the sea and rivers are evident even before the New Testament era, outside Christianity, not only amongst the Jews and Essenes, but even amongst the Gentiles such as the Babylonians, Indians, Egyptians, Romans, Greeks, etc. However, these purifications in the belief of all Greeks and barbarians concerned the necessity for moral catharsis, which physical cleanness and the washing of the body from its natural stains was always the visible sign.[209]

Tertullian[210] and St. Justin the Philosopher and Martyr[211] spoke of imitations and falsification of the Christian Sacraments by Satan. These external purifications were deprived of the power of the inner purification, which gave Life to the lifeless and were used as ways of magical and natural purification. Only in Judaism does one find that which is expressed in Psalm 50(51): *"Purge me with hyssop, and I shall be clean; wash me, and I shall be whiter than snow. Make me hear joy and gladness, that the bones You have broken may rejoice. Hide Your face from my sins, and blot out all my iniquities. Create in me a clean heart, O God, and renew a steadfast spirit within me."*[212]

The Prophets proclaimed repentance through washing on behalf of God's Name: *"Wash you, be clean; remove your iniquities from your souls before Mine eyes; cease from your iniquities; learn to do well; diligently seek judgment, deliver him that is suffering wrong, plead for the orphan, and obtain justice for the widow. And come let us reason together, said the Lord: and though your sins be as purple, I will make them white as snow; and though they be as scarlet, I will make them white as wool. And if you be willing, and hearken to Me, you shall eat the good of the land: but if you be not willing, nor hearken to Me, a sword shall devour you: for the mouth of the Lord has spoken this."*[213]

St. Justin the Philosopher and Martyr considered these admonitions to synchronise the washing of the body and inner cleanliness as prophetic announcements concerning Baptism, *"the*

---

[209] St Gregory of Nyssa, *To the day of Lights,* in Migne, *P.G.,* 46, 581.
[210] Tertullian, *De praescriptione haereticorum,* 40 and *De Baptismo,* 5, in migne, *P.L.,* 2, 66, 1312.
[211] St Justin the Philosopher and Martyr, *1 Apology,* 62, in **B**, v. 3, p. 195.
[212] Psalm 50(51):7-10.
[213] Is. 1:16-20.

only possible way to clean those who repent is the water of Life" "as it was proclaimed by Isaiah."[214]

In the Old Testament Greek (Septuagint, LXX) the Hebrew verb *"tabal"* is used to signify catharsis and washing as well as the verb *"to baptise."*[215] Through the mouth of Moses, speaking on behalf of God, these purifications, through water are determined as a means of purification according to Mosaic Law, which enable them to participate in public worship and communication with the people of God.[216] However, these purifications only *«had temporary purification of the body, but not the removal of sin."*[217] In later times the Baptism of proselytes was introduced as a way of bringing all those who were Gentiles into Judaism.

Pre-types of Christian Baptism were circumcision, the crossing of the Red Sea, the Salvation from the Cataclysm in Noah's Ark while the Baptism of St. John the Forerunner and Baptist was the preparation for Baptism in Christ

St. Paul observed that *"in Him you were also circumcised with the circumcision made without hands, by putting off the body of the sins of the flesh, by the circumcision of Christ, buried with Him in Baptism, in which you also were raised with Him through faith in the working of God, Who raised Him from the dead."*[218] *"All were baptised into Moses in the cloud and in the sea."*[219]

Upon the assurance of Moses to the people, the Red Sea was crossed and they were saved from the surrounding dangers. Likewise, we, being baptised in the water of the Baptismal Font and being buried in the depths of the waters, are freed from the imaginary of the slavery of Pharaoh. Moses *"baptised,"* although in simple and common water. Typically, this was, as Paul believed, *"the sea"* of the water of the Baptismal Font and *"the Cloud"* of the Holy Spirit Who Regenerates us. These were the symbols and the pre-figurations of Holy Baptism.[220]

---

[214] St Justin the Philosopher and Martyr, *Dialogue,* 14, § 1 and 44, § 4, in *B,* v. 3, pp. 220 and 247.

[215] 2 Kings (3 Kings) 5:14. Judith 12:7. Sirach 34:30.

[216] Lev. ch. 11-15. Num. ch. 19.

[217] St Gregory of Nazianzus, *To holy Baptism,* Homily 40, § 11, in Migne, *P.G.,* 36, 372.

[218] Col. 2:11-12.

[219] 1 Corinth. 10:2.

[220] St Gregory of Nazianzus, *To the holy Lights,* Homily 17, § 17, in Migne, *P.G.,* 36, 353.

The Holy Fathers refer to the Baptism of St. John the Forerunner and Baptist as a Judaic ceremony that was in use even before St. John's era but which was performed by him according to God's Commandment.[221] This is clearly evident from the words of the Lord Who, in order to soothe the reluctance of St. John, said: *"Permit it to be so now, for thus it is fitting for us to fulfil all righteousness."*[222] Whereas on the other hand, it is manifested from the question which He addressed to the Pharisees before His sufferings: *"The Baptism of John – was it from heaven or from men?"*[223]

Hence St. Gregory the Theologian of Nazianzus observed that *"John baptised not Judaically; for not only in water, but in repentance."*[224]

St. John Chrysostom observed that *"John was preaching Baptism of repentance"* but *"he does not say for the forgiveness of sins"* because the Sacrifice on the Cross *"was not yet offered neither had the Spirit descended, nor was sin forgiven, nor enmity wiped away, nor the curse abolished, so how could there be forgiveness?"* But what was the purpose of the Baptism of John? *"By preaching Baptism of repentance"* John *"was convincing"* those who approached him and received it *"to confess and repent of their sins, and by doing so would be easier to receive the forgiveness afterwards."* If in repentance they did not sincerely condemn themselves *"they could not have the Grace; by not requesting, they would not have the forgiveness"* when the Redeemer would offer it. So, St. John by baptising *"introduced a pedagogic Baptism by the washing in water of those who were polluted because of sin and through repentance teaching the higher and perfect things."*[225] Consequently, the Baptism of St. John *"prepared Christ's Baptism"* which was to be offered by the Lord to the faithful and which *"alone will have the Grace of the Spirit"*, whereas the Baptism of St. John *"lacked the Gift."* *"Jesus also baptised, but in the Spirit. This is the perfection."*[226]

St. Basil the Great characterised the two Baptisms as follows: that of John, which was an *"introductory Baptism"* and that of Jesus Christ which was *"conclusive,"* in other words *"the departure of sin."*

---

[221] John 1:33.
[222] Matth. 3:15.
[223] Mark 11:30. Matth. 21:25. Luke 20:4.
[224] St Gregory of Nazianzus, *To the holy Lights,* Homily 17, § 17, in Migne, *P.G.,* 36, 353.
[225] St John Chrysostom, *To Matthew,* Homily 10, §§ 1 and 2, in Minge, *P.G.,* 57, 185 and 186.
[226] Ibid, *To Mathew,* Homily 10, § 2 and 12, § 3, in Migne, *P.G.,* 57, 186 and 206.

"John preached Baptism of repentance; the Lord preached Baptism of adoption as sons."[227]

St. John continued to baptise after his witness that he gave at Christ's Baptism saying: *"Behold! The Lamb of God who takes away the sin of the world!"*[228] After the arrest and beheading of St. John by Herod, his disciples continued to baptise.[229] But this Baptism had fulfilled its purpose and ceased. St. John Chrysostom noted that *"what happened to the Passover, happened also to the Baptism."* Because, as the Lord eating the Passover with His Disciples, terminated it and *"gave a new beginning"* to the new Passover. Likewise, *"here again fulfilling the Judaic baptism together with that of the Church, He opened the doors."* When He instituted the Divine Mystery of the Eucharist *"He confirmed and fulfilled the Truth."*[230]

5. The Divine Institution and the Time of its Establishment

Although the Baptism of St. John was from Heaven, it was the shadow and preparation of the Baptism in the Spirit. Even St. John proclaimed: *"I indeed baptise you with water unto repentance, but He Who is coming after me is mightier than I, whose sandals I am not worthy to carry. He will baptise you with the Holy Spirit and fire."*[231]

There can be no doubt that the Baptism of the Orthodox Church was instituted by our Lord and Saviour Jesus Christ, the Son of God.[232] Taking into consideration the Commandment given to the Holy Apostles after the Lord's Ascension: *"Go therefore and make Disciples of all nations, baptising them in the Name of the Father and of the Son and of the Holy Spirit"*[233] as well as the assurance that *"he who believes and is baptised will be saved; but he who does not believe will be condemned"*[234] the Orthodox Baptism is the realisation of this Commandment.

Although no one doubted the fact that the Lord instituted the Holy Mystery of Baptism, questions arose concerning the time of its

---

[227] St Basil the Great, *To the Holy Baptism,* Homily 13, § 1, in Migne, *P.G.,* 31, 425.
[228] John 1:29.
[229] Acts 19:3.
[230] St John Chrysostom, *To Matthew,* Homily 12, § 3, in Minge, *P.G.,* 57, 206.
[231] Matth. 3:11. Luke 3:16.
[232] Mitsopoulos, *Themata,* pp. 306-307.
[233] Matth. 28:19.
[234] Mark 16:16.

institution. Some of the Holy Fathers expressed the opinion that it was at the time of Christ's Baptism in the river Jordan when, through His Baptism, He Sanctified the waters.[235] Others expressed the opinion that it was established at the discussion of Christ with Nicodemus when Christ proclaimed *"most assuredly, I say to you, unless one is born of water and the Spirit, he cannot enter the Kingdom of God."*[236]

The time of the establishment of the Holy Mystery of Baptism must be placed after the Resurrection when the Lord assured His Disciples that *"all authority has been given to Me in Heaven and on earth"*[237] and He commanded them to *"go therefore and make Disciples of all nations, baptising them in the Name of the Father and of the Son and of the Holy Spirit."*[238] The Holy Fathers of the Orthodox Church also supported the opinion that when the Lord had died on the Cross and was pierced by the soldier[239] there *"sprang out from His Holy and precious Side the Fountain of Forgiveness, the Water of Regeneration washing away sin and mortality"* and *" the Blood became the cause of the Drink of Life."* At that moment *"the beginning of the Sacraments took place"* *"and those who partake through water are Regenerated, through Blood and Flesh they are nourished."*[240]

The fact that our Lord and Saviour Jesus Christ, the Son of God, instituted the Holy Mystery of Baptism confirms its importance and the reason why the Holy Apostles and Disciples obeyed the instruction given by the Master. Truthfully, on the Day of Pentecost, when the people asked the Apostles: *"Men and brethren, what shall we do? Then Peter said to them, 'Repent, and let every one of you be baptised in the Name of Jesus Christ for the remission of sins; and you shall receive the Gift of the Holy Spirit."*[241] *"Then those who gladly*

---

[235] St John Chrysostom, *To Matthew,* Homily 12, § 2, in Minge, *P.G.,* 57, 205. Ibid, *Homily to the holy and saving Baptism of our Saviour Jesus Christ*, in Migne, *P.G.,* 49, 366. St Ambrosius, *In Luce,* c. II, 83, in migne, *P.L.,* 15, 1665. St Cyril of Jerusalem, *Catechesis,* III, 11, in Migne, *P.G.,* 33, 441. St John of Damascus, *Exposition. About faith and Baptism,* IV, 82, 9, in Migne, *P.G.,* 94, 1117. Theophilus of Antioch, *2 Autolycus,* § 16, in *B,* v. 5, p. 33.
[236] John 3:5. St John Chrysostom, *To John,* Homily 29, § 1, in Minge, *P.G.,* 59, 168.
[237] Matth. 28:19.
[238] Matth. 28:19.
[239] John 19:34.
[240] St John of Damascus, *Exposition. About faith and Baptism,* IV, 82, 9, in Migne, *P.G.,* 94, 1117.
[241] Acts 2:37-38.

received his words were baptised; and that day about three thousand souls were added to them."[242]   St Philip the deacon baptised in Samaria[243] as well as the eunuch of Ethiopia,[244]   while St. Paul and Silas baptised Lydia with all her household[245] as well as the Philippian Jailer *"with his entire household."*[246] Furthermore *"Crispus, the ruler of the synagogue "* and *"many Corinthians, hearing, believed and were baptised."*[247]   After his calling by the Lord on the road to Damascus St. Paul was baptised[248] and St. Peter baptised Cornelius together with his family.[249]

St. Paul in his Epistles related the Christian Baptism to the death and burial of the Lord proclaiming that *"as many of us as were baptised into Christ Jesus were baptised into His death"*[250] and that *"as many of you as were baptised into Christ have put on Christ."*[251] *"For by one Spirit we were all baptised into one body – whether Jews or Greeks, whether slaves or free"*[252] and *"in Him you were also circumcised with the circumcision made without hands, by putting off the body of the sins of the flesh, by the circumcision of Christ, buried with Him in Baptism."*[253]   St. Peter declared that *"there is also an antitype which now saves us – Baptism"*[254] as *"once the Divine longsuffering waited in the days of Noah, while the Ark was being prepared, in which a few, that is, eight souls, were saved through water."*[255]

The *Didache* noted: *"Now concerning Baptism, baptise as follows: after you have reviewed all these things, baptise 'in the Name of the Father and of the Son and of the Holy Spirit'*[256] *in running water. But if you have no running water, then baptise in some other water; and if you are not able in cold water, then do so in warm. But*

---

[242] Acts 2:41.
[243] Acts 8:12.
[244] Acts 8:27-38.
[245] Acts 16:14-15.
[246] Acts 16:25-34.
[247] Acts 18:8.
[248] Acts 9:18.
[249] Acts 10:1-48.
[250] Rom. 6:3.
[251] Rom. 3:27.
[252] 1 Corinth. 12:13.
[253] Col. 2:11-12.
[254] 1 Peter 3:21.
[255] 1 Peter 3:20.
[256] Matth. 28:19.

if you have neither, then pour water on the head three times 'in the Name of the Father and of the Son and of the Holy Spirit.' And before the Baptism, let the one baptising and the one who is to be baptised fast, as well as any others who are able. Also, you must instruct the one who is to be baptised too fast for one or two days beforehand."[257]

The Epistle of Barnabas noted that: "*there was river flowing on the right hand, and beautiful trees were rising from it, and whoever eats from them will live forever.'*[258] *By this he means that while we descend into the water laden with sins and dirt, we rise up bearing fruit in our heart and with fear and hope in Jesus in our spirits. 'And whoever eats from these will live forever' means this: whoever, He says, hears these things spoken and believes them will live forever.*"[259]

The Shepherd of Hermas also observed the following: "*The seal, therefore, is the water; so, they go down into the water dead and they come up alive. Thus, this seal was proclaimed to them as well, and they made use of it in order that they might enter the Kingdom of God.*"[260] "*Therefore they went down with them into the water, and came up again. But these went down alive and came up alive, whereas those who had previously fallen asleep went down dead and came up alive. So, they were made alive through them, and came to full knowledge of the name of the Son of God.*"[261]

St. Justin the Philosopher and Martyr declared that the Apostolic Tradition concerning Baptism continued.[262]

Thus, is it strongly proved that our Lord and Saviour Jesus Christ, the Son of God, is the Founder of Christian Baptism. Since the time of the Holy Apostles until this very day it continues to be officiated as the Mystery of Regeneration and the Renewal of souls. Through the Orthodox Christian Baptism the Holy Spirit is transmitted as the Gift of God regenerating all those who partake of it, assuring the adoption as sons and granting the Eternal Kingdom.

---

[257] *Didache,* 7, 1-4, in Lightfoot, *Apostolic Fathers,* p. 153.
[258] Ezek. 47:1-12.
[259] *Barnabas,* 11, 10-11, n Lightfoot, *Apostolic Fathers,* pp. 177-178.
[260] *Shepherd of Hermas,* Parable 9, 4, n Lightfoot, *Apostolic Fathers,* p. 276.
[261] Ibid, Parable 9, 6-7, n Lightfoot, *Apostolic Fathers,* p. 276.
[262] St Justin the Philosopher and Martyr, *1 Apology,* 61, in **B**, v. 3, p. 1

II.   THE PERCEPTIBLE SIGNS OF BAPTISM

The perceptible aspect of the Holy Mystery of Baptism is the thrice immersion and elevation of the body into and out of the water, accompanied by the invocation of the Name of the three Persons of the Holy Trinity. Thus, the use of water is required according to the Commandment of the Lord to activate and perfect the Baptism. This water receives the Power of Regeneration through the descent of the Holy Spirit Who bestows His Divine Grace upon it, for the water itself does not have this Power by nature. Thus, the Promise of our Lord and Saviour Jesus Christ, the Son of God, is fulfilled whereby He will baptise us *with water and the Holy Spirit."*

The thrice immersion and elevation of the Catechumen is also required, who is buried together with Christ and becomes of the same nature with Christ through the imitation of His death. Finally, the invocation of the Name of each Person of the Holy Trinity is required at each immersion, according to the instructions of the Master. The invocation is a confession of faith and acceptance of the teachings of Christ. This makes Baptism, a Baptism into Christ and the water is Sanctified through the calling of the Grace of the Holy Spirit. The thrice immersion and elevation in and out of the water symbolises, on the one hand, the three-day burial and Resurrection of the Son of God, while on the other hand symbolising the three Persons of the Holy Trinity. Due to the relationship between the Baptism of the Orthodox Church to the death, burial and Resurrection of our Lord and Saviour Jesus Christ, the Son of God, Baptism is performed once only and cannot be repeated. It is obvious that Baptism through sprinkling or pouring may be performed only due to great necessity and under exceptional conditions. Under no circumstances can the canonical way of Holy Baptism be replaced by the extraordinary ways of Baptism, having been instituted by the Founder and Master of the Orthodox Church, our Lord and Saviour Jesus Christ, the Son of God.

Finally, the type of invocation is Trinitarian, which is mentioned in the last chapter of the Holy Gospel according to St Matthew. The expressions mentioned in the New Testament such as *"the Baptism in the Name of Christ"* or *"in Christ Jesus"* or *"in Christ"* are not types of invocation but mean to be baptised according to the faith and teachings of Christ. Hence, it is obvious that any Baptism that is not performed with the invocation of the Names of the three Persons of the Holy Trinity is absolutely invalid and consequently must be repeated as it is not canonical.

1. The Use of Sanctified Water

The use of water[263] in Baptism was assigned by our Master Himself when He said to St Nicodemus: *"Most assuredly, I say to you, unless one is born of water and the Spirit, he cannot enter the Kingdom of God."*[264] This practice entered within the life of the Church, as witnessed in the case of the Baptism of the eunuch of Ethiopia by St Philip the deacon when *"they came to some water the eunuch said, 'See, here is water. What hinders me from being baptised?'"*[265] In the case of the Baptism of Cornelius, while St. Peter *"was still speaking these words"* he saw *"the Holy Spirit"* falling *"upon all those who heard the word"*[266] and he said: *"Can anyone forbid water, that these should not be baptised who have received the Holy Spirit?"*[267] St. Paul taught that the Church was Sanctified by the Lord cleansing *"her with the washing of water."*[268] *".Having our hearts sprinkled from an evil conscience and our bodies washed with pure water. Let us hold fast the confession of our hope."*[269]

The *Didache* instructs that Baptism should be done in living and *"running water"*[270] and in the case where there is *"no running water, then baptise in some other water; and if you are not able in cold water, then do so in warm. But if you have neither, then pour water on the head three times 'in the name of the Father and of the Son and of the Holy Spirit."*[271]

In the *Epistle of Barnabas* we read: *"Now concerning the water, it is written with reference to Israel that they would never accept the Baptism that brings forgiveness of sins, but would create a substitute for them."*[272] *"And: 'His water will never fail.*[273]*"*[274] *"Notice how he*

---

[263] Mitsopoulos, *Themata,* pp. 307-308. Georgopoulos, *Anthology,* p. 10.
[264] John 3:5. Cf. Evdokimov, *Orthodoxia,* pp. 371-372.
[265] Acts 8:36.
[266] Acts 10:44.
[267] Acts 10:47.
[268] Ephes. 5:26.
[269] Heb. 10:22-23.
[270] *Didache,* 7, 1 and 2, in Lightfoot, *Apostolic Fathers,* p. 153.
[271] Ibid, 7, 2-3, in Lightfoot, *Apostolic Fathers,* p. 153.
[272] *Barnabas,* 11, 1, in Lightfoot, *Apostolic Fathers,* p. 176.
[273] Cf. Is. 33:16-18.

pointed out the water and the cross together. For this is what he means: blessed are those who, having set their hope on the cross, descended into the water."[275] *"And there was a river flowing on the right hand, and beautiful trees were rising from it, and whoever eats from them will live forever.'*[276] *By this he means that while we descend into the water laden with sins and dirt, we rise up bearing fruit in our heart and with fear and hope in Jesus in our spirits. 'And whoever eats from these will live forever' means this: whoever, he says, hears these things spoken and believes them will live forever."*[277]

The *Shepherd of Hermas* also observed: *"The seal, therefore, is the water; so, they go down into the water dead and they come up alive."*[278]

St. Justin the Philosopher and Martyr assured the Apostolic Tradition of the use of water in Baptism. He informed us that the Catechumen were *"brought by us where there is water and are regenerated in the same way as we were regenerated."*[279]

Justifying the use of water in this Mysterious and Supernatural Ceremony, the Holy Fathers of the Orthodox Church explained that *"because we are accustomed to using water in order to clean the stain and dirt from the body and by submersing the body into the water it becomes clean, likewise in this Mystical act* (Baptism) *we receive the cleanliness from the filth of sin and through the perceptible the radiance of the bodiless is revealed."*[280] Because *"man is of two elements, soul and body" "and has visible and invisible nature, the cleansing through water and Spirit is double. The water is the visible and receives the body, the Holy Spirit Sanctifies the bodiless."*[281] *"Double is the cleansing: the bodiless through the bodiless, the body through the body. The water cleans the body whereas the Holy Spirit seals the soul regenerating 'in the image and likeness'*[282] *within us"*[283]

---

[274] *Barnabas,* 11, 5, in Lightfoot, *Apostolic Fathers,* p. 177.

[275] Ibid, 11, 8, in Lightfoot, *Apostolic Fathers,* p. 177.

[276] Cf. Ez. 47:1-12.

[277] *Barnabas,* 11, 10-11, in Lightfoot, *Apostolic Fathers,* pp. 177-178.

[278] *Shepherd of Hermas,* Parable 9, 16, 4, in Lightfoot, *Apostolic Fathers,* p. 276.

[279] St Justin the Philosopher and Martyr, *1 Apology,* 61, 3, in *B*, v. 3, p. 1

[280] St Gregory of Nyssa, *To the day of the Lights,* in Migne, *P.G.,* 46, 581.

[281] St John of Damascus, *Exposition. About faith and Baptism,* IV, 82, 9, in Migne, *P.G.,* 94, 1117.

[282] Gen 1:26.

[283] St Gregory of Nazianzus, *Homily* 40, § 11, in Migne, *P.G.,* 36, 372.

as the water *"through the Grace of the Spirit cleans the body from sin and frees it from mortality."*[284]

Also in modern testimonies we read that *"for Baptism the matter is the water"*[285] because *"the Holy Scriptures command to baptise in water."*[286] *"Even this must be preserved in Baptism, to be pure water, neither mixed with other things nor technical, nor other liquid but simple and natural water."*[287]

Obviously the *"water is nothing more than water"* which does not have the Supernatural Power in its own nature but receives it *"from the Grace which blesses from Above."* And as in ancient times *"the rod of Moses was out of common wood through which God wanted to perform the high and greater miracles"* and was *"changed into a serpent"* or *"was made into blood and separated the sea"* *"likewise one of the Prophets' mantles, although it was out of goat skin"* made Elisha a wonder worker and a great Prophet. *"All these were out of lifeless matter which received Divine Power to perform great Miracles."* Similarly, the water of Holy Baptism *"regenerates man into spiritual Regeneration."*[288] St. Basil concluded that *"if there is any Grace in the water, it is not from its nature, but because of the presence of the Holy Spirit."*[289] St. Cyprian believed that the water alone cannot Sanctify man if it does not have the Holy Spirit.[290]

From the teachings of the *Didache* and St. Justin the Philosopher and Martyr, one can conclude that the water which was used in Baptism was from a natural spring and did not require sanctification through prayer. This opinion was due to the belief that springs were Sanctified at the time of Christ's Baptism. [291] Consequently *"the simple water receives the power of sanctification"* and only *"the invocation of the Holy Spirit and of the Son and of the Father"* was necessary. The prayers and invocations for the descent of the Holy Spirit are essential to Sanctify the water. This we find in the

---

[284] St Cyril of Jerusalem, *Catechesis,* III, § 2, in Migne, *P.G.,* 33, 429.

[285] Jeremias, (A'), in Karmeris, *The dogmatics,* v. I, p. 388.

[286] Kritopoulos, ch. VII, in Karmeris, *The dogmatics,* v. II, p. 530.

[287] Mogilas, (A' 103), in Karmeris, *The dogmatics,* v. II, p. 636.

[288] St Gregory of Nyssa, *To the day of the Lights,* in Migne, *P.G.,* 46, 584.

[289] St Basil the Great, *About the Holy Spirit,* ch. 15, in Migne, *P.G.,* 32, 132.

[290] St Cyprian, *Epistola*74, § 5, in migne, *P.L.,* 3, 1178.

[291] St Cyril of Jerusalem, *Catechesis,* III, § 2, in Migne, *P.G.,* 33, 429. St John of Damascus, *Exposition. About faith and Baptism,* IV, 82, 9, in Migne, *P.G.,* 94, 1117. Tertullian, *De Baptismo,* 4, in migne, *P.L.,* 1, 1311.

ecclesiastical tradition even before the time of Tertullian[292] and St. Cyprian[293] who, in justifying this practice, refers to Ezekiel[294] according to which God promises to sprinkle the faithful with *"clean water."*[295] The same opinion is expressed by the Canons attributed to St Hippolytus.[296] In agreement with the above are the teachings of St. Ambrosius.[297]

According the above, water is an essential element for Baptism to be valid, since the Lord and the Apostolic Tradition commanded its use. St. Augustine asked: *"What is the Baptism of Christ? It is the washing with clean water and some invocation of words. If you remove the water, there is no Baptism; if you remove the words of invocation, and again there is no Baptism."*[298]

The Orthodox Church forbidden[299] the use of other liquid instead of water such as oil, sand, etc. [300] Also the opinion that Baptism is merely spiritual and internal and does not require to be performed in water was also condemned[301]. Mesoloras accepts the officiating of Baptism not only in water or in the oil of the oil-candles or by sand in the deserts, but also in the air by signing the infant with the sign of the cross and without any other element, but by simply through the invocation of the Divine Grace.[302] But again this opinion is not acceptable.

From the above one can understand that the ***"Baptism in the air"*** (Aerobaptism) is not considered to be completely canonical, but, if the infant survives it must be immersed and elevated in and out of the water according to the 51st Canon of Nicephorus of Constantinople. Also, the Holy Canons state that a man, who was baptised by the Baptism in the air or the clinical Baptism, cannot be ordained in priesthood, for his Baptism was by necessity[303] and not by his freewill.

---

[292] Tertullian, *De Baptismo,* 4 and 5, in migne, *P.L.,* 1, 1311 and 1313.
[293] St Cyprian, *Epistola*70, 1 and 3, in migne, *P.L.,* 3, 1077 and 1080.
[294] Ez. 36:24-29.
[295] Ez. 36:25.
[296] Canon 19, 112
[297] St Ambrosius, *De mysteriis,* III, 14, in migne, *P.L.,* 16, 410.
[298] St Augustine, *In Johannis evangelium. Tractatus* XV, 4, in migne, *P.L.,* 35, 1512.
[299] Trempelas, *Dogmatique,* v. III, p. 82. Cf. Ott, "Precis", p. 491.
[300] Moschus, *Leimon,* ch. 176, in Migne, *P.G.,* 87, 3014. Nicephorus, *Church History,* book 3, 27, in Migne, *P.G.,* 145, 973.
[301] Dyobouniotes, *The Mysteries,* p. 52.
[302] Mesoloras, *Symbolique,* II, p. 201.
[303] Synod of Neoceasaria, Canon 12.

2. The Three Immersions and Elevations Into & Out of the Water

The ancient practice of Baptism was always by three immersions and elevations into and out of the water.[304] This practice is not only implied by the Greek verb "*βαπτίζω*" ("*to baptise* ") which means to be immersed completely into the water but it is also witnessed by the Baptism of St. John, the Forerunner and Baptist, who "*was baptising in Aenon near Salim, because there was much water there*"[305] and when Jesus "*had been baptised He came up immediately from the water.*"[306] In the case of the Baptism of the eunuch of Ethiopia " *both Philip and the eunuch went down into the water*" and then "*they came up out of the water.*"[307] The full immersion into the water is required because it symbolises the crucifixion of the one who is baptised and his burial together with Jesus Christ, becoming "*of the same nature of the likeness of His death*"[308] and being "*buried with Him in Baptism.*"[309] In other words, we "*imitate the burial of Christ through Baptism. For the bodies of those who are baptised are buried*" and "*the water offers the image of death, as the tomb receives the body.*"[310] And the "*Leader of our life*" Christ's "*death was underground and became the common nature, the imitation of death is printed in the neighbouring matter*" that is in the water.[311] St. John Chrysostom observed that "*in the water are performed Divine symbols, tomb and death and resurrection and life, and all these are done together. As like in some tomb through water the old man is immersed and is buried and being immersed, he is completely hidden; then coming up the new is elevated. For, as it is easy for us to be baptised and to be raised, likewise it is easy for God to bury the old man and to raise the new.*"[312]

This immersion into the water is done three times and although is true that in the New Testament, right from the beginning, we do not have any proof of the thrice immersion into water, we do have the

---

[304] Mitsopoulos, *Themata,* p. 308.
[305] John 3:23.
[306] Matth. 3:16. Mark 1:10.
[307] Acts 8:38, 39.
[308] Rom. 6:5.
[309] Col. 2:12.
[310] St Basil the Great, *About the Holy Spirit,* ch. 15, in Migne, *P.G.,* 32, 129.
[311] St Gregory of Nyssa, *Catechesis,* ch. 35, in Migne, *P.G.,* 45, 88.
[312] St John Chrysostom, *To John,* Homily 25, § 2, in Migne, *P.G.,* 59, 151.

testimonies of Tertullian[313] and the *Didache*.[314] The 50th Canon of the Holy Apostles states that *"if any bishop or presbyter does not baptise thrice, but once, let him be deposed."*[315]

This thrice immersion into water, according to Tertullian, was performed in honour of the Holy Trinity.[316] St. John Chrysostom observed that *"thrice this (immersion and elevation) is performed, in order that you may learn that the Power of the Father and of the Son and of the Holy Spirit is fulfilling."* For this reason, it is understandable why in each immersion we call upon the Name of each Person of the Holy Trinity.[317] According to other Fathers, the thrice immersion and elevation signifies *"through symbol the three-day burial of Christ. For, as our Saviour remained three days and three nights in the earth, likewise"*[318] those who are baptised imitate through the thrice immersion this three day burial *"and the three days burial of the Master signifies the Baptism through the three immersions."*[319] *"And as He, the Man from Above"* our Lord from Heaven *"after the earthly position"* and *".three days burial, was raised again to life"* likewise everyone who is baptised to His death *"instead of the earth is poured with water and vested with the element three times* (imitating) *the three day Resurrection."*[320] St. Basil the Great observed that *"in the three immersions and the equal invocations, the great Mystery of Baptism is perfected, in order that the type of death be imprinted and the deliverance of the knowing of God be given to those souls who are being baptised."*[321]

---

[313] Tertullian, *Adversus Praxeam, 26,* in migne, *P.L., 2,* 213. Ibid, *De coron. militiae,* 3, in migne, *P.L., 2,* 98.

[314] *Didache,* 7, 2-3, in Lightfoot, *Apostolic Fathers,* p. 153.

[315] 50th Canon of the Holy Apostles. , Pedalion, p.81-91

[316] Tertullian, *Adversus Praxeam, 26,* in migne, *P.L., 2,* 213.

[317] St John Chrysostom, *To John,* Homily 25, § 2, in Migne, *P.G., 59,* 151.

[318] St Cyril of Jerusalem, *Catechesis Mystagogy,* II, § 4, in Migne, *P.G., 33,* 1080.

[319] St John of Damascus, *Exposition. About faith and Baptism,* IV, 82, 9, in Migne, *P.G., 94,* 1117.

[320] St Gregory of Nyssa, *Catechesis,* ch. 35, in Migne, *P.G., 45,* 88.

[321] St Basil the Great, *About the Holy Spirit,* ch. 15, in Migne, *P.G., 32,* 132. Cf. Jeremias, Answer II, § 4; Kritopoulos, ch. 7; Mogilas, A' 103, in Karmeris, *The dogmatics,* v. II, pp. 459, 530 and 636. Callistus I, Patriarch of Constantinople, in Miclosich, *Acta,* v. I, p. 439.

3. One Baptism, Not Repeatable

The teachings of the Orthodox Church are based upon this relationship between Baptism and the death, the burial and the Resurrection of our Lord and Saviour Jesus Christ, the Son of God. In addition, the Baptism is performed once only and under no circumstances, as long as it is canonical Baptism, can it be repeated. In the New Testament it is clearly proclaimed that there is only *"one Lord, one faith, one Baptism."*[322]

There is only one Lord Who was crucified for us and was buried and was raised. Hence *"we know the saving Baptism; because one is the death for the entire world and one is the resurrection of the dead, of which the type is the Baptism."*[323] *"The Baptism is also a cross. Our old man was crucified together and we became in the likeness of the death of Christ and we were buried together with Christ through Baptism. As Christ died on the cross, likewise we die in Baptism, not in flesh, but to sin. See death and death; He died in flesh; we die to sin."*[324]

Precisely for this reason, as well as the death of Christ, Baptism became important since the one death of Christ and His one Sacrifice was more than sufficient to perfect those who are Sanctified. Being one it must remain one. *"Those who are initiated* (and who) *attempt to be baptised for the second time re-crucify the Lord, killing Him twice, mocking the Divine, scoffing at the Holy, blaspheming the Holy Spirit and dishonouring the Sacred Blood as* (though it were) *common."*[325]

Truthfully, since we accept that the death of Christ was offered as a Sacrifice once and for all, *"one offering perfecting through the Lord those who are Sanctified for ever"* we must accept that Baptism, which draws its Power from the death of Christ, since it is officiated canonically, is absolutely and under no circumstances repeatable. *"For, as Christ suffered once, likewise we cannot have communion with His sufferings but only once and alone."*[326] *"As Christ cannot be*

---

[322] Ephes. 4:5.
[323] St Basil the Great, *About the Holy Spirit,* ch. 15, in Migne, *P.G.,* 32, 129.
[324] St John Chrysostom, *To Hebrew,* Homily 9, § 3, in Migne, *P.G.,* 63, 79.
[325] *Apostolic Orders,* VI, 15, 4, in *B,* v. 2, p. 104.
[326] Theodoretus of Cyrus, *To Hebrews,* 6:6, in Migne, *P.G.,* 82, 717.

crucified twice (for this is the example to him) likewise neither (are we) *to be baptised* (twice)."[327]

Undoubtedly, those who do not accept one canonical Baptism cleansing and regenerating them only once, are under the blasphemous belief that it is not enough to partake in the death of Christ, having been (spiritually) crucified together with Him. Their faith in Holy Baptism and its sacred benefits appears to be erroneous because of their indirect disbelief in the Power of the death of Christ on the Cross.

4. Baptism by Sprinkling and Pouring

The practice of the Roman Catholic Church, whereby she replaced the three immersions and elevations in and out of the water and the generalisation of Baptism by sprinkling or pouring, was known in the ancient Church as it is mentioned in the *Didache*[328] although it was only practiced in extraordinary circumstances, especially upon the bed-ridden or extremely ill, when it was impossible for them to be immersed into water. This is the Baptism of the ill (*"Baptismus clinicorum"*). However, the fact that Baptism by immersion and elevation was canonical, is witnessed by the many Baptismal fonts that are preserved in Italy and generally in Western Europe.

But, even in the West, Baptism by sprinkling or pouring was considered doubtful as evident from the specific writings of St. Cyprian.[329] In the East, Baptism by pouring or clinical Baptism was recognised although those who received such Baptism were forbidden from entering into Priesthood.[330]

5. The Only Canonical and Valuable Type of Invocation

The type of invocation during Baptism is according to the Gospel of St Matthew [331] whereby *"the words of Christ to baptise in the Name*

---

[327] St John Chrysostom, *To Hebrew,* Homily 9, § 3, in Migne, *P.G.,* 63, 79.

[328] *Didache*, 7, 3, in Lightfoot, *Apostolic Fathers,* p. 153.

[329] St Cyprian, *Epistola*76, 12-13, in migne, *P.L.,* 3, 1195-1196.

[330] Synod of Neoceasasria, Canon 12. Pope Cornelius, *Epistle to Photius bishop of Antioch,* in Eusebius, *Church History,* VI, 43, 14, in Migne, *P.G.,* 20, 621.

[331] Matth. 28:19. Cf. Plato of Moscow, *Orthodox Teaching,* pp. 146-147. Dositheus of Jerusalem, *Confession,* ch. 16, p. 39. Mitsopoulos, *Themata,* p. 308.

of the Father and of the Son and of the Holy Spirit" were obeyed while *"all those who were not baptised in the Holy Trinity must be re-baptised."*[332]

St. Athanasius of Alexandria stated that *"he who misappropriates something from the Holy Trinity and is baptised only in the Name of the Father or only in the Name of the Son or without the Holy Spirit but only in the Father and the Son, does not receive anything, but remains empty and imperfect. For the perfection is achieved only in the Holy Trinity".*[333]

Truly from the beginning, the words of Christ were the type of invocation, which He introduced after His Resurrection, as witnessed in the Didache and which literally states *"to baptise 'in the Name of the Father and of the Son and of the Holy Spirit."*[334]

St. Justin the Philosopher and Martyr confirmed that *"in the Name of the Father of all and the despot God and of our Saviour Jesus Christ and of the Holy Spirit perform the washing in water."*[335]

Tertullian with regard to this Trinitarian type of invocation during Baptism, reminded us that this was introduced by the Lord Himself Who instructed His disciples in the Law of Baptising in water and the type,[336] clearly setting forth the manner of invocation.[337]

St. Cyprian declared that Baptism which is performed only in the Name of our Lord Jesus is insufficient because Christ Himself instructed that the nations be baptised in the full and united Trinity.[338]

Origen recognised the only legal Baptism, which is performed in the Name of the Holy Trinity.[339]

The *Apostolic Orders* reminds us that *"our Lord instructed us, saying: 'Make disciples of all nations and then instructed to baptise them in the Name of Father and of the Son and of the Holy Spirit."*[340] Elsewhere the faithful are urged to receive *"not the Baptism of the*

---

[332] St John of Damascus, *Exposition. About faith and Baptism,* IV, 82, 9, in Migne, *P.G.,* 94, 1117.
[333] St Athanasius the Great, *To Serapion,* Epistle I, § 30, in Migne, *P.G.,* 26, 597.
[334] *Didache*, 7, 1, in Lightfoot, *Apostolic Fathers,* p. 153.
[335] St Justin the Philosopher and Martyr, *1 Apology,* 61, 3, in *B*, v. 3, p. 194.
[336] Tertullian, *De Baptismo,* XIII, in migne, *P.L.,* 1, 1323.
[337] Ibid, *Adversus Praxeam,* XXVI, in migne, *P.L.,* 2, 213.
[338] St Cyprian, *Epistola*LXXIII, 18, in migne, *P.L.,* 3, 1166.
[339] Origen, *To Romans,* 5, 8, in Migne, *P.G.,* 14, 1039. Ibid, *To John,* 6, 17, in Migne, *P.G.,* 14, 257.
[340] *Apostolic Orders*, VII, 40, 3, in *B*, v. 2, p. 134.

heretics, but that which is given by the faultless priests in the Name of Father and of the Son and of the Holy Spirit."[341]

Thus, this type of Trinitarian invocation in Baptism appears to be continuous and unbroken since the time of the writers of the *Apostolic Fathers* (*Didache*) until the 4th century. Thereafter it was continued by the Holy Fathers to this very day.

In the New Testament it is mentioned variously that Baptism was performed "*in the Name of Jesus Christ*"[342] "*in the Name of the Lord Jesus*"[343] "*in the Name of the Lord*"[344] "*into Christ Jesus*"[345] or "*into Christ.*"[346] Nonetheless, St. John of Damascus correctly observed that "*the Baptism in Christ manifests to baptise those who believe in Him for if the Divine Apostle says that in Christ and in His death we were baptised, then the invocation should not be done as it is, but that the type of Christ's death is the Baptism.*"[347]

Consequently, to be baptised in the Name of the Lord Jesus or in Christ Jesus does not mean that the Baptism was bestowed on the invocation of our Lord's Name alone but that this was according to the order and full acceptance of Jesus Christ's Teachings and upon the faith of those who believed in Him.

According to the *Didache,* Baptism was characterised as "*into the Name of the Lord*"[348] having been performed according to the description in the 7th chapter that literally commanded it be done upon the invocation of the Name of three Persons of the Deity.[349] Besides that, as we have mentioned before, a bishop or a priest who baptises only in "*one Baptism, that which is given to the death of the Lord*" is accursed by the 50th Canon of the Holy Apostles.[350]

St. Irenaeus commented that in the Name of Christ, the whole Trinity is understood to be included: He Who is anointed and He Who was anointed and He through Whom He was anointed. While the Father anointed, the Son was anointed in the Spirit Who is the

---

[341] Ibid, VI, 15, 1, in **B**, v. 2, p. 104.
[342] Acts 2:38.
[343] Acts 8:16; 19:5.
[344] Acts 10:48.
[345] Rom. 6:3.
[346] Gal. 3:27.
[347] St John of Damascus, *Exposition. About faith and Baptism,* IV, 82, 9, in Migne, *P.G.,* 94, 1117.
[348] *Didache,* 9, 5, in Lightfoot, *Apostolic Fathers,* p. 154.
[349] Ibid, 7, 1 and 3, in Lightfoot, *Apostolic Fathers,* p. 153.
[350] *Pedalion,* p.81

Anointment.[351] This was also the proclamation of St. Ambrosius of Mediolan (Milan), according to whom, he who names only one Name declares the entire Trinity.[352] However, these opinions do not necessarily imply that Baptism could be canonically celebrated with the invocation of the Name of Christ alone, as St. Irenaeus bore witness to the fact that at the time of Baptism the invocation is done in the Names of the three Persons of the Holy Trinity.[353]

St. Basil the Great supported the opinion that the Name of Christ is simultaneously a confession of the entire Deity because it implies, at the same time, the Father Who anointed and the Son Who was anointed and the Holy Spirit through Whom He was anointed. Furthermore, Baptism should not be bestowed upon the invocation of the Name of Christ alone but in the Names of the three Persons of the Holy Trinity.[354]

St. Cyril of Alexandria wrote: *"We have been baptised truly in the Name of the Father and of the Son and of the Holy Spirit. If you shall say that we were baptised in Christ, you are not out of the truth."* In other words, St. Cyril verified that the term *"in the Baptism of Christ"* means the calling upon Baptism in the Names of the Holy Trinity. Explaining this he concluded that *"because in the Father is the Son, in the Son the Father, really in both the Holy Spirit, because of the sameness of the essence, and even if someone names by power the theorems, he made the implication of all."*[355]

Taking into consideration that the type of Trinitarian invocation is absolutely vital for the validity of Baptism, it is understandable that *"anyone who was not baptised in the Name of the Holy Trinity must be re-baptised."*[356] A Baptism that was not performed in the Name of the Holy Trinity is absolutely invalid and cannot be accepted even through the *Economia* of the Church. *"The invocation of the Name of the Holy Trinity is the necessary treaty."*[357]

---

[351] St Irenaeus, *Heresies,* book III, ch. 18, § 3, in Migne, *P.G.,* 7, 934. Cf. Ibid, in Hadjephraimides, p. 240.

[352] St Ambrosius, *De Spiritus Sanctus,* I, 44, in Tixeront, *Histoire,* v. II, p. 113.

[353] St Irenaeus, *Heresies,* book III, ch. 17, § 1, in Migne, *P.G.,* 7, 929. Cf. Ibid, in Hadjephraimides, p. 237.

[354] St Basil the Great, *About the Holy Spirit,* XXII, § 28, in Migne, *P.G.,* 32, 116.

[355] St Cyril of Alexandria, *To Romans,* in Migne, *P.G.,* 74, 792.

[356] St John of Damascus, *Exposition. About faith and Baptism,* IV, 82, 9, in Migne, *P.G.,* 94, 1117.

[357] Androutsos, *Dogatique,* p. 333.

III. THE SUPERNATURAL RESULTS OF BAPTISM AND ITS NECESSITY

Accordingly, the Regeneration of man *"by water and the Spirit"*is the assurance in Baptism of the Lord[358] that takes place.[359] Without this Regeneration or Rebirth no one can enter the Kingdom of Heaven.[360] Hence, the Holy Apostles referred to Holy Baptism as *"the washing of regeneration and renewing of the Holy Spirit."*[361] The negative attributes of Regeneration are exalted such as the forgiveness of sins, the justification and the release from the punishments of sins while the positive aspect is exalted whereby those who are baptised vest (puts on) Christ in the Newness of Life with Him, having been raised together, becoming sons by adoption[362] and joint heirs with Christ.[363]

To this teaching of Holy Scripture, all Holy Fathers are in full agreement, clarifying to better the internal and pure spiritual and mysterious side of Baptism and the recreation of the old man who is reformed within the Holy Baptismal fount to the new man in Christ.

But, if these are the Supernatural results of Baptism in Christ, then one can understand its importance and necessity according to the words of Christ Who clearly stated that if one is not born from water and the Spirit, it is impossible to be Saved.[364] Baptism is the only entrance through which one enters the Path of Salvation.

1. Negative and Positive Results of Baptism

Our Lord and Saviour Jesus Christ, the Son of God, described the Saving results of Baptism with few words, characterising them as *"Rebirth from Above"* which guaranteed one's entrance into the Kingdom of God.[365] This means spiritual Rebirth, Regeneration and Newness of Life through Baptism. The Rebirth from Above is a Heavenly and Supernatural action of the Grace of God that occurs in

---

[358] John 3:5.
[359] Labadarios, *Sermons,* v.1, pp. 105-106.
[360] Cf. John 3:3.
[361] Tit. 3:5.
[362] Cf. Rom. 8:15, 23. Gal. 4:5. Ephes. 1:5.
[363] Cf. Rom. 8:17. Gal. 3:29; 4:7. Tit. 3:7. James 2:5. Cf. Damalas, *Catechesis,* pp. 83-84.
[364] Cf. John 3:3, 5, 7.
[365] Cf. John 3:3.

the soul of the one who is being baptised. Through the words *"unless one is born again"*[366] Christ verified that through Holy Baptism the old sinful way of life is banished and the renewal of the old man transpires through his Regeneration, simultaneously introducing him to the Newness of Life in Christ.[367] In other words Regeneration in Christ that happens only through Baptism, appears as the putting to death of the old man according to its negative aspect. Consequently, it is the forgiveness of sins[368] and Justification[369] as well as being freedom from the punishments of sin, while, according to its positive aspect, it is Sanctification,[370] adoption as sons[371] and the Newness of Life[372] that springs up from our incorporation into Christ.

Thus, St. Peter, when he addressed people who were under the great sin of having contributed to Christ's crucifixion, naturally exalted the negative effects of Holy Baptism by exhorting them *"repent, and let every one of you be baptised in the Name of Jesus Christ for the remission of sins."* In addition, by means of saying *"and you shall receive the Gift of the Holy Spirit"* he reassured them by implying the positive side of Baptism.[373]

St. Paul stressed the negative results of Baptism by connecting Baptism to the death of Christ on the Cross. He presented it as symbolising the participation of the one who is being baptised to the death of Christ and who is buried together with Him through Baptism: *" do you not know that as many of us as were baptised into Christ Jesus were baptised into His death? Therefore, we were buried with Him through Baptism into death, that just as Christ was raised from the dead by the glory of the Father, even so we also should walk in Newness of Life. For if we have been united together in the likeness of His death, certainly we also shall be in the likeness of His Resurrection, knowing this, that our old man was crucified with Him, that the body of sin might be done away with, that we should no longer be slaves of sin."*[374] When he again proclaimed that the Lord *"saved us, through the washing of regeneration and renewing of the*

---

[366] John 3:3, 7.
[367] Cf. Rom. 6:4; 7:6.
[368] Cf. Acts 10:43; 13:38; 26:18. Eph. 1:7. Col. 1:14.
[369] Cf. Acts 13:39. Rom. 3:24; 8:30, 33. 1 Corinth. 6:11. Gal. 2:16-17; 3:8, 24. Tit. 3:7.
[370] Cf. 1 Corinth. 6:11. 2 Tim. 2:21. Heb. 2:11.
[371] Cf. Rom. 8:15, 23. Gal. 4:5. Eph. 1:5.
[372] Cf. Rom. 6:4; 7:6.
[373] Acts 2:38.
[374] Rom. 6:3-6.

Holy Spirit"[375] he stressed the positive results of the Holy Mystery of Baptism. Furthermore, both results are manifested in his Epistle to the Corinthians, when he wrote: " *you were washed, you were sanctified, you were justified in the name of the Lord Jesus and by the Spirit of God.*"[376] And in his letter to the Ephesians, referring to the Church he emphasised: "*Christ also loved the Church and gave Himself for her, that He might Sanctify and cleanse her with the washing of water by the Word.*"[377] When he declared that "*as many of you as were baptised into Christ have put on Christ*"[378] he added "*you are all in one in Christ Jesus.*"[379] He presented the new form and image, which those who are baptised through the washing of Regeneration receive, being vested with "*the new man which was created according to God, in true righteousness and holiness*"[380] and he concluded: "*Therefore you are no longer a slave but a son, and if a son, then an heir of God through Christ.*"[381]

2. The Supernatural Results of Baptism

The teachings of the Holy Fathers of the Orthodox Church are in agreement with the teachings of Holy Scripture concerning Baptism. Thus, amongst the Apostolic Fathers in the *Shepherd of Hermas,* we read that those who were to be baptised went "*down into the water dead and came up alive.*"[382] Likewise in the Epistle of Barnabas, it is assured that "*while we descend into the water laden with sins and dirt, we rise up bearing fruit in our heart and with fear and hope in Jesus in our spirits.*"[383]

Amongst the Apologists, St. Justin the Philosopher and Martyr characterised Baptism as "*the only means which can clean those who repent.*"[384] It is "*the water of Life*" in which those who are baptised are "*Regenerated,*" having been "*washed for the forgiveness of sins*

---

[375] Tit. 3:5.
[376] 1 Corinth. 6:11.
[377] Ephes. 5:25-26.
[378] Gal. 3:27.
[379] Gal. 3:28.
[380] Ephes. 4:24.
[381] Gal. 4:7.
[382] *Shepherd of Hermas, Parable* 9, 4, in Lightfoot, *Apostolic Fathers,* p. 276.
[383] *The Epistle of Barnabas*, 11, 11, in Lightfoot, *Apostolic Fathers,* p. 178.
[384] St Justin the Philosopher and Martyr, *Dialogue,* 14, § 1, in *B*, v. 3, p. 220.

through the bath which was spoken of by Isaiah"[385] and which is the only "*path, through which the forgiveness of our sins is accomplished and the hope of the inheritance of the good things which were promised.*"[386]

Theophilus of Antioch considered that at the beginning of Creation God gave the blessing to the waters from which the animals came as a Sign of the "*forgiveness of sins*" and the washing of Regeneration, which men were to receive "*being Regenerated*" in the waters of Baptism "*and receiving the Blessing from God.*"[387]

Tertullian proclaimed, "*Oh blessed Mystery of our water, through which our sins are washed away and from our previous deafness we are freed in the Eternal Life.*"[388] According to Leeming, Tertullian's teachings of Baptism clearly assert that:

1) the Holy Mystery of Baptism is marvellous, manifesting the Power of God

2) the Holy Spirit Sanctifies the waters and grants the Power to accomplish its purpose

3) the Baptism can be compared to the fountain of Bethesda, restoring man "*in the likeness*"[389] of God, in which condition he was originally created

4) the Baptism of St. John did not forgive the sins but only gave the reason for repentance, whereas the Baptism of Christ gives true forgiveness and Sanctification.[390]

St. Cyprian, in addition, observed that Baptism cleans sins and Sanctifies man not because of its nature but because it has the Holy Spirit.[391]

Clement the Alexandrian stated that "*being baptised, we are Enlightened, being Enlightened we become sons, becoming sons we are Perfected, being Perfected we become Immortal.*"[392]

---

[385] Ibid, *1 Apology*, 61, § 3, in **B**, v. 3, p. 194.

[386] Ibid, *Dialogue*, 44, § 4, in **B**, v. 3, p. 247.

[387] Theophilus of Antioch, *2 Autolycus*, 16, in **B**, v. 5, p. 33.

[388] Tertullian, *De Baptismo*, 1, 4, in migne, *P.L.*, 1, 1197.

[389] Gen. 1:26.

[390] Leeming, *Principles*, p. 45.

[391] St Cyprian, *Epistola*74, § 5, in migne, *P.L.*, 3, 1178.

[392] Clement the Alexandrian, *Pedagogus*, I, 6, in **B**, v. 7, p. 92. Origen, *To John*, VI, 7, in Migne, *P.G.*, 14, 225.

St. Cyril of Jerusalem, expanding on the opinion expressed by Hermas, commented that *"he comes down in the water dressed with sins, but the invocation of the Grace seals the soul allowing it not to be devoured by the frightful dragon. He came down dead in sins but is made alive in righteousness and in some way, he was buried in the water, as Jesus was in the tomb Who took up the universal sins, and was raised* (and) *walks again in the Newness of Life."* *"And in the same* (water) *you die and are reborn; and that saving water became for us tomb and mother"*.[393]

St. Basil the Great determined the two goals of Baptism:

1)   to cease *"the body of sin in order not to be fruitful in death"*
2)   to live according *"to the Spirit and to have the fruit in holiness"*

Furthermore, he observed that *"the water gives the image of death, as the body is surrendered to the burial"* while the Holy Spirit is *" the Life-giving Power"* that Regenerates *" the souls from the deadness of sin to the beginning of Life."*[394] Thus he who is baptised *"is Regenerated without being digested; he is reformed without being crushed, he is healed without feeling pain"* and *"without a mother he is reborn and the old man perishes according to the desires of deceit and relives and becomes a new true flower of youth."*[395]

St. Gregory of Nyssa expressed the belief that in Baptism *"through the presence of the Divine Power, it changes him to immortality who became mortal in nature."* Thus, *"the birth from Above becomes the Recreation of man."*[396]

St. Gregory the Theologian of Nazianzus pointed out that this Divine Bath is called *"the Baptism as burying sin in the water."* Thus Baptism *"becomes a helper to the first birth, working new instead of old and Divine instead of the beings, without fire refining and*

---

[393] St Cyril of Jerusalem, *Catechesis,* III, § 9; and *Catechesis Mystagogy,* II, § 4, in Migne, *P.G.,* 33, 444 and 1080.

[394] St Basil the Great, *About the Holy Spirit,* ch. 15, in Migne, *P.G.,* 32, 129.

[395] Ibid, *Homily* 13, *To the holy Baptism,* §§ 3, 5, in Migne, *P.G.,* 31, 429 and 433.

[396] St Gregory of Nyssa, *To the day of Lights,* in Migne, *P.G.,* 46, 580 and 584. Ibid, *Catechesis,* ch. 33 and ch. 40, in Migne, *P.G.,* 45, 84 and 101. Ibid, *To the Epitaphius,* 7, in Migne, P.G., *46, 793.*

recreating without crushing." Through this "*change*" "*all the old characters are changed in the one form of Christ.*"[397]

St. John Chrysostom addressed the question of why, since Baptism frees us from all our sins, is it not called "*the washing of the forgiveness of sins*" rather than "*the washing of Regeneration.*" He explained that it is indeed the washing of Regeneration "*not simply because it removes the offences, but it creates and makes us from Above, not forming us again from the earth*" as once God made the body of Adam out of dust "*but creating us from the element of the water's nature.*" Therefore, it is the washing of Regeneration because "*it does not clean the vessel, but refines it once again completely.*"[398]

3. Total Change in Baptism

According to the forementioned, the Regeneration of Baptism consists of a deep and total change in human nature. It is a new birth that removes the relics of sin which are put to death in the Sanctified water.[399] What remains is the desire to sin or "*concupiscentia,*" a sensitive condition in which the one who is baptised is like an invalid recovering from a long period of sickness or like the weakness of a new born infant in Christ, not having anything polluted in him, but going from strength to strength and slowly progressing.[400] This condition does not carry the guilt of ancestral sin, but consists of the reason for cultivating virtues and simultaneously being strengthened by Divine Grace.

Because of this total change that Regenerates inner man, Baptism once received canonically, can never be repeated. As one is physically born only once and undergoes physical changes throughout his entire life, likewise and even more so, the Rebirth and Regeneration by the Holy Spirit occurs only once. It is a blasphemy against the Holy Spirit should one doubt the perfect and complete

---

[397] St Gregory of Nazianzus, *Homily* 40 *to holy Baptism*, §§ 4, 7, 8 and 47, in Migne, *P.G., 36*, 364, 368 and 397.

[398] St John Chrysostom, *Catechesis,* I, § 3, in Migne, *P.G., 49,* 227. Ibid, *To Isaiah,* book A', Homily II, in Migne, *P.G., 70,* 96. Ibid, *About the "in the spirit and truth",* in Migne, *P.G., 68,* 752. Ibid, *To John,* book II, in Migne, *P.G., 59,* 245. Ibid, *About the "in the spirit and truth",* in Migne, 68, 273.

[399] St Symeon, *Euriskomena,* Homily LI, pp. 255-258.

[400] Cf. Kritopoulos, ch. VIII, in Karmeris, *The dogmatics,* v. II, p. 531. Jeremias, B', 4, in Karmeris, *The dogmatics,* v. II, p. 459. Dositheus of Jerusalem, *Confession,* ch. 16, p. 31.

recreation given to us through our Baptism by seeking a second and more perfect Baptism.

Moreover, since we are Regenerated and recreated in Baptism, it has an indelible and thus irreplaceable nature characterising Holy Baptism as a permanent *"Seal"* through which *"the Stamp of the Lord is assigned"* upon the one who is baptised. *"The Light of the Lord's Face"* is bestowed upon one through which one is recognised as belonging to Christ. If anyone does not have this Seal, *"how can the Angel fight for him? How can he be detached from the enemies, if the Seal is not recognised? How can he say that 'I am God's,' not having the characteristics?"* However, should one manage *"to seal his soul and body with the anointment and the Spirit as Israel once sealed their homes with the blood of the animal and saved their firstborn, he will be without fear. For as a sealed sheep he will not be attacked easily, and the thieves do not see him as an easy prey."* This Seal remains *"alive for the security even after the departure (from this life). It is as a bright vestment, more honourable than gold and greater than a majestic tomb."*[401]

4.   The Necessity of Baptism

The necessity of Baptism[402] was accentuated by our Lord and Saviour Jesus Christ, the Son of God, Who guaranteed that it is impossible for those who are not Regenerated through Baptism and have not participated in the saving change and recreation, to enter the Kingdom of God. *"Most assuredly, I say to you, unless one is born again, he cannot see the Kingdom of God."*[403] *"He who believes and is baptised will be saved; but he who does not believe will be condemned."*[404]

Dositheus of Jerusalem accurately verified that *"the Holy Baptism, which was ordered by the Lord, and performed in the Name of the Holy Trinity, is one of great importance. For without this no one can be saved, as the Lord said, that whoever is not born by water*

---

[401] St Gregory of Nazianzus, *Homily* 40, §§ 4 and 15, in Migne, *P.G.,* 36, 364 and 377. St Basil the Great, *Homily* 13, § 4, in Migne, *P.G.,* 31, 432.
[402] Mitsopoulos, *Themata,* p. 310.
[403] John 3:3.
[404] Mark 16:16.

and the Spirit, he cannot enter the Kingdom of Heaven. And for this reason, it is necessary for the new born infants."[405]

Jeremias declared that "even the infants must be baptised and should not be left for a long time; for if one is not Regenerated by water and the Spirit he cannot enter into the Kingdom of Heaven."[406]

According to Mogilas, through Baptism "the entrance into the Kingdom of Heaven is allowed, according to the words of our Saviour Who said: 'Unless one is born again, he cannot see the Kingdom of God.'"[407]

Kritopoulos numbered Baptism first among the three necessary Holy Sacraments, counting the "threats and the promises" that Christ pronounced such as: "If one is not Regenerated by water and the Spirit, he cannot enter into the Kingdom of Heaven" and "he who believes and is baptised will be saved."[408]

It is also most essential to note that in the case of Cornelius, although the Holy Spirit descended upon all those who heard the words of St. Peter, it was considered important for them to be baptised in water "in the Name of the Lord" as St. Peter not only instructed but commanded them.[409]

That which was always believed by the Orthodox Church is expressed in the ancient writings of the *Shepherd of Hermas* whereby "they go down into the water dead and they come up alive."[410] It is also understandable that those who were not made alive through Baptism remained dead. "For before a man bears the name of the Son of God, he is dead, but when he receives the seal, he lays aside his deadness and receives Life."[411]

Origen confirmed that "there is no forgiveness of sins without Baptism."[412]

St. Cyril of Jerusalem strongly declared that "if one does not receive Baptism, he cannot have Salvation" no matter how good he is because "he who does not receive the Seal of the water, cannot enter into the Kingdom of Heaven."[413]

---

[405] Dositheus of Jerusalem, *Confession,* Term XVI, in Karmeris, *The dogmatics*, v. II, p. 759.
[406] Jeremias, (A'), in Karmeris, *The dogmatics*, v. II, p. 394.
[407] Mogilas, (A' 102), in Karmeris, *The dogmatics*, v. II, p. 636.
[408] Kritopoulos, ch. 5, in Karmeris, *The dogmatics*, v. II, p. 525.
[409] Cf. Acts 10:44-48.
[410] *Shepherd of Hermas*, Parable 9, 16, § 4, in Lightfoot, *Apostolic Fathers,* p. 276.
[411] Ibid, Parable 9, 16, § 3, in Lightfoot, *Apostolic Fathers,* p. 276.
[412] Origen, *Admonition to Martyrdom,* 30, in *B,* v. 9, p. 52.
[413] St Cyril of Jerusalem, *Catechesis,* III, §§ 7 and 2, in Migne, *P.G.,* 33, 440 and 432.

Also, the practice of the Orthodox Church whereby new born infants who face the threat of death may be baptised through Baptism in air (Aero-baptism), demonstrates the importance and necessity of Baptism for Salvation.[414]

5. The Baptism of Martyrdom

The Baptism of Martyrdom[415] was considered as the only type of Baptism that was able to replace Baptism in water. This belief was based on the teachings of our Lord and Saviour Jesus Christ, the Son of God, Who declared: "*Whoever confesses Me before men, him I will also confess before My Father Who is in Heaven*"[416] as well as His assurance that "*for whoever desires to save his life will lose it, but whoever loses his life for My sake will save it.*"[417] The Baptism of Martyrdom was called the "*Baptism of Blood*" as Christ called His death on the Cross "*Baptism.*"[418]

Tertullian mentioned that there is a second Baptism among us, which is the Baptism of Blood and of which the Lord said: "*I have a Baptism with which I will be baptised*"[419] even though He had already been baptised.[420]

Origen certifying "*that Martyrdom is given to us as Baptism*" justified Baptism of Blood by observing that it "*is called in this way because it manifests*" the question asked by our Lord: "*Are you able to drink the cup that I am about to drink, and be baptised with the Baptism that I am baptised with?* [421] Elsewhere our Lord pronounced: "*I have a Baptism to be baptised with, and how distressed I Am until it is accomplished!*" [422] [423]

St. John Chrysostom, referring to the words of St. Paul according to which "*we were buried with Him through Baptism into death*" and "*we have been united together in the likeness of His death*"[424] called

---

[414] Androutsos, *Dogmatique,* p. 324.
[415] Mitsopoulos, *Themata,* p. 310.
[416] Matth. 10:32.
[417] Luke 9:24. Matth. 16:25.
[418] Matth. 20:22-23.
[419] Cf. Matth. 20:22.
[420] Tertullian, *De Baptismo,* c. 16, in migne, *P.L.,* 1, 1326.
[421] Matth. 20:22.
[422] Luke 12:50.
[423] Origen, *Admonition to Martyrdom,* 30, in *B,* v. 9, p. 52.
[424] Rom. 6:4, 5.

"the Baptism a cross" concluding that *"the cross is a Baptism"* because *"the Baptism with which I am to be baptised"* He said, *"you will also be baptised with"* and again *"the Baptism which I have to be baptised with, you do not know."*[425]

What inner inspiration and Divine Visitation presupposes in order that one suffers death for Christ's sake, one can understand if he recalls the God-inspired words of St. Paul, according to which *"no one can say that Jesus is Lord except by the Holy Spirit."*[426]   Hence St. John Chrysostom observed that *"do not admire if the Baptism is called Martyrdom; for here the Spirit flies over with great attention."*[427]

Generally speaking, right from the beginning within the Orthodox Church it was believed that Martyrs *"without water receive the Kingdom"*[428] *"and as those who are baptised in water, likewise those who are Martyred are washed within their own blood."*[429] During the persecutions when a Catechumen was killed, although before his death he had been forbidden to participate in any of the Holy Sacraments of the Church, through Martyrdom he would be justified by God *"because he received the Baptism with his own blood."*[430]

According to St. Cyprian, these Catechumens received Baptism in their own blood of which Christ had spoken and which is greater in Grace, higher in Power and more valuable in honour because with it no one sins. It perfects our faith and transmits us from this life directly to God and while Baptism in water bestows forgiveness of sins, that of Baptism of Blood bestows crowns of virtue.[431]

St. Gregory of Nazianzus said that Baptism *"through Martyrdom and blood with which Christ was baptised"* is characterised as *"more respectable than any other type of Baptism because no one is polluted with the stain (of sin)."*[432]

Tertullian believed that this Baptism of Martyrdom replaces that of the washing through water, even if the latter has not yet been

---

[425] St John Chrysostom, *To John,* Homily 25, § 2, in Migne, *P.G.,* 59, 151.
[426] 1 Corinth. 12:3.
[427] St John Chrysostom, *To saint Lucianus the Martyr,* § 2, in Migne, *P.G.,* 50, 522.
[428] St Cyril of Jerusalem, *Catechesis,* III, § 7, in Migne, *P.G.,* 33, 440.
[429] St John Chrysostom, *To saint Lucianus the Martyr,* § 2, in Migne, *P.G.,* 50, 522.
[430] St Hippolytus, *Egyptian Order,* ch. 44.
[431] St Cyprian, *Ad Fortum. praef.* 4, in migne, *P.L.,* 4, 680. Cf. Ibid, *Epistola*73, 22, in migne, *P.L.,* 3, 1170.
[432] St Gregory of Nazianzus, *To the holy Lights,* Homily 17, in Migne, *P.G.,* 36, 356.

received but, if lost because of a renouncement of faith or due to serious sins, it reinstates the Blessings of Holy Baptism.[433]

The question of whether *"those who died in battle* (could) *be considered as Martyrs of Christ"*[434] is answered in the light of history and theology and not from a political aspect. Martyrs were greatly honoured as they were considered to be like other Christs (*"alter Christus"*). Christ died not simply as the only Innocent One but He faced death with absolute patience, longsuffering and without any resistance or defence. He is the First-Martyr, *"the faithful Witness."*[435] Consequently, those who died for Christ's sake, enduring Martyrdom with tremendous patience were always considered as Holy Martyrs by the Orthodox Church. A Martyr is proclaimed not because of death but because of the reason for which that death is enforced; not the passion itself, but the intension of him who endures it, according to the teachings of St. Paul who wrote " *though I give my body to be burned, but have not love, it profits me nothing."*[436] Thus those who die in battle for the protection of their nation may be considered Martyrs and heroes of the nation but they are not Martyrs of Christ except when one is captured and refusing to be forced to renounce his Orthodox Christian Faith is killed for Christ's sake. Then he would be considered a Holy Martyr of the Faith as well as a Martyr of the nation - an ethno-Martyr.

IV. THE OFFICIATORS OF BAPTISM

The officiator of the Holy Mystery of Baptism is the bishop followed by the presbyters. If necessary and in the absence of a presbyter, the deacon or even a layman, man or woman, who are already members of the Orthodox Church and uphold the true Faith, may conduct a Baptism. In order for anyone to be accepted in the Orthodox Church it is necessary for him to go through the indispensable preparation, which is the Catechism, the renouncement of the old sinful life, the acceptance of the Truth of the Orthodox Christian Faith and the Confession of this Faith. However, when the one is baptised as an infant or a young child, they are immediately

---

[433] Tertullian, in Trempelas, *Dogmatique,* v. III, p. 103, note 26.
[434] Bartmann, *Theologie Dogmatique,* v. II, p. 290.
[435] Rev. 1:5.
[436] 1 Corinth. 13:3.

accepted in Holy Baptism by relying on parents and God-parents to seriously undertake the responsibility of teaching them the Orthodox Faith.

1. The Officiators of Holy Baptism

The Commandment and Authority was given by our Lord and Saviour Jesus Christ, the Son of God, to His Holy Apostles and Disciples to *"go therefore and make disciples of all the nations, baptising them in the Name of the Father and of the Son and of the Holy Spirit, teaching them to observe all things that I have commanded you"*[437] and to *"go into all the world and preach the gospel to every creature."*[438] Since the early years of the Church this Authority has been passed down by the Holy Apostles to others, as in the case of the Ordination of the seven deacons,[439] the Baptism of the Samaritans by St Philip the deacon,[440] the Baptism of Cornelius and his household by St. Peter.[441] St. Paul however, informing us that he did not baptise anyone *"except Crispus and Gaius"* and *"the household of Stephanas"* stated that *"Christ did not send* (him*) to baptise, but to preach the gospel."*[442] St. Paul himself received Holy Baptism[443] not from any of the Apostles but from St Ananias who is described in the Book of Acts as being a simple *"disciple."*[444]

Consequently, it was believed that bishops had the duty and the right to baptise. For this reason, St. Ignatius of Antioch exhorted the Christians to *"all follow the bishop, as Jesus Christ followed the Father, and follow the presbyter as you would the Apostles; respect the deacons as the commandment of God. Let no one do anything that has to do with the Church without the bishop. Only that Eucharist which is under the authority of the bishop (or whomever he himself designates) is to be considered valid. Wherever the bishop appears, there let the congregation be; just as wherever Jesus Christ is, there is the catholic Church. It is not permissible either to baptise or to hold a*

---

[437] Matth. 28:19-20.
[438] Mark 16:15.
[439] Cf. Acts 6:2-6
[440] Cf. Acts 8:12.
[441] Cf. Acts 9:44-48.
[442] Cf. 1 Corinth. 1:14-16, 17.
[443] Cf. Acts 9:18.
[444] Acts 9:10.

love feast[445] *without the bishop. But whatever he approves is also pleasing to God, in order that everything you do may be trustworthy and valid.*"[446]

Tertullian confirmed the bishops' s right to baptise and that it was later permissible for the presbyters and deacons to do so but not without the bishop's permission.[447]

In agreement with the 47th, 49th and 50th Canons[448] of the Holy Apostles,[449] which confer that bishops and presbyters should baptise, are the Canons of the *Apostolic Orders* which forbid those in the lower priesthood (readers, chanters etc.) to baptise, permitting "*only the bishops and presbyters being served by the deacons.*" Elsewhere they order exactly that the "*Deacon does not baptise, neither offers; for only the bishop offers or the presbyter,* (while) *he (the deacon) gives to the people, not as a priest but as serving the priests.*"[450]

Conversely, although this was the canonical practice of the Orthodox Church, when in time of extreme danger and threat of death it was impossible to find a canonical officiator to conduct the Holy Mystery of Baptism, it was allowed for a deacon or any Orthodox member of the Church to do so.[451]

Tertullian forbade women from officiating the Mystery of Baptism based upon the teachings of St. Paul[452] whereby women were not allowed either to speak, to teach or to baptise at the gatherings of the Church.[453]

St. Epiphanius pointed out that if it was allowed for women to baptise, our Lord would have had received Baptism from His Mother and Ever-Virgin Mary and not from St. John the Forerunner and Baptist[454] although this argument was used to prove that women are not allowed "*to officiate or to act anything canonical in the Church.*"

---

[445] Cf. Jude 12. 1 Corinth. 11:17-34.

[446] St Ignatius, *To Smyrnaeans,* 8, 1-2, in Lightfoot, *Apostolic Fathers,* p. 112-113.

[447] Tertullian, *De Baptismo,* 17, in migne, *P.L.,* 1, 1218.

[448] See Pedalion, pp. 68, 76, 80-81, 81-91.

[449] Rallis, Canons 2, p. 66.

[450] *Apostolic Orders,* III, 11, and VIII, 28, 4, in *B*, v. 2, pp. 64 and 162. Georgopoulos, *Anthology*, p. 10.

[451] Cf. Tertullian, *De Baptismo,* c. 17, in migne, *P.L.,* 1, 1218. Owen, *Theology,* p. 401. St Augustine, *Contra EpistolaParmenia,* II, 13, 29, in migne, *P.L.,* 43, 71. St Hieronymus, *Dialogus contra Lucif.,* 9, in migne, *P.L.*, 23, 173.

[452] 1 Corinth. 14:34.

[453] Tertullian, *De virg. Veland.,* in migne., *P.L.,* 2, 950.

[454] St Epiphanius, *Panarion, Heresy* 79, 3, in Migne, *P.G.,* 42, 744.

This forbiddance of women ceased in the West only after the year 1,000.

In the East until the 4th century Baptism by laymen was regarded with great reluctance. St. Basil the Great under no circumstances accepted Baptism of heretics, officiated by laymen. St. Gregory of Nazianzus believed that anyone could receive Baptism from any canonical bishop or presbyter although he did not mention that if necessity arose it could be officiated by a layman.[455] In any case, in the 51st Canon of Nicephorus, Patriarch of Constantinople, it is stated that *"if an infant was baptised by a layman through immersions in the Name of the Holy Trinity and recovers from the danger of death, the ecclesiastic canons determine that the priest should perform the entire service of the Holy Baptism upon the infant which is to be baptised except not to repeat the three immersions and the invocation of the Holy Trinity."*[456] Concerning the Baptism in air (Aerobaptism), since the three immersions and elevations are not performed in water, if infants survived, the Service must be repeated[457].

It is clearly understandable that under no circumstances can anyone who is not canonically baptised and who is not a member of the Orthodox Church, baptise.

2. Who Are Accepted in Baptism?

The question of who are accepted in Holy Baptism[458] was addressed by St. Justin the Philosopher and Martyr who said: *"Anyone who is convinced and believes truthfully in our teachings and promises to live accordingly, and prays and asks with fasting from God to be forgiven of their previous sins and afterwards are presented where water is"* may receive Baptism. Initially Catechesis preceded the evangelism of those who were to be baptised. Hence from the 2nd century we have the Order of Catechumen. After expressing their steadfast faith and promising to follow the moral teachings of the Holy Gospel they were accepted in Holy Baptism. This was practiced according to the teachings of our Lord and Saviour Jesus Christ, the Son of God, Who instructed His Holy Apostles to

---

[455] St Gregory of Nazianzus, *Homily* 40 *to holy Baptism*, § 26, in Migne, *P.G.*, 36, 396
[456] According to quotation in Androutsos, *Dogmatique*, p. 534.
[457] Trempelas, *Dogmatique*, v. III, p. 109.
[458] Labadarios, *Sermons*, v. 1, p. 107. Georgopoulos, *Anthology*, p. 15.

"teach"[459] the nations and afterwards to baptise them, promising that *"he who believes and is baptised will be Saved."*[460]

The hearing of the word of the Gospel, faith in it, repentance for their previous way of life and disbelief, renouncement of Satan and joining with Christ, official Confession of Faith and the promise to follow the virtuous and new Life, were the requirements from those who were prepared to receive the Holy Mystery of Baptism. Hence St. Cyril of Jerusalem in his 1st Catechesis characterised that period of Catechesis as *"a period of confession"* according to which Catechumen were called to confess *"their sins which they committed in deeds, in words, during night or in day."*[461] Tertullian[462] and St. Ambrosius[463] greatly appreciated Repentance before Baptism.

3. Infant Baptism

It is uncertain but very possible that from the Apostolic Era infants and children were accepted in Baptism.[464] Thus, the Book of Acts and St. Paul mention entire families accepting Baptism such as Cornelius and *"his household,"*[465] Lydia and *"her household,"*[466] the Philippian Jailor *"and all his family,"*[467] *"Crispus, the ruler of the synagogue with all his household"*[468] and the *"household of Stephanas"*[469] while in the case of St Timothy, St. Paul mentioned that *"from childhood you have known the Holy Scriptures."*[470] In these families it is quite possible that children were included. Baptism was considered by St. Paul as *"the circumcision of Christ,"*[471] which replaced the circumcision of the flesh according to Judaic Law. Besides, our Lord and Saviour Jesus Christ, the Son of God, proclaimed the necessity of Baptism regardless of one's age and

---

[459] Matth. 28:19.

[460] Mark 16:16. Cf. Acts 2:38, 41; 8:12; 9:37; 10:34-38; 16:14.

[461] St Cyril of Jerusalem, *Catechesis,* I, § 5, in Migne, *P.G.,* 33, 376.

[462] Tertullian, *De poenitentia,* 6, in migne, *P.L.,* 1, 1349.

[463] St Ambrosius, *In Luce,* VI, 2, in migne, *P.L.,* 16, 1754.

[464] Dositheus of Jerusalem, *Confession,* ch. 16, pp. 39-41. Labadarios, *Sermons,* v. 1, p. 110. Mitsopoulos, *Themata,* pp. 289-290. Pedalion, pp.688-690.

[465] Acts 11:14

[466] Acts 16:15.

[467] Acts 16:33.

[468] Acts 18:8.

[469] 1 Corinth. 1:16.

[470] 2 Tim. 3:15.

[471] Col. 2:11.

expressed a special love towards the *"little children,"* instructing the Holy Apostles not to forbid mothers who presented them to Him, in order that He may bless and pray for them. *"Then little children were brought to Him that He might put His hands on them and pray, but the disciples rebuked them. But Jesus said, 'Let the little children come to Me, and do not forbid them; for such is the Kingdom of Heaven.' And He laid His hands on them and departed from there."*[472] Furthermore, St. Paul referred to the children of mixed marriages declaring that *"they are Holy"* too.[473]

St. Irenaeus remarked that Christ came to Dave all, especially those who through Him will be Regenerated in God: children, infants, youths and the elderly.[474]

Tertullian proclaimed even more clearly that the innocent state of infants makes the acceptance of Baptism unnecessary, while others must receive Baptism after having been taught the Christian Faith. This he believed because our Master had warned not to forbid children when they came to Him. Rather let them come to Him and when they are adolescent, after they had been taught, let them become Christians, when they are able to know Christ.[475]

On the contrary, St. Cyprian felt that it is not permissible to forbid recently born children from receiving Holy Baptism as they have no other sins besides that with which they were born according to Adam, bearing the pollution of death of the ancient Offence and which is forgiven so easily.[476]

Origen, bearing in mind the practice of the Church during his time with regard to infant Baptism, commented that *"the children are baptised for the forgiveness of sins"* and when the question arose *"What sins? When have they sinned?"* he replied *"because no one is free from sin, the stain is placed aside through Baptism, and for this reason the children are baptised."*[477]

St. Gregory of Nazianzus more than anyone else dealt with infant Baptism. He would ask: *"Do you have an infant? Do not give time to the evil one. Let it be Sanctified from infancy, in the Spirit."* He

---

[472] Matth. 19:13-15. Mark 10:13-16. Luke 18:15-17.
[473] 1 Corinth. 7:14.
[474] St Irenaeus, book II, ch. 22, § 4, in Migne, *P.G.,* 7, 784. Cf. Ibid, in Hadjephraimides, p. 156.
[475] Tertullian, *De Baptismo,* 18, in migne, *P.L.,* 1, 1330.
[476] St Cyprian, *Epistola*59, 5, in migne, *P.L.,* 3, 1054.
[477] Origen, in Trempelas, *Dogmatique,* v. III, p. 114.

reminded people of St Anna who *"before Samuel was born promised him to God*[478] *and when he was born, (promised) to make him a priest immediately and sowed the priestly vestments.*[479]*"* He also dealt with the argument that infants do not have a conscience nor suffer damage that occurs when being deprived of Holy Baptism or the Grace which those who are baptised receive. He expressed the opinion that infants should be three years old *"or younger or older than this"* so that *"even if they do not understand completely they are imprinted"* in the memory of the little child *"thus being Sanctified and the souls and the bodies being perfected in the great Mystery."* He further emphasised that it is advisable to baptise infants *"for if a danger occurs. It is greater to be Sanctified unconsciously rather than to depart without being Sealed."* He referred to the eight days circumcision as a typical Seal. He pointed out *"the use of the anointing of the lintel"*[480] with the blood of lambs during the time of the exodus of the Israelites from the land of Egypt, which *"through the use of the unconscious"* the first-born of the Jews was saved.[481]

The subject of infant Baptism was seriously dealt with during the 4th century between St. Augustine and the Pelagianism. St. Augustine was searching for a reason to justify Original or Ancestral Sin through infant Baptism, since Baptism is offered for the forgiveness of sins. The Pelagianism refused to accept the inheritance of this sin, for their own reason, believing that it was to their benefit to deny that infant Baptism was a universal and ancient practice of the Orthodox Church. They believed that infants were baptised, not to be healed from sin but to become greater in goodness from whatever they were for should they die without being baptised, they believed that infants would not go to the Kingdom of Heaven but instead would be introduced to Eternal Life.

It is obvious that Baptism is offered only to the living. Consequently, Baptism for the dead is a misinterpretation of the Apostolic verse: *"What will they do who are baptised for the dead, if the dead do not rise at all? Why then are they baptised for the dead? And why do we stand in jeopardy every hour"*[482] which was correctly

---

[478] Cf. 1 Samuel (1 Kings) 1:11; 2:11.
[479] Cf. 1 Samuel (1 Kings) 2:18-19.
[480] Ex. 12:22.
[481] St Gregory of Nazianzus, in Trempelas, *Dogmatique,* v. III, p. 114.
[482] 1 Corinth. 15:29-30.

condemned by the Church.[483] In Africa, according to the witness of St Augustine[484] and Fulgentius,[485] this practice was in use especially by the heretics. However, these heretics were correctly characterised by St. John Chrysostom as *"playing in a tent."* Theophylactus of Bulgaria observed that *"those who believed that there is Resurrection of the dead bodies and are baptised for such hope, what are they doing since they are deceived? Why are they completely baptised men for the Resurrection, in other words for the hope in the Resurrection, if the dead are not risen?"*[486]

CHAPTER SIX
THE MYSTERY OF HOLY CHRISMATION

I. DEFINITION, NAMES AND DIVINE INSTITUTION

The Holy Mystery of Chrismation is given immediately after the Holy Mystery of Baptism by the Anointing and Signing of the Cross on the different parts of the one who has been baptised to transmit the Strength and various Gifts or Charismata of the Holy Spirit.[487] These Gifts are necessary for the strengthening and arming of those who have been baptised in order to grow and perfect them in the newness of Life in Christ It is an individual and separate Holy Mystery the nature and meaning of which is clarified by the different names applied to it. The Divine institution is evident from the promises of our Lord and Saviour Jesus Christ, the Son of God, concerning the richness of the Gifts or Charismata of the Holy Spirit bestowed upon the faithful. It is clearly witnessed by the laying on of hands of the Holy Apostles that followed Baptism for the purpose of transmitting the Holy Spirit to the faithful as well as by the Apostolic Proclamations of assurance, anointing and engagement of the Holy Spirit. The *Apostolic Proclamations* refer to the inner Visitation and

---

[483] St John Chrysostom, *To 1 Corinthians,* Homily 40, § 1, in Monfaucon, v. 10, p. 440.
[484] St Augustine, *Opus imperfectum contra Julianem,* VI, 38, in migne, *P.L.,* 45, 1597.
[485] Fulgentius, *Epistola*XI, 4, in migne, *P.L.,* 65, 379. Ibid, *Epistola*XII, 20, in migne, *P.L.,* 65, 383.
[486] Theophylactus of Bulgaria, *To 1 Corinthians*, in Migne, *P.G.,* 124, 768.
[487] Cf. Plato of Moscow, *Orthodox Teaching,* p. 148. Evdokimov, *Orthodoxia,* pp. 374-388. Kefalas, *Catechesis,* pp. 182-183. Frangopoulos, *Christian Faith,* pp. 197-199. Mitsopoulos, *Themata,* p. 312. Labadarios, *Sermons,* v. 1, pp. 111-114. Georgopoulos, *Anthology,* pp. 17-20.

Action of the Holy Spirit but they do not exclude the external use according to ancient Ecclesiastic Tradition of oil.

1.   The Meaning of the Holy Mystery of Chrismation

When one is baptised, one arises from the Baptismal Font Regenerated from Above, clean, Justified and Sanctified just like infants in Christ. As the newly born in their natural life, regardless of their health, have need of air, light and nourishment for their strengthening, growth and progress towards adulthood, likewise in spiritual life. Those who arise from the Baptismal Font have the need of the Life-giving atmosphere and Protection of the Holy Spirit in order that through the various Gifts they be strengthened in the newness of Life in Christ, armed against sin, enabling them to grow into perfection according to the measure of the stature of Christ It is offered to those who are baptised *"the Divine power which gives all things pertaining to Life and Godliness"*[488] through the Divine Mystery of Holy Chrismation, which at the beginning was inseparably joined to the Holy Mystery of Baptism.

The Holy Mystery of Chrismation is the God-instituted Ceremony, according to which those who are recently Baptised and Regenerated in Christ, being anointed with the Sanctified Myrrh on the various parts of their bodies, by the Signing of the Holy Cross and the invocation of the *"Seal of the Gift of the Holy Spirit"* they receive the Charismata or Gifts of the Holy Spirit, which are necessary for strengthening and growth in the newness of Life in Christ

2.   Names of the Holy Mystery and its Divine Institution

The meaning of the Holy Mystery of Chrismation more or less manifests its nature and the various names with which it is ascribed, expresses either the external aspect, the internal action or influence upon the depths of the soul of the one who is anointed. Thus, in relation to the external and perceptible sign of Holy Chrismation, it is referred to in the New Testament as the *"laying on of the hands*[489] *"manus imposition," "chrism," or "unction," "mystical chrism," "Holy chrism," "Heavenly chrism," "Mystery of the chrism," "Sacramentum*

---

[488] 2 Peter 1:3.
[489] Acts 8:17-18. Heb. 6:2. *Apostolic Orders*, II, 32, 3, in *B*, v. 2, p. 38.

Chrismatis," "Myrrh," "oil of God," "Holy Oil," "Chrism of Eucharist," "Mystery of the Ceremony of the Myrrh."[490]

In relation to the internal Supernatural and invisible action upon the soul of the Anointed by the Grace of the Holy Spirit, the action is called *"the dose of the Spirit," "Christ's Charisma," "the antitype of the Holy Spirit," "the assurance of the Confession,"*[491] *"Confirmation," "the perfect," "the perfection"* and *"Perfectio consummation."* Both aspects of the Holy Mystery are expressed by the terms: *"Signaculum Dominicum, "Signaculum spiritale"* and *"Signaculum vitae aeternae."*[492]

The contemporary books of confession refer to Holy Chrismation as the Mystery *"of assurance of the Holy Myrrh and of the Holy chrism,"*[493] *"the Myrrh of Chrismation,"*[494] *"Holy Chrism"*[495] or *"Holy Myrrh,"*[496] *"the chrism"*[497] or *"Mystery of the Divine Myrrh."*[498]

The New Testament does not contain direct information with regard to the Divine institution of the Holy Mystery of Chrismation by our Lord Himself. However, it is signified by the Promise of Christ to send the Holy Spirit to the Disciples by Whom all those who come to Him and who thirst would be quenched: *"If anyone thirsts, let him come to Me and drink. He who believes in Me, as the Scripture has said, out of his heart will flow rivers of living water. But this He spoke concerning the Spirit, Whom those believing in Him would*

---

[490] St Augustine, *De baptismo contra Donatus,* III, 16, 21, in migne, *P.L.,* 43, 149. Tertullian, *De baptismo,* 7. St Cyprian, *Epistola*LXX. St Cyril of Jerusalem, *Catechesis Mystagogia,* III, 1, 4, 3, in Migne, *P.G.,* 33, 1088, 1092 and 1089. Canons 48 and 7 of the Laodicia Synod. St Augustine, *Contra lit. Petiliani,* III, civ, 239, in migne, *P.L.,* 43, 342. St Cyril of Alexandria, *To Isaiah,* 25, 6, in Migne, *P.G.,* 70, 561. Theophilus of Antioch, *1 Autolycus,* § 12, in *B*, v. 5, p. 19. St Dionysius the Aeropagite, *About Ecclesiastic Hierarchy,* IV, 3, 12, in Migne, *P.G.,* 3, 485.

[491] St Isidorus of Pelusium, *book I, Epistolale* 450, in Migne, *P.G.,* 78, 429. St Cyril of Jerusalem, *Catechesis Mystagogia,* III, 3 and 1, in Migne, *P.G.,* 33, 1092 and 1088. *Apostolic Orders,* III, 17, *B,* v. 2, p. 67.

[492] Clement the Alexandrian, *Pedagogus,* I, 6. St Ambrosius, *De sacramentis,* III, 2 and 8, in migne, *P.L.,* 16, 450. St Cyprian, Epistola*ad Jubaien,* 73, 9, in migne, *P.L.,* 3, 1160. St Ambrosius, *De mysteriis,* c. VII, 41, in migne, *P.L.,* 16, 453 and 419. Didymus the Blind, *About the Holy Spirit,* book II, ch. XIV, in Migne, *P.G.,* 39, 712. *Apostolic Orders,* VII, 22, 2-3.

[493] Dositheus of Jerusalem, *Confession,* Term 15, in Karmeris, *The dogmatics,* v. II, p. 757.

[494] Mogilas, A' 104, in Karmeris, *The dogmatics,* v. II, p. 637.

[495] Kritopoulos, ch. 5, in Karmeris, *The dogmatics,* v. II, p. 526..

[496] Ibid, ch. 8, in Karmeris, *The dogmatics,* v. II, p. 531.

[497] Jeremias, A', in Karmeris, *The dogmatics,* v. II, p. 389.

[498] Ibid, B', § 4, in Karmeris, *The dogmatics,* v. II, p. 390 and 459.

receive."[499]   Obviously this Divine Promise refers not only to a few charismatics, as mentioned in 1st Corinthians,[500] who, according to the needs of the first Church, received special Charismata that eventually ceased, but those who from generation to generation re-appeared, being fulfilled particularly through the Holy Mystery of Chrismation. This can be understood from the teachings and practices of the Holy Apostles, who neither practiced nor taught anything unless they had heard it from or been guided by their Master and Teacher, our Lord and Saviour Jesus Christ, the Son of God.

Jeremiah declared that *"the Divine Mystery of the sacred Myrrh is not found in the Holy Scripture, but is delivered by the disciples of the Word."*[501]

Mogilas added that *"the second Mystery is the Myrrh of Chrismation, which began from that period, when the Holy Spirit descended upon the Apostles. This anointing with Myrrh or this action was performed at the time of the Apostles by the laying on of the hands; because the Scripture says: 'then they laid the hands upon them and received the Holy Spirit.' Afterwards it was performed with the anointing with Myrrh."*[502]

That the Holy Mystery was initially established by the Holy Apostles is witnessed in the case of those who believed and were baptised in Samaria, according to which " *as yet He (the Holy Spirit) had fallen upon none of them"* so they had sent for St Peter and St John who *"when they had come down, prayed for them, that they might receive the Holy Spirit then they laid hands on them, and they received the Holy Spirit."*[503] There was another instance in Ephesus when St. Paul *"having passed through*(found) *some disciples"* who were baptised according to the Baptism of St. John but had not received the Holy Spirit for they had *"not so much heard whether there is a Holy Spirit."*. For this reason, *"they were baptised in the Name of the Lord Jesus. And when Paul had laid hands on them, the Holy Spirit came upon them, and they spoke with tongues and prophesied."*[504]

---

[499] John 7:37-38, 39.
[500] 1 Corinth. 12:29.
[501] Jeremias, A', in Karmeris, *The dogmatics,* v. II, p. 390.
[502] Mogilas, A' 104, in Karmeris, *The dogmatics,* v. II, p. 637.
[503] Acts 8:14-17..
[504] Acts 19:1-7.

In both cases Baptism is clearly distinguished from the laying on of hands by means of which the Gifts or Charismata of the Holy Spirit were granted. This differentiation is also very clear in the Epistle to the Hebrews, which speaks of *"the doctrines of Baptisms"* and *"laying on of hands."*[505]

Biblical references referring to the teachings of the Holy Apostles are: *"the Love of God has been poured out in our hearts by the Holy Spirit Who has been given to us"*[506] *"you did not receive the spirit of bondage again to fear, but you received the Spirit of Adoption by Whom we cry out, 'Abba, Father'"*[507] *"Now we have received, not the spirit of the world, but the Spirit Who is from God, that we might know the things that have been freely given to us by God"*[508] *"This only I want to learn from you: Did you receive the Spirit by the works of the law, or by the hearing of faith?"*[509] and *" because you are sons, God has sent forth the Spirit of His Son into your hearts"*[510]. Classic verses are: *"Now He Who established us with you in Christ and has anointed us in God, Who also has sealed us and has given us the Spirit in our hearts as a guarantee"*[511] *"in Him you also trusted, after you heard the word of truth, the gospel of your salvation; in Whom also, having believed, you were sealed with the Holy Spirit of promise, Who is the guarantee of our inheritance until the redemption of the purchased possession, to the praise of His glory"*[512] *" do not grieve the Holy Spirit of God, by Whom you were sealed for the day of redemption"*[513] *" you have an anointing from the Holy One, and you know all things"*[514] *" the anointing which you have received from Him abides in you, and you do not need that anyone teach you; but as the same anointing teaches you concerning all things, and is true, and is not a lie, and just as it has taught you, you will abide in Him."*[515]

No one can deny that both of the abovementioned Holy Apostles were referring to the inner action of the Holy Spirit, by means of

[505] Heb. 6:2.
[506] Rom. 5:5.
[507] Rom. 8:15.
[508] 1 Corinth. 2:12.
[509] Gal. 3:2.
[510] Gal. 4:6.
[511] 2 Corinth. 1:21-22.
[512] Ephes. 1:13-14.
[513] Ephes. 4:30.
[514] 1 John 2:20.
[515] 1 John 2:27.

which the Lord *"as by a Seal gave us the Gift of the Holy Spirit"*[516] and anointed and sealed us *"together as Prophets and priests and kings."*[517] These Offices were anointed by Blessed Oil and in a very early stage, the laying on of hands upon those who were baptised was replaced by the Holy Apostles with the anointing with Holy Myrrh, reminiscent of the anointing of the high priests and kings in the Old Testament.

3.   The Teachings of the Holy Fathers

It must be noted that since the second century, the teachings of the Holy Fathers and ecclesiastic writers of the Orthodox Church dealt with the Holy Mystery of Chrismation. Neither the Didache nor St. Justin the Philosopher and Martyr mention anything about the transmitting of the Gifts of the Holy Spirit through the laying on of the hands although they speak of Baptism and the Divine Eucharist This could be explained by the fact that in the beginning, as Christian communities were small, all Holy Sacraments were officiated by the local Bishops.   Holy Chrismation was immediately given after Baptism as a continuation of the latter. Since the right of officiating the Mystery of Baptism was given to priests, obviously the right of anointing with the Holy Myrrh was passed down as well.

Thus, the first witness of Holy Chrismation is that of Theophilus of Antioch, who explaining the reason why *"we are called Christians"* observed that *"we are anointed with the Oil of God."*[518]

St. Irenaeus, referring to the ways that were used by heretics in Baptism and Chrismation, observed that the Holy Spirit is not given by magic, as believed by Simon the magician, but through the laying on of hands. According to St. Irenaeus the Holy Spirit Who is the Bread of Life, is received by those who the Apostles laid their hands upon.[519]

Tertullian, referring to the three Holy Sacraments of Baptism, Chrismation and Eucharist, clearly distinguishes Chrismation from Baptism. The latter Regenerates by water whereas the former bestows the Holy Spirit. Baptism, according to Tertullian, does not give the

---

[516] Theodoretus of Cyrus, *To Ephesians 1:13*, in Migne, *P.G.,* 82, 513.

[517] St John Chrysostom, *To 2 Corinthians,* Homily III, § 4, in Migne, *P.G.,* 61, 411.

[518] Theophilus of Antioch, *1 Autolycus,* § 12, in **B,** v. 5, p. 19.

[519] St Irenaeus, *Heresies,* book I, ch. 21, §§ 3-5 and ch. 23, § 1; and book IV, ch. 38, § 2, in Migne, *P.G.,* 7, 614-615. Cf. Ibid, in Hadjephraimides, pp. 87-89, 90, 352.

Holy Spirit but only prepares the faithful to receive Him through Holy Chrismation.[520] He considers Baptism as a kind of contract whereby he who is being baptised is sealed with proclamations and promises by God.[521] He does not clarify exactly how the Holy Spirit bestows His Gifts through the laying on of hands or through the anointment. Although he noted that these Gifts are bestowed through the blessing and invocation of the Holy Spirit,[522] elsewhere he observed that the flesh is anointed, in order that the soul be Sanctified, the flesh is Signed, in order that the soul be armed and the flesh, through the laying on of the hands, is overshadowed so that the soul be Enlightened through the Holy Spirit.[523]

Pope Cornelius (circa 250) in his letter to Photius of Antioch accused Novatianus that because he was baptised with clinical Baptism but was not sealed "*by the bishop* "he did not receive "*the Holy Spirit.* "[524]

St. Cyprian distinguishing Chrismation from Baptism, ascribed them as Sacraments, for each one he observed that it is necessary for the one who is baptised to be anointed through Chrismation in order to become anointed of God and thus enabling him to have the Grace of Christ within him.[525] Elsewhere he emphasised that "*two Sacraments rule in the Christian perfect birth, the one which regenerates man, Baptism, and the other which gives to him the Holy Spirit.*"[526] It is not impossible for men to be Sanctified and to become children of God on condition that they are Regenerated by both Holy Sacraments. Exalting the Mystery of the laying on of the hands, he determined that through Baptism one is Regenerated and through the laying on of the hands one receives the Holy Spirit.[527] Referring to the Book of Acts[528] referring to the Samaritans, he noted that the practice of the local church is the same as ours, for those who are baptised are presented to the Elders of the Church so as through prayer and the

---

[520] Tertullian, *De praescriptione haeritcorum* 40, in migne, *P.L.,* 2, 54-55. Ibid, *De baptismo,* IV, in migne, *P.L.,* 1, 1206.
[521] Leeming, *Principles,* p. 197.
[522] Tertullian, *De baptismo,* VIII, in migne, *P.L.,* 1, 1207.
[523] Ibid, *De resurrection carne,* VIII, in migne, *P.L.,* 2, 806.
[524] Eusebius, *Church History,* VI, 43, in Migne, *P.G.,* 20, 624.
[525] St Cyprian, Epistola*ad Januarium 70*, in migne, *P.L.,* 3, 1078.
[526] Ibid, *Epistola*72, 1, in migne, *P.L.,* 3, 1083. Ibid, *Epistola*73, 21-22, in migne, *P.L.,* 3, 1170.
[527] Ibid, *Epistola*74, 7, in migne, *P.L.,* 3, 1132.
[528] Acts 8:14-17.

laying on of the hands they may receive the Holy Spirit and through the Sign of the Lord, they might be perfected.[529]

In the epistle of Phirmilianus of Caesarea addressed to St. Cyprian,[530] he revealed that the same order and teaching concerning the second Holy Mystery was practiced in Carthage. The transmitting of the Charismata of the Holy Spirit, the giving of Baptism and the Ordination of priests were preserved to be officiated only by the bishop. These were performed by the laying on of hands.[531]

In the Alexandrian Church, Origen first informs us that the Gift of the Grace of the Holy Spirit is manifested through the imagery of the Blessed Oil, so that he who returns from sin would not only be able to receive forgiveness of sins but also to be filled with the Holy Spirit.[532]

The *Egyptian Order*, as well as the Canons ascribed to St Hippolytus, bears witness not only of the practice in Rome but that of Alexandria as well. According to both writings, he who was baptised was immediately anointed *"with oil which was Sanctified."* The Catechumen was anointed by the presbyter who said: *"I anoint you with Holy Oil in the Name of Jesus Christ."* He was then presented to the bishop who laid his hand on him and called upon Divine Grace while pouring the Sanctified Oil upon his head.[533]

St. Cyril of Jerusalem, who dealt with the Mystery of Chrismation in his writings, *Mystagogy Catechisis*, observed that as Christ *"in Jordan was washed in the river"* He emerged from the waters *"and the Holy Spirit descended upon Him."* Likewise, we emerge from the Baptismal font and receive Sacred Chrismation which is the antitype of that by which Christ was Anointed and which is the Holy Spirit.[534]

St. Ambrosius, the author of the *"De Sacramentis,"* mentioned the Spiritual Sign (*"signaculum spiritale"*) by means of which, with the invocation of the priest, the Holy Spirit with the seven Gifts or Charismata is poured upon those who are baptised.[535]

---

[529] St Cyprian, *Epistola*73, 9, in migne, *P.L.,* 3, 1115.

[530] Ibid, *Epistola*75, 7-8, in migne, *P.L.,* 3, 1161-1162.

[531] Acts 19:2-6.

[532] Origen, *To Leviticus,* Homily VIII, 11, in Migne, *P.G.,* 12, 507-508.

[533] Hauler, *Didascaliae Apostolorum,* p. 110. Achelis, *Die ältesten Quellen,* v. I, *Canones Hippoliti,* p. 98. Canon 19, §§ 134, 136 and 139.

[534] St Cyril of Jerusalem, *Catechesis Mystagogia,* III, § 1, in Migne, *P.G.,* 33, 1089.

[535] St Ambrosius, *De mysteriis,* in migne, *P.L.,* 16, 419. Ibid, *de Sacramentis,* III, c. 2, § 8, in migne, *P.L.,* 16, 453.

St. Basil the Great observed that concerning the blessing of *"the Oil of Chrismation"* and *"the anointing of the Oil"* we have been taught *"from silent and mystic tradition."*[536]

St. Gregory of Nazianzus wondered what would happen to the one who has been armed with Baptism *"and signed with Chrismation and the Spirit."*[537]

St. John Chrysostom advised that one should cry for *"those departed without the enlightenment, those without the seal."*[538]

Didymus the Blind taught that *"the anointing of Aaron "* was sacred *"and all those who are anointed are called anointed ones because they bear the Sanctified Chrismation, which we receive."*[539]

St. Cyril of Alexandria observed that *"we are anointed with Myrrh at the time of Baptism, which is the seal of the Holy Spirit."*[540]

St. Augustine noted that the visible anointment is the Mystery of the spiritual anointment by the Holy Spirit[541] and this Mystery of Chrismation is equal to the Holy Baptism.[542]

II. EXTERNAL ASPECT, OFFICIATORS AND TIME OF RECEIVING HOLY CHRISMATION

In the early period, with the invocation and special prayer for the calling of the Holy Spirit and the laying on of hands, the use of Sanctified Myrrh appeared. The Newly Illumined was anointed in a cross-shape sign on different parts of the body. The invocation was: *"Seal of the Gift of the Holy Spirit. Amen."* This use was also common in the Old Testament and appeared to be in general use within the Orthodox Church since the Apostolic era. The person who was baptised was immediately anointed with Sanctified Myrrh followed by the laying on of the right hand of the Bishop upon his head. Special prayers recited for the preparation and making of the Holy Myrrh, which takes place every seven years. The invocation and the cross-shape anointing are the external and visible aspects of the Holy

---

[536] St Basil the Great, *About the Holy Spirit*, XXVII, § 66, in Migne, *P.G.*, 32, 188.
[537] St Gregory of Nazianzus, *Homily* 40 *to holy Baptism*, § 15, in Migne, *P.G.*, 36, 377.
[538] St John Chrysostom, *To Philippians*, Homily 3, § 4, in Migne, *P.G.*, 62, 203.
[539] Didymus the Blind, *About the Holy Spirit*, II, 14, in Migne, *P.G.*, 39, 712.
[540] St Cyril of Alexandria, *To Isaiah*, book III, 1, Migne, *P.G.*, 70, 561.
[541] St Augustine, *In Epistolal Johannis, Tractatus* III, § 5, 12, in migne, *P.L.*, 35, 2002 and 2004.
[542] Ibid, *Contra lit. Petiliani*, II, 104 and 239, in migne, *P.L.*, 43, 312.

Mystery of Chrismation. Since the beginning, it was officiated by the Holy Apostles and afterwards by the bishops. After many centuries the right of anointing with Holy Myrrh in the service was given by the Bishops to the Presbyters. Thus, the preparation of the Holy Myrrh is only conducted by the gathering of all the bishops of the universal Orthodox Church. This Service of the Making of the Holy Myrrh takes place at the Ecumenical Patriarchate of Constantinople (Istanbul) every seven years.

1. The Transmission of the Holy Spirit Through the Laying on of Hands with Prayer

The laying on of the hands for the receiving of the Gifts of the Holy Spirit accompanied by a special invocation and prayer to God, is witnessed by Holy Scripture such as in the case of the Holy Apostles who were sent from Jerusalem to Samaria. Before they lay their hands upon those who were baptised, *"they prayed that they might receive the Holy Spirit."*[543]

Tertullian stated that by the laying on of hands and prayer the Holy Spirit was called to come upon the Newly Illuminated.[544]

St. Cyprian assured that the Holy Spirit is given *"by our prayers."*[545]

The *Egyptian Order*, the Canons of St Hippolytus, the *Apostolic Orders* and the *Testamentum Domini nostri Jesu Christi* witness the liturgical practice of the 3rd century and refer to a special prayer that accompanied the laying on of the hand by the bishop. To this day, within the Orthodox Church, the Holy Myrrh is anointed in a cross-shape sign on different parts of the Newly Illuminated, together with prayer, by the Bishop or Presbyter.[546]

The prayer accompanying the laying on of the hands differs from the prayer used for the Sanctification of the Myrrh.

St. Cyril of Jerusalem commented in his *Mystagogy Catechisis* addressed the Newly Illuminated: *"Be watchful that you do not think that Myrrh is simple. Because, as the Bread of the Eucharist after the invocation of the Holy Spirit, is no longer simple bread, but the Body*

---

[543] Acts 8:14,15.
[544] Tertullian, *De baptismo,* 8, in migne, *P.L.,* 1, 1316.
[545] St Cyprian, *Epistola*LXXIII, 9, in migne, *P.L.,* 3, 1160.
[546] *Apostolic Orders*, VII, 22, 2, in *B,* v. 2, p. 123. Ibid, VII, 44, 1, in *B,* v. 2, p. 136.

of Christ, likewise this Holy Myrrh is not simple nor should anyone say that is something common with invocation but that it is the Gift of Christ and the Presence of the Holy Spirit."[547] In other words St. Cyril believed that through the anointing with the Holy Myrrh a mystical change occurs such as at the Consecration in the Divine Eucharist

The importance of prayer together with the anointing of Sanctified Myrrh is expressed in the *Apostolic Orders* that stress *"if the pious priest does not pray with the laying on of the hands upon him who is baptised, then the latter is like going down in water only"*[548] just as in the baptismal purifications of the Jews.

2. The Anointing with Myrrh

The use of Sanctified Myrrh appeared to be in use since the end of the 2nd century. There is no doubt *"the anointing"* in the Old Testament is similar to the Holy Mystery of Chrismation. *"Aaron was anointed with chrism by Moses and all those who were anointed from the hieratic horn were called the anointed ones." "Solomon, becoming king, was anointed by the high priest after he washed in Geon."* This chrism of the Old Testament is considered to be a prefiguration *"of Sanctified Myrrh which we receive."* Hence in the Old Testament *"these took place typically for them* (Jews) *but for us truthfully because we are truly anointed by the Holy Spirit."*[549]

The practice of the anointing with Holy Myrrh was generally accepted by the entire Orthodox Church. We must take into consideration that the early Fathers were very strict in keeping the instructions of the Holy Apostles.[550] The question of how this practice was accepted by the universal Church is answered by the fact that the Holy Apostles, seeing the Church expanding, introduced the use of Holy Myrrh.

---

[547] St Cyril of Jerusalem, *Catechesis Mystagogia*, III, § 3, in Migne, *P.G.*, 33, 1092.
[548] *Apostolic Orders*, VII, 44, 3, in **B**, v. 2, p.136.
[549] Didymus the Blind, *About the Holy Spirit*, II, 14, in Migne, *P.G.*, 39, 712. St Cyril of Jerusalem, *Catechesis Mystagogia*, III, § 4, in Migne, *P.G.*, 33, 1093. Mogilas, A' 105, in Karmeris, *The dogmatics*, v. II, p. 637. Jeremias, II, § 4, in Karmeris, *The dogmatics*, v. II, p. 459. Kritopoulos, ch. VIII, in Karmeris, *The dogmatics*, v. II, p. 531. Evdokimov, *Orthodoxia*, pp. 375-376. Mitsopoulos, *Themata*, p. 313.
[550] 1 Tim. 6:20. 2 Thess. 2:15.

The Sanctification of the Myrrh is witnessed by Tertullian[551] as well as by St. Cyprian.[552] St. Basil the Great characterised it as *"being received from the silent and mystical tradition"* the Apostolic Tradition.[553] It is also mentioned in the New Testament.[554]

The laying on of hands with invocation of prayer took place after the prayer of anointing by the Elders. The Newly Illuminated were presented to the bishop who then lay his right hand upon those who had been anointed by the Presbyter with Myrrh.

3. The Officiator of the Mystery

If we take into consideration the Book of Acts the officiator of the Holy Mystery of Chrismation was at that time only the Holy Apostles. Later this authority was passed down to the bishops. [555]

According to the *Egyptian Order* the Myrrh is blessed by the bishop but the Newly Illuminated are anointed by Presbyters.[556] In addition, the *Apostolic Orders* recognise different authorities between that of the bishops and those of the Presbyters.[557]

St. John Chrysostom speaking of the authorities of the bishop commented that *"through the ordination alone they* (bishops) *are considered to be higher than the Presbyters."*[558] The same observation was expressed by St Hieronymus.[559]

In the West, the anointing with Holy Myrrh was preserved only for the bishop whereas in the East this authority, as that of Baptism, was passed down to the Presbyters.

---

[551] Tertullian, *De baptismo,* 7, in migne, *P.L.,* 1, 1315.

[552] St Cyprian, *Epistola*70 *ad Januarium,* 2, in migne, *P.L.,* 3, 1078.

[553] St Basil the Great, *About the Holy Spirit,* XXVII, § 66, in Migne, *P.G.,* 32, 188.

[554] 1 John 2:20 and 2 Corinth. 1:21, 22.

[555] St John Chrysostom, *To Acts,* Homily XVIII, § 3, in Migne, *P.G.,* 60, 144. St Isidorus of Pelusium, *Book A',* Epistle 450, in Migne, *P.G.,* 78, 429. St Cyprian, *Epistola*Jubaien 73, § 9, in migne, *P.L.,* 3, 1115. Georgopoulos, *Anthology,* p. 18.

[556] St Hippolytus, *Canon* 19, §§ 134 and 139. *Testamentum Domini,* book II, ch. VIII and IX.

[557] *Apostolic Orders,* VII, 42, 22 and 44, in *B,* v. 2, pp. 135, 123 and 136. Cf. Kritopoulos, ch. 8, and Mogilas, A' 105, in Karmeris, *The dogmatics,* v. II, pp. 531 and 637-638.

[558] St John Chrysostom, *To 1 Timothy,* Homily 11, § 1, in Migne, *P.G.,* 62, 553.

[559] St Hieronymus, *Epistola*146, § 1, in migne, *P.L.,* 22, 1194.

III. THE RESULTS AND NECESSITY OF THE HOLY MYSTERY OF CHRISMATION

St. Cyril of Jerusalem stressed that *"through the visible Myrrh the body is anointed, through the Holy and Life-giving Spirit the soul is Sanctified."*[560] In other words, through the Holy Mystery of Chrismation the Gifts or Charismata of the Holy Spirit are transmitted, which are necessary for the strengthening of the Regenerated in the Baptismal font. Through these Gifts the faithful become invincible soldiers of Christ and are able to face the assaults of the invisible enemy. This Holy Mystery is absolutely necessary for one's perfection in the Newness of Life in Christ.

1. The Perfection of Baptism through the Gift of Holy Chrismation

The main invisible result of the Holy Mystery of Chrismation imprinted on the soul is the transmission of the Gifts or Charismata of the Holy Spirit.[561] The Regeneration that occurs in Holy Baptism is achieved through the Holy Spirit. According to St. Cyprian there can never be Baptism without the Holy Spirit.[562] In any case our Lord and Saviour Jesus Christ, the Son of God, taught us that Rebirth takes place *"by water and the Spirit."*[563] It is a common belief of all Holy Fathers and ecclesiastic writers that the fruit of Baptism is the Holy Spirit.[564]

Only Tertullian believed that in Baptism *"we do not receive the Holy Spirit, but in the water, we are cleansed by the angels and we are prepared for the Holy Spirit."*[565] He also argued that if the Baptism of St. John, the Forerunner and Baptist, was from Above as that of our Lord Jesus, it would have granted forgiveness of sins.

St. Cyprian observed that through Baptism we receive the Holy Spirit.[566] However, if we receive the Holy Spirit through Baptism,

---

[560] St Cyril of Jerusalem, *Catechesis Mystagogia,* III, § 3, in Migne, *P.G.,* 33, 1092.

[561] Mitsopoulos, *Themata,* pp. 313-314.

[562] St Cyprian, *Epistola*74, § 5, in migne, *P.L.,* 3, 1178.

[563] John 3:3, 5.

[564] St Irenaeus, *Heresies,* book III, ch. 17, §§ 2-4, in Migne, *P.G.,* 7, 929-930. Cf. Ibid, in Hadjephraimides, pp. 237-239. Justin the Philosopher and Martyr, *Dialogue,* 29, in ***B,*** v. 3, p. 233.

[565] Tertullian, *De baptismo,* 6, in migne, *P.L.* 1, 1314.

[566] St Cyprian, *Epistola*63, 8, in migne, *P.L.,* 4, 391.

what do we receive through Holy Chrismation? St Dionysius the Aeropagite explained that *"the Myrrh is the perfection of the anointing."*[567]

St. Ambrosius commented that after Baptism the Spiritual Seal follows for the purpose of perfection when, with the invocation by the priest, the outpouring of the Holy Spirit takes place.[568]

St. Cyril of Alexandria, referring to the initiation and to the three Holy Sacraments, remarked that Holy Chrismation *"is given to us as the rain gives us the living water of the Holy Baptism, as the wheat gives us the Bread of Life and as the wine gives us the Blood. Similarly, the Sanctified Oil works towards the perfection of those who are Justified in Christ through Holy Baptism."*[569]

The putting to death of the old man that occurs in Baptism as well as the Rebirth of the new man with the outpouring of the richness of the Gifts of the Holy Spirit through Holy Chrismation, strengthens and leads to perfection. The Myrrh *"through the presence"* of the Holy Spirit *"becomes active"* transmitting to the new born in Christ, through Baptism, strength and power *"in order that the fragrance of Christ remains certain and consolidated in him."* The *"Reborn and recreated through the Washing of Regeneration partakes of the Gift of the Holy Spirit and is secured so that through this Seal he will remain strong and unmoveable, unharmed and unlooted, uninfluenced, unschemed, living according to the faith and with the knowledge of the truth until the end."*[570]

St. Augustine believed that *"He anointed us, because He made us fighters against demons."*[571]

St. Cyril of Jerusalem added that Chrism *"is Holy"* because *"it is the spiritual safe keeper of the body and the salvation of the soul."*[572]

---

[567] St Dionysius, the Aeropagite, *Ecclesiastic Hierarchy,* ch. II, § 8, in Migne, *P.G.,* 3, 404.

[568] St Ambrosius, *De sacramentis,* III, 2, 8, in migne, *P.L.,* 16, 453.

[569] St Cyril of Alexandria, *To Joel,* II, 21-24, in Migne, *P.G.,* 72, 452. Ibid, *To John,* books VII and VIII, in Migne *P.G.,* 74, 49. Ibid, *To Isaiah,* book III, 1, in Migne, *P.G.,* 70, 561.

[570] St Cyril of Jerusalem, *Catechesis Mystagogia,* III, § 3, in Migne, *P.G.,* 33, 1092.

[571] St Augustine, *In Johannis evangelium, Ttractatus.* XXXIII, 3, in migne, *P.L.,* 35, 1648.

[572] St Cyril of Jerusalem, *Catechesis Mystagogia,* III, § 5, in Migne, *P.G.,* 33, 1092.

2. The Gifts Transmitted Through the Holy Mystery of Holy Chrismation

St. Ambrosius, determining the Charismata which are transmitted through the second Holy Mystery in more detail, referred to the Prophet Isaiah who said: *"And there shall come forth a rod out of the root of Jesse, and a blossom shall come up from his root: and the Spirit of God shall rest upon him, the spirit of wisdom and understanding, the spirit of counsel and strength, the spirit of knowledge and godliness shall fill him; the spirit of the fear of God."*[573] The Holy Father urged each newly Illuminated to always remember that he had received the spiritual seal, the *"Spirit of wisdom and understanding, the Spirit of counsel and strength, the Spirit of knowledge and godliness."*[574]

St. Cyril of Jerusalem believed that the newly Illuminated *"became Christs of the Holy Spirit by receiving the antitype because you are images of Christ."*[575]

St. John Chrysostom declared that God, through the Anointment and His Spirit *"made us together Prophets and priests and kings."* Hence *"not one, but three offices we have."*[576]

In other words, we become *"taught by God"* by receiving the Charisma of God and receiving the Prophetic Charisma through the Spirit of Wisdom and Understanding that is transmitted to us. Alternatively, we rule over the passions and ourselves through the Spirit of Counsel and Strength, according to the imitation of Christ the King. Furthermore, through the Communion with Christ we are elevated to kingship and through the Spirit of Knowledge and Godliness as well as the Spirit of the fear of God, we are consecrated to Him as priests in all godliness, worshipping Him and offering logical sacrifices with humbled hearts before Him.

Thus, according to St. Cyprian, each one who is baptised becomes Christ of God containing the Grace of Christ within him.[577] Being in the complete image of Christ he is related to Him, just like the dough is to the Holy Dough. Christ is *"the beginning of our*

---

[573] Is. 11:1-3.
[574] St Ambrosius, *De mysteriis,* c. VII, § 42, in migne, *P.L.,* 16, 419. Ibid, *Sacramentis,* III, c. 2, §§ 8 and 10, in migne, *P.L.,* 16, 453.
[575] St Cyril of Jerusalem, *Catechesis Mystagogia,* III, § 1, in Migne, *P.G.,* 33, 1092.
[576] St John Chrysostom, *To 2 Corinthians,* Homily 3, § 4, in Migne, *P.G.,* 61, 411.
[577] St Cyprian, *Epistolaad Januarium,* 70, 2, in migne, *P.L.,* 3, 1078.

Salvation" because "*He is truly the beginning and we are the dough. If the beginning is Holy, it is obvious that Holiness will be transmitted to the dough.*"[578]

These Charismata of the Holy Spirit are deeply and indelibly imprinted in the soul of the anointed one. Hence, Holy Chrismation under no circumstance can be repeated for an Orthodox Christian who remains steadfast in his Orthodox Faith. The Holy Canons demand those who return from heresy to be be anointed "*first with Holy Myrrh*" and sealed with the invocation "*Seal of the Gift of the Holy Spirit.*" This is due to the fact that " *heretics do not have Holy Chrismation*" and being deprived of canonical Priesthood, "*the Bishop alone officiates the Chrismation with the Grace from Above.*"[579] In other words, if for some heretics their Baptism is recognised, this is done out of the *Economia*, (e.g. the Roman Catholics are accepted in the Orthodox Church only through the Holy Sacrament of Chrismation whereas all other Protestant Christian denominations require canonical Baptism). The rest of the heretics' Sacraments are completely invalid. All Orthodox Christians who have fallen into heresy or schism simultaneously fall from Priesthood, as all those who are ordained by heretics do not receive the Grace of Priesthood. Consequently, the heretics or schismatics do not have consecrated Chrismation nor do those who are anointed by them receive the Gift of the Holy Spirit.

Those who have renounced their Orthodox Faith and joined heretics or schismatics, when they repent and return, they are reinstated in the canonical Church of Christ with the anointing of the Mystery of Holy Chrismation. This does not mean that the Holy Mystery is repeated.[580]

The anointing of kings is performed according to the imitation of the Old Testament anointing. Furthermore, the anointing of Holy Images (Icons), Holy Altar, and other ecclesiastic items used in the Divine Services is to signify their Liturgical importance.

From the aforementioned, one can understand the significance of the Holy Mystery of Chrismation for Salvation. If anyone is baptised but willingly disregards this Holy Mystery and rejects it, then he excludes himself from Salvation because he commits the sin of the

---

[578] St Cyril of Jerusalem, *Catechesis Mystagogia,* III, § 6, in Migne, *P.G.,* 33, 1093.
[579] Didymus the Blind, *About the Holy Spirit,* ch. 15, in Migne, *P.G.,* 39, 720.
[580] Androutsos, *Dogmatique,* pp. 340-341.

blasphemy against the Holy Spirit, since it is He Who grants the Gifts and Sanctifies man. However, if anyone was baptised but for specific reasons had not the opportunity to be anointed, then he would not be excluded from Salvation. Consequently, the Holy Mystery of Chrismation is necessary for the further perfection of the Newness of Life in Christ.

CHAPTER SEVEN
THE MYSTERY OF HOLY EUCHARIST

I. DEFINITION, IMPORTANCE, PREFIGURES AND DIVINE ESTABLISHMENT

The Holy Eucharist is the Mystery of the Orthodox Church in which the presence of our Lord and Saviour Jesus Christ **is real and essential**. The bread and wine are offered as a Sacrifice without the shedding of blood and in remembrance of that unique Sacrifice that was offered on the Cross once and for all. The Holy Eucharist is offered as the Life-giving food and communion to all the faithful. Thus, the Holy Eucharist has two aspects, according to which it is a Mystery as well as a Sacrifice. These two aspects are manifested through the many and various names ascribed to Eucharist by Holy Scripture and Sacred Tradition of the Orthodox Church. Through these names the Mystery is exalted. It nourishes the souls of the faithful and unites them through the one Bread and the one Body to Christ and to one another. As a Sacrifice it is a re-enactment, without the shedding of blood, mysteriously and realistically of that Blood offered on the Cross by the High Priest Since in this Holy Mystery the exact Body and Blood of our Lord and Saviour Jesus Christ, the Son of God, is offered for eating and drinking, its supreme and special importance is obvious. It becomes the centre of all other Holy Sacraments and Christian Life. Therefore, as the greatest of all New Testament Holy Sacraments, it is prefigured in the Old Testament and undoubtedly was directly instituted by our Lord and Saviour Jesus Christ, the Son of God.[581]

---

[581] Cf. Kefalas, *Catechesis,* pp. 183-186. Frangopoulos, *Christian Faith,* pp. 199-201. Dositheus of Jerusalem, *Confession,* ch, 17, part 4, pp. 51-58. Mitsopoulos, *Themata,* pp. 315-320. Labadarios, *Sermons,* pp. 17-18, 69-81. Sophrony, *His Life,* pp. 87-90. Meyendorff, *Theology,* pp. 201-210. Georgopoulos, *Anthology,* pp. 20-42. Schmemann, *Eucharist,* translated by Joseph Roelides, Athens, 2000.

1. Supernatural Nourishment and Sacrifice

If through the Holy Mystery of Holy Baptism we enter into the Kingdom of Grace, Justified and Regenerated in Christ, through the Holy Mystery of Chrismation the Gift of the Holy Spirit is bestowed upon us. This is essential in order to strengthen us in the Newness of Life. The third Holy Mystery of Holy Eucharist nourishes us by eating and drinking the actual Body and Blood of our Lord and Saviour Jesus Christ, the Son of God. Partaking in this Holy Mystery, although our senses inform us that we eat and drink the offered bread and wine, we are assured by the undoubtable Faith that we have communion with the actual Body and Blood of the Lord, which was shed on the Cross for the Life and Salvation of the entire world. *"We do not judge the thing from its taste, but from faith we are informed without hesitation that the Bread which is seen is not bread, although its taste is perceptible, but it is the Body of Christ; and the wine which is seen is not wine, but it is the Blood of Christ."*[582]

We are guaranteed by the word of our Lord and Saviour Jesus Christ, the Son of God Who said: *"This is My Body' and we are convinced and believe and see this with the conceivable eyes."*[583]

Through the invocation of the Holy Spirit a Supernatural, unspeakable and an above all human understanding change takes place in these elements, which are presented, offered and officiated by the officiators who presents them to the Lord Who initially had been offered. He commanded us to do this in remembrance of Him, when on that unique night He blessed the Bread and gave the Cup with His own hands to His Holy Disciples.[584] As then, likewise now, He uses the officiator as a logical instrument to officiate this High Mystery. He Himself on the Christian Altars invisibly blesses and changes the offerings of bread and wine in an indescribable manner through the Grace of the Holy Spirit, into the His actual Body and Blood. This offering is performed in remembrance of His Sacrifice on the Cross. He Himself was the One Who was offered and is being offered. He is distributed to the faithful as a Spiritual Nourishment and Life-giving Source of Immortality.

---

[582] St Cyril of Jerusalem, *Catechesis,* XXII, *Mystagogia* I, § 9, in Migne, *P.G.,* 33, 1104.

[583] St John Chrysostom *To Matthew,* Homily 82, §§ 4 and 1, in Migne, *P.G.,* 58, 743. Mogilas, A' 106, in Karmeris, *The dogmatics,* v. II, p. 638. Dositheus of Jerusalem, *Confession*, Term 17, in Karmeris, *The dogmatics,* v. II, p. 761.

[584] Matth. 26:26-30. Mark 14:22-26. Luke 22:15-20. Evdokimov, *Orthodoxia,* pp. 328-335.

St. John Chrysostom observed that *"He made these in that Supper and He Himself now works these."* We who are standing before the Altar *"serve; but it is He Himself Who Sanctifies and changes these."*[585]

Thus, the Holy Eucharist has two important and vital aspects. It is on the one hand the Mystery that nourishes us through the Body and Blood of the Lord; and on the other hand, it is the Sacrifice without the shedding of blood. This Sacrifice is the same as that which was offered by the Saviour and High Priest once and for all. Jesus Christ as the sinless Lamb of God was Sacrificed for the Salvation of the world and the forgiveness of its sins, which are wiped away through His precious Blood.

2.   The Names of the Mystery

In relation to the double aspect of the Holy Mystery of Eucharist there are many names ascribed to it. We find these names in Holy Scripture and in the Tradition of the Orthodox Church. Thus, this Holy Mystery is called *"Eucharist"* according to its institution when *"Jesus took the bread and giving thanks He broke"* then *"He took the Cup and giving thanks He gave it"* to His Disciples.[586] This Mystery is the remembrance of Christ's death, which is the extreme benefit and expression of Divine Love and the inexpressible Mercy of God Who shows mercy to us.[587]

St. John Chrysostom taught that *"it is a perfect guardian of the benefit, the remembrance of the benefit and a constant thanksgiving. For this reason, the Mystery, which is full of Salvation, is celebrated daily in the gatherings and is called Eucharist because it is a remembrance of many benefits, the beginning of God's Providence is manifested and it prepares thanksgiving through all."*[588]

From the moment that our Lord and Saviour Jesus Christ, the Son of God, instituted and delivered this Holy Mystery, it was called the *"Lord's Supper,"*[589] the *"Mystical and Divine Supper"* because *"on the night in which He was betrayed as they ate"* Jesus *"took bread and when He had given thanks, He broke it"* then *"He also took the Cup*

---

[585] St John Chrysostom, *To Matthew,* Homily 82, § 5, in Migne, *P.G.,* 58, 744.
[586] Matth. 26:26-27. Mark 14:23. Luke 22:19 and 1 Corinth. 11:24.
[587] Owen, *Theology,* p. 413.
[588] St John Chrysostom, *To Matthew,* Homily 25, § 3, in Migne, *P.G.,* 57, 331.
[589] 1 Corinth. 11:20. Theodoretus of Cyrus, *To 1 Corinthians 11:20,* in Migne, *P.G.,* 82, 316.

after supper."[590]   It is also called the *"Lord's Table,"* *"Cup of the Lord,"*[591] the *"Despotic Table"* and *"Table of Christ"*[592] being presented by Christ Himself. His Body and Blood are offered to be eaten and drunk by all those who believe in Him. It is also called the *"breaking of the Bread"*[593] from the *"bread which we break"* which is *"the communion of the Body of Christ."*[594]

From the use of the elements in this Holy Mystery it is also called the *"Living Bread,"*[595] *"the bread which comes down from Heaven"*[596] and the *"Lord's Bread"*, *"Bread of God,"*[597] the *"Heavenly Bread and the Cup of Salvation,"*[598] the *"daily Bread,"*[599] and the *"Cup of blessing"*[600] because of the prayer of thanksgiving through which *"we bless"* this. The Latin Fathers refer to it as *"Sacramentum Calicis."*[601]

From the Supernatural change that takes place, it is called *"Body of Christ"* and *"Blood of Christ,"* Mystical Table and the *"Lord's Body."*[602]   Due to the effect upon those who partake, it is called *"Communion of the Body of Christ," "Communion of the Blood of Christ," "Cup of Life,"*[603] *"Medicine of Immortality," "the antidote we take in order not to die"*[604] and *"Viaticum."* It is also called: *"Altar,"*[605] *"Sacrifice without the shedding of blood," "Prosphora" ("Offering"),*[606] *"Holy Sacrifice," "Mystical"* and *"Logical"*[607] Sacrifice.

---

[590] 1 Corinth. 11:23, 24, 25.

[591] 1 Corinth. 10:21.

[592] Eusebius, *Evangelic Proof,* in Migne, *P.G.,* 22, 92.

[593] Acts 2:42, 46.

[594] 1 Corinth. 10:16.

[595] John 6:51.

[596] John 6:50.

[597] St Ignatius, *To Romans,* 7, 3, in Lightfoot, *Apostolic Fathers,* p. 105.

[598] St Cyril of Jerusalem, *Catechesis Mystagogia,* 4 and 5, § 12, in Migne, *P.G.,* 33, 1100 and 1120.

[599] St Basil, the Great, *About the Holy Spirit,* ch. 27, in Migne, *P.G.,* 32, 188.

[600] 1 Corinth. 10:16.

[601] St Cyprian, *Epistola63, ad Ceacil. De lapsis,* in migne, *P.L.,* 3, 391-397.

[602] *Apostolic Orders* VIII, 13, 15, in *B,* v. 2, p. 158. St Cyril of Jerusalem, *Catechesis Mystagogia,* 4, § 3, in Migne, *P.G.,* 33, 1100.

[603] St Isidorus of Pelusium, *Book I, Epistolale 109,* in Migne, *P.G.,* 78, 256.

[604] St Ignatius, *To Ephesians,* 20, 2, in Lightfoot, *Apostolic Fathers,* p. 93.

[605] Heb. 13:10

[606] Heb. 8:3.

[607] *Apostolic Orders* V, 19, 7; VIII, 5, 7 and 46, 15 and 13, 15, in *B,* v. 2, pp. 90, 144, 172 and 158. Theodoretus of Cyrus, *To Hebrews 8:4,* in Migne, *P.G.,* 82, 736. Eusebius, *Evangelic Proof,* in Migne, *P.G.,* 22, 92.

3. The Superiority of the Holy Mystery

From the above names, which manifest the essence of the Divine Eucharist, one can understand the extreme importance of this Mystery as well as its superiority to the rest of the Holy Sacraments. This Holy Mystery is not only a Supernatural channel through which Divine Grace is transmitted to the faithful but the Saviour and Redeemer Himself exists within it.[608]   In Baptism and Holy Chrismation the Sanctified water and Myrrh become the way through which Divine Grace is transmitted to those who are baptised and anointed, whereas in Eucharist, the use of bread and wine are essentially changed into the exact Body and Blood of our Lord and Saviour Jesus Christ. This change occurs in such a manner that *"it cannot be understood but only through faith"* because invisibly *"the Holy Spirit descends and works those things that are above nature and above word and meaning."*[609] No one can deny that through the Holy Sacraments the Divine Grace acts and transmits in a Supernatural way, which surpasses all understanding. The veil of the Mystery and the Supernatural secrecy, which covers the Divine Eucharist, is above any other Holy Mystery. In the Divine Eucharist the way of change, the Presence of Christ in all the parts of the Holy Communion, the unbreakable union of the Body and the Blood of the Lord in all the Holy Altars and its sameness to the human nature of the Lord, the re-enacting of the one, unique Sacrifice which was offered *"once and for all"* are Sacraments that will remain always unapproachable to the human mind. Only through Faith are these accepted and received.

Through this Mystery the Lord accepts to descend and *"not only to be seen but to be touched, to be eaten and to be engaged."* All these reveal His Love and *"desire which He has for us."* Because of this inexpressible humility of the Lord, man is nourished through His Body, which *"being nailed* (on the Cross) *wiped out death and the sun*

---

[608] Mogilas, *A' 106*, in Karmeris, *The dogmatics,* v. II, p. 389. Jeremias, *A'*, in Karmeris, *The dogmatics,* v. II, p. 638. Dositheus of Jerusalem, *Confession,* Term 16, in Karmeris, *The dogmatics,* v. II, p. 761.

[609] St John of Damascus, *Exposition. To those who ask, if the Theotokos brought forth two natures, and if two natures were hanged on the Cross,* IV, 80, 13, in Migne, *P.G.,* 94, 1141.

seeing Him crucified did not hide its radiance" and *"the angels seeing* (these events) *were horrified and dared not see without shame."*[610]

Truthfully and in reality, man partakes of Heavenly and Angelic Bread. This Bread we will also eat in Heaven for the Lord is Food for all the Heavenly Powers.[611]

The Lord offers equally to all those who believe in Him His Body and Blood. He does not give *"part of His Body to you, and another part is nourished by the other, but from the same Body everyone partakes"* uniting all in Him and to one another. Thus *"we all become noble because He wants."*[612] St. John Chrysostom stated that: *"When you see this Body before you, say to yourself, this Body is no longer earth and dust and I am no longer a prisoner."*[613]

4. The Bond between the Christian Flock and Eucharist

Right from the beginning of the Apostolic era the importance and distinguishable bond that existed between the Christian Flock and the Supernatural and Mystical Table was emphasised. Around this Mystical Table the faithful gathered as members of one Family and one Body. Thus, according to the teachings of the Book of Acts, the faithful *"continued steadfastly in the apostle's doctrine and fellowship, in the breaking of bread, and in prayers"*[614] and *"continuing daily with one accord in the temple, and breaking bread from house to house, they ate their food with gladness and simplicity of heart, praising God and having favour with all the people."*[615]

Didache gives us instructions for officiating the Holy Mystery every Sunday, forbidding the offerings to non-Christians. *"But let no one eat or drink of your Eucharist except those who have been Baptised into the Name of the Lord, for the Lord has also spoken concerning this: 'Do not give what is Holy to dogs.'*[616] *"*[617]

---

[610] St John Chrysostom, *To John,* Homily 46, § 3, in Migne, *P.G.,* 59, 261. Ibid, *To 1 Corinthians,* Homily 24, § 4, in Migne, *P.G.,* 61, 203. Ibid, *To Matthew,* Homily 82, § 5, in Migne, *P.G.,* 58, 743.
[611] St Athanasius the Great, *Epistle* 7, in Migne, *P.G.,* 26, 1395.
[612] St John Chrysostom, *To 1 Corinthians,* Homily 24, § 2, in Migne, *P.G.,* 61, 201-203.
[613] St John Chrysostom, *To 1 Corinthians,* Homily 24, § 4, in Migne, *P.G.,* 61, 203.
[614] Acts 2:42.
[615] Acts 2:46-47.
[616] Matth. 7:6.
[617] *Didache,* 9, 5, in Lightfoot, *Apostolic Fathers,* p. 154.

St. Justin the Philosopher and Martyr, verified the teachings of *Didache* but added that *"on the day of the sun"* which is the *"Lord's Day,"* the faithful gather to partake of the Eucharistic Food, which was *"not received as common bread nor as common drink."*[618]

Very early daily Communion is mentioned. St. Basil the Great noted that *"it is good and beneficial"* to have Communion every day. He assured us that in his community the faithful were receiving Holy Communion *"four times"* a week, on Wednesday, Friday, Saturday and Sunday.[619]

St. Cyprian also noted that every day the Eucharist was received as the nourishment of Salvation.[620]

St. Ambrosius referred to the practice of the Church in Mediolan (Milan), whereby Christ was offered to him every day.[621]

Tertullian also witnessed that the Divine Eucharist was officiated every day, especially on Wednesday and Friday.[622] The Bread of Eucharist was considered by him to be *"our daily bread"*[623] *"which was placed upon the essence of the soul"*[624] or the daily bread *"panis quotidianus"* as being received daily. He gave the reason to the author of the *De Sacramentis* to ask: *"If it is a daily bread, why do you receive it after a year? Receive it every day. Thus, you will live, in order that you will be worthy of partaking of it daily. Whosoever is not worthy to take of it every day is not worthy either to receive it after a year."*[625]

The Newly Illuminated were encouraged to partake of Divine Eucharist regularly. For a whole week, after their baptism, vested in white, they participated in the Liturgy, not only to be guided in the Mystagogy of the Divine Truths, but to have communion of the Divine Sacraments, being taught the Newness of Life in which they were *"born again"* through Baptism. To survive in this natural life we need daily nutrition, likewise in the spiritual life, once Baptised and Regenerated, we are called to participate in the Divine Mystery of Eucharist. We constantly need spiritual nourishment to preserve and

---

[618] St Justin the Philosopher and Martyr, *1 Apology,* 66, 2, in *B*, v. 3, p. 197.
[619] St Basil the Great, *Epistle 93 to sister Patricia*, in Migne, *P.G.,* 32, 484.
[620] St Cyprian, *De oratio Dominica,* 18, in migne, *P.L.,* 4, 549.
[621] St Ambrosius, *In Psalm 118(119), Sermo* 18, 26, in migne, *P.L.,* 15, 461.
[622] Tertullian, *De idol.*, 7, in migne, *P.L.,* 1, 745.
[623] Tertullian, *De oratione,* 6, in migne, *P.L.,* 1, 1263.
[624] St Cyril of Jerusalem, *Catechesis Mystagogia,* 5, § 15, in Migne, *P.G.,* 33, 1120.
[625] St Ambrosius, *De sacramentis*, V, 25, in migne, *P.L.,* 16.

grow in the New Life of Grace. Precisely for this reason the Lord said: *"Whoever eats My flesh and drinks My blood has eternal life."*[626] Consequently the whole life of the faithful is led towards this Holy Mystery by which we are exalted and Sanctified.

As the confirmation of the Mystery of Holy Baptism is the Mystery of Holy Chrismation, likewise the confirmation of Holy Chrismation is the participation in the Holy Mystery of the Divine Eucharist. This Divine Mystery is the centre of all others, for in the Divine Eucharist the ordinations take place; within it the union of those who are joined in the Mystery of Marriage is fulfilled and partake of the offering Gifts; those who turn with repentance are led to the Body and Blood of the Lord; even the Mystery of Holy Unction, the Mystery of healing spiritual wounds, is united with Divine Eucharist

Gennadius of Constantinople stated: *"Oh, Mystery more sacred than any other Sacraments, and surpassing even that of baptism; for through that (baptism) our Master according to power alone, through this (Eucharist) in essence He has communion with us. In this Mystery the creature is changed to the Creator."*[627]

5. Prophetic Announcements and Prefigurations

The Holy Fathers and ecclesiastic writers attempted to find Prophetic announcements and prefigurations concerning the Mystery of Eucharist in the Old Testament. Thus, in Malachi we read: *"For from the rising of the sun even to the going down thereof My Name has been glorified among the Gentiles; and in every place incense is offered to My Name, and a pure offering: for My Name is great among the Gentiles, says the Lord Almighty."*[628] Again we read: *"Cursed is the man who had the power, and possessed a male in his flock, and whose vow is upon him, and who Sacrifices a corrupt thing to the Lord: for I Am a great King, says the Lord Almighty, and My Name is glorious among the nations."*[629]

The Prophet Zephaniah announced *"then will I turn to the peoples a tongue for her generation, that all may call on the Name of*

---

[626] John 6:54.

[627] Gennadius of Constantinople, *About the mysterious body of our Lord Jesus Christ,* in Migne, *P.G.,* 160, 357 and 377.

[628] Mal. 1:11

[629] Mal. 1:14.

the Lord, to serve Him under one yoke. From the boundaries of the rivers of Ethiopia will I receive My dispersed ones; they shall offer Sacrifices to Me."[630]

The Prophet Habakkuk announced that "God shall come from Thaeman, and the Holy One from the dark shady mount Pharan. His excellence covered the Heavens, and the earth was full of his praise. And His brightness shall be as light; there were horns in His hands, and He caused a mighty love of His strength. Before His face shall go a report, and it shall go forth into the plains, the earth stood at His feet and trembled: He beheld, and the nations melted away: the mountains were violently burst through, the everlasting hills melted at His everlasting going forth."[631]

Didache states: "On the Lord's own day gather together and break bread and give thanks, having first confessed your sins so that your Sacrifice may be pure. But let no one who has a quarrel with a companion join you until they have been reconciled, so that your Sacrifice may not be defiled. For this is the Sacrifice which the Lord said, "In every place and time offer Me a pure Sacrifice, for I Am a great King, says the Lord, and My Name is marvellous among the nations.[632]"[633]

St. Irenaeus used the whole verse of the Prophet Malachi and accepted it as an announcement of the Sacrifice within the Divine Eucharist. He observed that through these words, the Prophet noticed that the people would first cease offering other Sacrifices to God and then the Sacrifice in all places would follow and His Name would be glorified in all nations.[634]

St. Cyril of Alexandria noted that the prophecy of the Prophet Malachi was being fulfilled "and churches everywhere, shepherds and teachers, scholars and those who lead to Mystagogues and Divine Altars, the Lamb is Sacrificed conceivably by the Holy officiators."[635]

---

[630] Zephan. 3:9-10.

[631] Hab. 3:3-6.

[632] Mal. 1:14.

[633] Didache, 14, 1-3, in Lightfoot, Apostolic Fathers, p. 157.

[634] St Irenaeus, Heresies, book IV, ch. 17, § 5, in Migne, P.G., 7, 1023. Cf. Ibid, in Hadjephraimides, pp. 296-297.

[635] St Cyril of Alexandria, To Zephaniah 3:10, book II, in Migne, P.G., 71, 1008.

St. John of Damascus commented *"this is the pure Sacrifice without the shedding of blood, which from sunrise to sunset is offered as the Lord said through the Prophet."*[636]

St. John Chrysostom insisted that the announcement of the offering of this Sacrifice from sunrise to sunset raised the question of *"When did these take place?"* to which he responded: *"You do not have any other appointed time but rather after the appearance of Christ."* *"For not only in one city as the Jews"* is this Sacrifice offered but *"from sunrise to sunset."* He continued: *"He says a pure Sacrifice"* explaining that if someone wanted to compare this to those Sacrifices offered in the Old Testament *"he will find the differences great and infinite concerning why this is mainly said to be pure, for not because of smoke nor through blood, but through the Grace of the Holy Spirit is it presented."*[637]

The Old Testament Sacrifices ceased and were replaced by the Eucharist. The former were pre-announcements and prefigurations according to the observations of St Augustine.[638] Before the coming of Christ, the Flesh and Blood of His Sacrifice was announced and prefigured. At the sufferings of Christ, this Truth was proclaimed. After Christ's Ascension the Mystery of remembrance is performed.[639] When those Sacrifices ceased *"the power of worship was in shadows and types"* and through the replacement of these by the Sacrifice of the Eucharist, *"the nature of the thing was moved to the greater."* It remains *"unconceivable, the liturgy of God. For the elders of the Holy Churches approach God and offer to Him the Sacrifice without the shedding of blood."*[640] For this reason, *"at the time of Passover the Lord officiated this Divine Mystery, so that you would learn all that in the Old Testament these were pre-figured."* Whereas the Lord in the New Testament *"placed the truth."* As the Passover was celebrated by the Jews *"in remembrance of the miracles in Egypt"* likewise, the Divine Eucharist, which replaces the Judaic Passover according to the assurance of St. Paul, *"for indeed Christ,*

---

[636] St John of Damascus, *Exposition. About the holy and glorious mysteries of the Lord,* IV, 86, 13, in Migne, *P.G.,* 94, 1152.

[637] St John Chrysostom, *Against Jews*, Homily 4, § 12, in Migne, *P.G.,* 48, 902.

[638] St Augustine, *De civitate Dei,* X, 20, in migne, *P.L.,* 41, 295.

[639] Ibid, *Contra Faustum,* XX, 21, in migne, *P.L.,* 42, 385. Ibid, VI, 5, in migne, *P.L.,* 42, 251.

[640] St Cyril of Alexandria, *To Habakkuk* 3:6, in Migne, *P.G.,* 71, 916.

our Passover, was Sacrificed for us."[641] We officiate in remembrance of the Lord. The blood of the sacrificed lamb in Egypt[642] *"was shed for the salvation of the firstborns*[643]*"* whereas the Blood of the Lamb of God was shed *"for the forgiveness of sins of the entire world. For this is My Blood, He said, which is shed for the forgiveness of sins.*[644]*"*[645]

St. Ambrosius said *"the Apostle spoke about this type; that our fathers ate spiritual food and drank spiritual water."*[646]

Concerning the prefigurations of the Holy Mystery of Eucharist, the Holy Fathers initially exalted the offering of *"bread and wine"*[647] by Melchizedek. They believed *"that table prefigured this mystical table, as Melchizedek the Priest was the type and image of the true High Priest Christ."*[648] Furthermore, the *"showbread"*[649] as well as the *"manna,"* prefigured *"this Bread"* of Eucharist by means of which the Jews were fed in the desert[650] together with the waters that sprang forth from the rock in Choreb.[651] Christ spoke of the manna by comparing it to the true *"Bread of Life"* saying: *"Our fathers ate the manna in the desert; as it is written, 'He gave them bread from Heaven to eat.' Then Jesus said to them, "Most assuredly, I say to you, Moses did not give the bread from Heaven, but My Father gives you the true bread from Heaven. For, the Bread of God is He Who comes down from Heaven and gives Life to the world." Then they said to Him, 'Lord, give us this bread always.' And Jesus said to them, "I Am the Bread of Life. He who comes to Me shall never hunger, and he who believes in Me shall never thirst."*[652]

---

[641] 1 Corinth. 5:7.
[642] Gen. 12:3, 5-13.
[643] Gen. 12:21-23.
[644] Matth. 26:28.
[645] St John Chrysostom, *To Matthew*, Homily 82, § 1, in Migne, *P.G.*, 58, 739.
[646] St Ambrosius, *De mysteriis*, c. IX, 58, in migne, *P.L.*, 16, 426.
[647] Gen. 14:18.
[648] St John of Damascus, *Catechesis*, IV, 13, in Migne, *P.G.*, 94, 1149. St Epiphanius, *Heresis*, 55, § 6, in Migne, *P.G.*, 41, 981.
[649] Lev. 24:5-9. Ex. 29:32. Matth. 12:4. Heb. 9:2.
[650] Ex. 16:4, 16. John 6:31, 49, 58. Nehemiah. 9:15. Psalm 77(78):24. Heb. 9:4. Rev. 2:17.
[651] Ex. 17:5-7. 1 Corinth. 10:4.
[652] John 6:31-35.

6. The Divine Institution

The Divine Institution is clearly expressed in the New Testament. Our Lord and Saviour Jesus Christ, the Son of God, pre-announced the establishment of this Holy Mystery, preparing His Holy Disciples to receive the new Christian Passover that He would deliver to them. This Institution of the most Divine and Sacred Mystery was not an inspiration of the moment but an essential act of Divine Providence. This pre-announcement was declared because of the Miracle of the feeding of the five thousand.[653] Christ mentioned the *"living bread"* by proclaiming:

"I Am the living bread which came down from Heaven. If anyone eats of this bread, he will live forever; and the bread that I shall give is My flesh, which I shall give for the life of the world."[654] He continued. *"Most assuredly, I say to you, unless you eat the flesh of the Son of Man and drink His blood, you have no life in you. Whoever eats My flesh and drinks My blood has eternal life, and I will raise him up at the last day. For My flesh is food indeed, and My blood is drink indeed. He who eats My flesh and drinks My blood abides in Me, and I in him. As the living Father sent Me, I live because of the Father, so he who feeds on Me will live because of Me. This is the bread which came down from Heaven – not as your fathers ate the manna, and are dead. He who eats this bread will live forever."*[655]

We have four narrations concerning the establishment of the Divine Mystery of Eucharist in the New Testament, which can be divided into two groups. The first group can be incorporated in the tradition according to St. Paul, which consists of the narration of St. Paul in his Epistle to the Corinthians[656] and that which is found in the Holy Gospel according to St Luke.[657] The second group represents the tradition of St. Peter, which is found in the narration of St Mark and is almost similar to that found in the Holy Gospel of St Matthew.[658] Although one can distinguish differences between these

---

[653] Matth. 14:13-21. Mark 6:30-44. Luke 9:10-17. John 6:1-14. CF. Mitsopoulos, *Themata,* p. 317.
[654] John 6:51.
[655] John 6:53-58.
[656] 1 Corinth. 11:23-25. Cf. Plato of Moscow, *Orthodox Teaching,* p. 153-155.
[657] Luke 22:19-20.
[658] Mark 14:22-24 and Matth. 26:26-28.

two groups, they are secondary and non-essential. The essential agreement of the four narrations is not contradictory.

Dositheus, Patriarch of Jerusalem, remarked that *"the most Holy Mystery of the Sacred Eucharist, the Lord delivered Himself on that night for the life of the world. He took bread and blessed, gave to His Holy disciples and apostles saying: 'Take, eat; this is My body, drink from it, all of you. For this is My blood of the New Covenant, which is shed for many for the remission of sins.*[659]*"*[660]

Mogilas referred to the words of St. Paul in 1st Corinthians whereby he *"received from the Lord that which I also delivered to you: that the Lord Jesus on the same night in which He was betrayed took bread; and when He had given thanks, He broke it and said, 'Take, eat; this is My body which is broken for you; do this in remembrance of Me.' In the same manner He also took the Cup after supper, saying, 'This Cup is the New Covenant in My blood. This do, as often as you drink it, in remembrance of Me.' For as often as you eat this bread and drink this Cup, you proclaim the Lord's death until He comes. Therefore, whoever eats this bread or drinks this Cup of the Lord in an unworthy manner will be guilty of the Body and Blood of the Lord. But let a man examine himself, and so let him eat of the bread and drink of the Cup. For he who eats and drinks in an unworthy manner, eats and drinks Judgement to himself, not discerning the Lord's Body. For this reason, many are weak and sick among you, and many sleep.*[661]*"*[662]

Kritopoulos mentioned that *"all the Evangelists speak about the Lord that He took bread."*[663]

Jeremias also noted that *"the Lord on the night that He was delivered, took bread and giving thanks He broke and said Take, eat."*[664]

Our Lord and Saviour Jesus Christ, the Son of God, gave this Divine and Heavenly Mystery so that it may be officiated forever until His Second glorious Coming.[665] In the tradition of St. Paul it includes

---

[659] Matth. 26:26, 27-28.
[660] Dositheus of Jerusalem, *Confession*, ch. 17, pp. 41.
[661] 1 Corinth. 11:23-30.
[662] Mogilas, *A' 107*, in Karmeris, *The dogmatics*, v. II, p. 532.
[663] Kritopoulos, ch. 9, in Karmeris, *The dogmatics*, v. II, p. 639.
[664] Jeremias, *A'*, in Karmeris, *The dogmatics*, v. II, p. 761.
[665] Cf. Plato of Moscow, *Orthodox Teaching*, pp. 149-152.

the instruction: *"Do this in remembrance of Me."*[666] When the end of the world comes and the Kingdom of God is established, the relation and communion between the Lord and the faithful will be perfected, the Mystery of the Holy Eucharist will not only continue, but will be perfected in such a manner that the Cup of the Eucharist will be drunk in perfect communion with the Lord as *"new"*[667] *"until it is fulfilled in the Kingdom of God."*[668]

Eusebius declared that *"we who are on earth partake of the bread which came down from Heaven and partake of the Word Who emptied Himself and became lesser. Those in the Kingdom of Heaven perfectly partake of Him, being nourished through His Divinity and enjoying the theories of the wisdom."*[669]

The Mystery of Divine Eucharist as the communion of the faithful with the Lord and as the inauguration of the close relationship with Him, as between that of the head and the rest of the body, will never cease, but beginning from this life, it will be perfected in the future Kingdom.

II. THE VISIBLE ASPECT OF THE HOLY MYSTERY, TERMS OF ITS PERFECTION AND PARTICIPATION

The visible elements that are used in the Divine Eucharist are the bread and wine mixed with a small portion of water. These elements are Sanctified by the invocation of the Holy Spirit, which follows immediately after the reciting of the words of institution and the instruction of remembrance. Although the Divine Eucharist is a Sacrifice offered by the whole Orthodox Church, the officiator in the Sanctification as the instrument of the Great and High Priest Who unites and offers and is received, is the Bishop or Presbyter being served and assisted by the Deacon. Participators of the Holy Mystery, by means of both elements, are all those who are Baptised, regardless of their age, who must examine themselves and thus, partake in the Mystery through true repentance.

---

[666] 1 Corinth. 11:24, 25.
[667] Luke 22:20.
[668] Luke 22:16.
[669] Eusebius, *To Psalm 33:6-8,* in Migne, *P.G.,* 23, 296.

1. The Use of Leavened Bread

The use of leavened bread in the Divine Eucharist was the general practice in the entire Orthodox Church since the Apostolic era until this day. None of the ancient Holy Fathers or ecclesiastic writers used the term *"unleavened bread"* (***"azyma"***) concerning the bread of the Eucharist. All spoke of leavened bread (***"artos"***). This Eucharistic bread through the Eucharist *"is no longer considered common bread"*[670] nor is it *"received as such."*[671] These phrases imply that before the Eucharist, it was simple and ordinary bread. The bread which Melchizedek offered to Abraham was highlighted very early as the prototype of the Eucharistic Bread and was obviously not *"unleavened bread"* (*"azyma"*) but *"leavened"* (*"artos"*), which was used in the Divine Eucharist.[672]

In the Synoptic Gospels, the Lord ate with His Disciples at Passover. However, we must not think that that Passover was Judaic since, according to the Gospel of St. John, it is clearly and undoubtedly stated that *"before the Feast of the Passover"*[673] the Last Supper took place and therefore on *"the Preparation Day"*[674] before the Judaic Passover, the Lord was crucified.[675] This is evident from the Synoptics according to which, on the day of Christ's Crucifixion, Simon the Cyrenian,[676] if it had been the Day of the Judaic Passover, certainly would not have been working or travelling, thus disregarding the Law concerning the Sabbath. Consequently, the Lord by eating the New Christian Passover with His Holy Apostles and Disciples abolished *"the chief feast"* of Judaism, *"transferred it to a more frightening Table and leads* (the Apostles) *away from the Judaic costumes."* It was obvious that by celebrating a New Passover, completely He had put aside the use of the shadowy *"unleavened bread"* (*"azyma"*).

The first Christian Church consisted of Jews who used *"unleavened bread"* (*"azyma"*) during the week of the Judaic

---

[670] St Irenaeus, *Heresies,* book IV, ch. 18, § 5, in Migne, *P.G., P.G.,* 7, 1023. Cf. Ibid, in Hadjephraimides, pp. 299-300.

[671] St Justin the Philosopher and Martyr, *1 Apology,* 66, 2, in ***B***, v. 3, p. 197.

[672] Cf. Bryennios, *Paralipomena,* ch. XXX, v. III, pp. 103-104. Mitsopoulos, *Themata,* pp. 317-318.

[673] John 13:1.

[674] Matth. 26:17. Mark 14:12. Luke 22:7. John 19:31. John 18:28

[675] Matth. 27:32-44. Mark 15:21-32. Luke 23:26-43. John 19:17-37.

[676] Mark 15:21. Matth. 27:32. Luke 23:26.

Passover. In Holy Scripture it is stated that the Lord, at *"the breaking of bread"* used normal, leavened bread. It must therefore be very strongly emphasised that Holy Scripture clearly differentiates the use of the terms *"unleavened bread"* (*"azyma"*)[677] and *"leavened bread"* (*"artos"*)[678] and under no circumstance can there be any confusion. According to the author of the *Sacramentis*, the Bread of Eucharist was always ordinary bread (*"panis usitatus"*).[679]

2.   The Use of Wine

Wine is the second element used by our Lord and Saviour Jesus Christ, the Son of God, in the Divine Eucharist, according to the testimonies of the Evangelists.[680] This is witnessed by St. Justin the Philosopher and Martyr,[681] St. Irenaeus[682] and St. Cyprian[683] who condemned the heretics for using plain water in their Eucharist.[684]

From the beginning, the wine was mixed with water according to Palestinian tradition whereby wine was not drunk without mingling with water. This is reminiscent of the liturgy recorded in the *Apostolic Orders*, according to which the Lord *"mixed in the Cup wine and water and Sanctified gave it to them saying, 'Drink of it.'"* [685] It reminds us also of the piercing of the Lord's side on the Cross from which water and blood came out.[686]

St. Cyprian saw this mixing of the wine with water as the symbolic union of Christ with His Church. He observed that when the water is poured in the Cup (Chalice), the people are united with Christ. He explained that if one uses only wine in the Eucharist then

---

[677] Matth. 26:17. Mark 14:1, 12. Luke 22:1, 7. Acts 12:3. 1 Corinth. 5:7, 8.

[678] **Matth.** 4:3, 4; 6:11; 7:9; 12:4. 14:17,19; 15:2, 26, 33, 34, 36; 16:5, 7, 8, 9, 10, 11, 12; 26:26. **Mark** 3:20; 6:8, 36, 37, 38, 41, 44, 52; 7:2, 5, 27; 8:4, 5, 14, 16, 19; 14:22. **Luke** 4:3; 7:33; 9:3, 13, 16; 11:3, 5, 11; 14:1, 15; 15:17; 22:19; 24:30, 35. **John** 6:5, 7, 9, 11, 13, 23, 26, 31, 32, 33, 34, 35, 41, 48, 50, 51, 58; 13:18; 21:9, 13. **Acts** 2:42, 46; 20:7, 11; 27:35. **1 Corinth.** 10:16, 17; 11:23, 26, 27, 28.   **2 Corinth.** 9:10. **2 Tim.** 3:8, 12. **Heb.** 9:2.

[679] St Ambrosius, *Sacramentis*, IV, § 14.

[680] Matth. 26:28. Mark 14:25. Luke 22:18.

[681] St Justin the Philosopher and Martyr, *1 Apology*, 65, 2, in *B*, v. 3, p. 197.

[682] St Irenaeus, *Heresies*, book V, ch. 2, § 3, in Migne, *P.G.*, 7, 1125. Cf. Ibid, in Hadjephraimides, pp. 364-365.

[683] St Cyprian, *Epistola*63, in migne, *P.L.*, 4, 392.

[684] St John Chrysostom, *To Matthew*, Homily 82, § 2, in Migne, *P.G.*, 58, 740.

[685] *Apostolic Orders*, VIII, 12, 37, *B*, v. 2, p. 155. Clement the Alexandrian, *Pedagogus*, II, ch. 2, in Migne, *P.G.*, 8, 409.

[686] Cf. John 19:34.

the Blood of Christ excludes the Faithful, whereas if there is only water in the Cup, this would exclude Christ.[687]

3.   The Sanctifying Words

In the ancient Church one does not find any specific prayer which Sanctifies the offering Gifts of Eucharist.[688]

Didache instructs the faithful *"on the Lord's own day gather, break bread and give thanks, having first confessed your sins beforehand so that your Sacrifice may be pure."*[689]

St. Justin the Philosopher and Martyr spoke of *"Eucharistic bread and wine and water"* and of *"Eucharistic nourishment through prayer"*[690] without determining which prayer Sanctifies them.

St. Irenaeus generally observed that *"the mixed Cup and the bread receive the Word of God and become the Body of Christ in the Eucharist."*[691]

Origen reached the same conclusion, observing that we *"thank the Creator of all with prayers presenting bread which becomes the Body (of Christ)."* Elsewhere he noted *"that which is Sanctified is by the Word of God and prayer."*[692]

St. Gregory of Nyssa on the other hand repeated that *"the bread is Sanctified by the word of God and prayer."*[693]

St. Athanasius of Alexandria, in a fragment saved by Eulogius of Constantinople, noted *"the Levites carrying the breads and cup of wine, placed them upon the altar accompanied by many prayers and petitions. This was a pre-figuration of what takes place now. In the Divine Liturgy the bread and the cup are ordinary but when the great and admirable prayers are fulfilled the Word comes down upon the Bread and the Cup and they become His Body."*[694]

St. Augustine referring to the words which Sanctify the Holy Mystery are characterised by Bartmann as being *"symbolic and*

---

[687] St Cyprian, *Epistola*63, 13, in migne, *P.L.,* 4, 395.

[688] Bartmann, *Theologie Dogmatique,* v. II, p. 349.

[689] *Didache,* 14, 1, in Lightfoot, *Apostolic Fathers,* p. 157.

[690] St Justin the Philosopher and Martyr, *1 Apology,* 65, *B*, v. 3, p. 197.

[691] St Irenaeus, *Heresies,* book V, ch. 2, § 3, in Migne, *P.G.,* 7, 1125.   Cf. Ibid, in Hadjephraimides, p. 364.

[692] Origen, *Against Celsus,* VIII, 33, in *B*, v. 10, p. 199.

[693] St Gregory of Nyssa, *Catechesis,* 37, in Migne, *P.G.,* 45, 97.

[694] St Athanasius the Great, *Fragment in Eulogius of Constantinople,* in Migne, *P.G.,* 26, 1325.

unclear."[695] He spoke of the Bread on the Altar, which is Sanctified by the Word of God into the Body and the Cup into the Blood of Christ.[696] This Mystery is Sanctified by Christ Who changes the two elements into His Body and Blood. Again he spoke of the essence that is taken from the fruits of the earth and Sanctified through the Mysterious prayer into the Body of Christ.[697]

In the "*Anaphora*" of St Hippolytus the words of institution were combined with the invocation,[698] which were recited mainly for the faithful in order that they be filled with the Holy Spirit. This "*Anaphora*" beseeches the Holy Spirit to descend upon the offered Gifts of the Holy Church and Sanctify them. As a result, the faithful are "*filled with all blessings and Grace.*"[699]

All the Holy Fathers from the 4th century onwards, unanimously declared that in the Eucharist the change of the bread and wine takes place after the invocation.[700] St. Cyril of Jerusalem repeatedly stressed that "*the Bread of the Eucharist, after the invocation of the Holy Spirit, is no longer ordinary bread but the Body of Christ.*" "*We ask God Who loves man to send the Holy Spirit upon the presented Gifts and to make the bread the Body of Christ and the wine the Blood of Christ. Whatever the Holy Spirit touches, is changed and Sanctified.*"[701]

St. Basil the Great referred to "*the words of the invocation which blesses the Eucharistic Bread and Cup.*" He stated that we received this tradition "*from the unwritten teachings.*"[702] Whereas the invocation and prayer are addressed in order that the Holy Spirit be sent to "*bless and sanctify and make*" the presented Gifts into the Body and Blood of Christ.

Not only the Christian East, but the West as well, insisted that the Sanctification is caused by the invocation.[703] Only St. Ambrosius

---

[695] Bartmann, *Theologie Dogmatique*, v. II, p. 350.

[696] St Augustine, *Sermo* 227, in migne, *P.L.*, 38, 1099.

[697] Ibid, *De Trinitate*, III, 4, § 10, in migne, *P.L.*, 42, 874. Ibid, *Epistola*149 *ad Paulinum*, c. 2, § 16, in migne, *P.L.*, 33, 636-637.

[698] St Hippolytus, in Bartmann, *Theologie Dogmatique*, v. II, p. 379.

[699] Bartmann, *Theologie Dogmatique*, v. II, p. 350.

[700] Evdokimov, *Orthodoxia*, pp. 337-353.

[701] St Cyril of Jerusalem, *Catechesis*, XXI, § 3; XXIV, § 7; and XIX, § 7, in Migne, *P.G.*, 33, 1089, 1092, 1113, 1116 and 1072.

[702] St Basil the Great, *About the Holy Spirit*, ch. XXVII, § 66, in Migne, *P.G.*, 32, 188.

[703] Bartmann, *Theologie Dogmatique*, v. II, p. 350. Hieronymus, *Epistola*146, § 1, in migne, *P.L.*, 22, 1193. St Isidorus of Pelusium, *Book I, Epistolale 109*, in Migne, *P.G.*, 78, 256. Theodoretus of Cyrus, *Dialogue*, II, in Migne, *P.G.*, 83, 165-168.

declared that Sanctification takes place with the reciting of the words of institution.[704] Tertullian did not refer to the Sanctification at the time of the celebration of the Eucharist but in the change during the Last Supper, according to which the Lord, taking the bread in His Hands and distributing it to His Disciples made it His Body by saying: *"This is My Body."*[705]

St. John Chrysostom stressed that *"the same Christ Who was crucified for us is present"* during the celebration of the Divine Eucharist. He assured us that *"the saying 'This is My body' changes the present. And as the Commandment of God to 'Increase and multiply and fill the earth' was said once, but through time became work strengthening our nature for child-bearing, likewise the New Commandment concerning the institution of the Divine Eucharist was also said once and affects every Altar until His Second Coming."* Through these teachings he emphasised the irrefutable institution of the Holy Mystery as well as the invisible and continuous perfection of the Great High Priest. However, he does not exclude the importance of the invocation. This is clearly manifested from the fact that he repeatedly refers to it.[706]

St. John of Damascus, following St. John Chrysostom, assured us that the *"bread of the prothesis (preparation table) and the wine and the water through the invocation and descent of the Holy Spirit are changed Supernaturally into the Body and Blood of Christ."* He also stressed that *"the Holy Spirit descends and makes them above any word and understanding."*[707]

According to the above, we can say that the Sanctification of the precious Gifts (bread and wine) are perfected through the invocation and prayer. No one can deny that the invocation is enough to perfect the whole Mystery of Eucharist as this occurs in Holy Baptism where the calling upon the Name of the Father and of the Son and of the Holy Spirit is sufficient to perfect the Holy Mystery of Baptism. In the Divine Eucharist the invocation is based *"upon the saving*

---

[704] St Ambrosius, *De Sacramentis,* IV, cap. 4, § 14, in migne, *P.L.,* 16, 459. Ibid, *De mysteriis,* IX, 54, in migne, *P.L.,* 16, 424.

[705] Tertullian, *Adversus Marcianem,* IV, 40, in migne, *P.L.,* 2, 491.

[706] St John Chrysostom, *To the betrayal of Judas,* § 6, in Migne, *P.G.,* 49, 380. Ibid, *About priesthood,* III, § 4 and VI, § 4, in Migne, *P.G.,* 48, 642 and 681. Ibid, *To the name of the cemetery and to the Cross,* § 3, in Migne, *P.G.,* 49, 398. Ibid, *To the understanding of the apostle and high priest of our faith,* in Migne, *P.G.,* 64, 489.

[707] St John of Damascus, *Exposition. About the holy and glorious mysteries of the Lord,* IV, 86, 13, in Migne, *P.G.,* 94, 1145.

Commandment 'Do this in My remembrance," in order to have the exact re-enactment of that which the Lord delivered at the Last Supper. It is necessary to recite the words of institution followed by invocation."[708]

The words of institution and invocation consist of two important parts of the whole "*Anaphora*" and without the words of institution, we risk not having whatever Christ delivered. Furthermore, without the invocation we are in danger of not having the Sanctification and change of the two elements (Bread and Wine).

"*The bread is changed into the exact Body and the wine is changed into the exact Blood of the Lord through the invocation and sacred prayers by the Grace of the Almighty Spirit.*"[709] "*The bread and the wine and water of the prothesis through the invocation and visitation of the Holy Spirit are changed into the exact Body and Blood of Christ.*"[710] The change is accomplished "*through the action of the Holy Spirit Who is called at that moment to perfect this Mystery, praying and saying: 'Send down your Holy Spirit upon us and upon these presented Gifts and make ' After these words the change immediately takes place and the bread changes into the real Body and the wine into the real Blood of Christ.*"[711]

4. The Officiators of the Holy Mystery of Eucharist

The Bishop or the Presbyter is the officiator and instrument who serves the invisible High Priest, Christ our God, in order to perfect the Holy Mystery.[712] Neither the Bishop nor the Presbyter "*who is present*" before the Altar "*acts, but God acts through him.*" This act is not of any "*human nature but is the achievement of the Grace of the Spirit Who is present, oversees and prepares the Mystical Sacrifice.*" This is the fundamental teaching of the Orthodox Church, which refers to the entire perfection of the Holy Sacraments. This great truth is stressed in the prayers of the Divine Liturgy whereby "*no man makes the offering of bread and wine to become the Body and Blood of Christ*" but "*the Priest standing and reciting those words*" which were said in the "*upper room at that Supper*" Christ "*changes and*

---

[708] Karmeris, *Synopsis,* p. 101, note 1.
[709] Jeremias, A', in Karmeris, *The dogmatics,* v. II, p. 394.
[710] Ibid, B', in Karmeris, *The dogmatics,* v. II, p. 460.
[711] Mogilas, A' 107, in Karmeris, *The dogmatics,* v. II, p. 638.
[712] Frangopoulos, *Christian Faith,* pp. 201-204. Georgopoulos, *Anthology,* pp. 22-23.

Sanctifies them." The officiator prays to the Lord as our High Priest as He Who offers and is being offered and Who accepts the Sacrifice of the Eucharist, which is distributed to the faithful. Christ is He Who invisibly unites those who surround the Holy Altar to Himself in order to offer the Sanctified Gifts not only to them but also through them to all His people. Hence, St. John Chrysostom urged the faithful *"to partake of the Divine Body by approaching, not as receiving from man, but as in the case of the Prophet Isaiah[713] who saw the Seraphim touching his lips with the burning coal, and thus partaking of the saving Blood."[714]*

Besides the above, only the Bishop or the Presbyter serve the invisible High Priest and only they are used by Him as the instruments for the perfection of the Divine Eucharist.[715] The Eucharist is simultaneously a Sacrifice that is offered by the whole Orthodox Church. The plain bread and wine are Sanctified and changed into the actual Body and Blood of Christ by the Grace of the Holy Spirit and through the officiator. They are changed into the Sacrifice of Golgotha, becoming the Sacrifice of the entire Holy Orthodox Church and as such, refer to the Holy Trinity, the only and True God.

The Bishop or Presbyter is the only officiator of the Holy and Heavenly Mystery. The Lord delivered this Mystery to His Apostles and gave them the Commandment *"do this in remembrance of Me."[716]* The instruction *"Take, eat"* and *"drink of it all of you"* was addressed only to His Holy Apostles. This is supported by the practice and Tradition of the Orthodox Church.

In the *Didache* we find the instruction: *"Appoint for yourselves Bishops and Deacons worthy of the Lord, men who are humble and not avaricious and true and approved, for they too carry out for you the ministry of the Prophets and Teachers."[717]*

In the Letter of St. Clement of Rome to the Corinthians the Bishops and Deacons are compared to the Priests and Levites of the Old Testament and are recognised as the only officiators. *"Let each of*

---

[713] Is. 6:6-7.

[714] St John Chrysostom, *To the holy Pentecost,* Homily 1, § 4, in Migne, *P.G.,* 50, 49. Ibid, *To the betrayal of Judas,* § 6, in Migne, *P.G.,* 49, 380. Ibid, *To Matthew,* Homily 82, § 5, in Migne, *P.G.,* 58, 744 . Ibid, *About repentance,* Homily 2, § 1, in Migne, *P.G.,* 49, 345.

[715] Mogilas, *A'* 107, in Karmeris, *The dogmatics,* v. II, p. 638. Dositheus of Jerusalem, *Confession,* Term 16, in Karmeris, *The dogmatics,* v. II, p. 763.

[716] Luke 22:19.

[717] *Didache,* 15, 1, in Lightfoot, *Apostolic Fathers,* p. 157.

you, brothers, in his proper order, give thanks to God, maintaining a good conscience, not overstepping the designated rule of his ministry, but acting with reverence. Not just anywhere, brothers are the continuous officiators of the daily Sacrifices which are offered. And even there (Jerusalem) *the offering is not made in every place, but in front of the sanctuary at the altar, the offering having been first inspected for blemishes by the high Priest and the previously mentioned ministers. Those, therefore, who do anything contrary to the duty imposed by his will receive death as the penalty. You see, brothers, as we have been considered worthy of greater knowledge, so much the more are we exposed to danger."*[718] *"The Apostles received the gospel for us from the Lord Jesus Christ; Jesus the Christ was sent forth from God. So then Christ is from God, and the Apostles are from Christ. Both, therefore, came of the Will of God in good order. Having therefore received their orders and being fully assured by the Resurrection of our Lord Jesus Christ and full of faith in the Word of God, they went forth with the firm assurance that the Holy Spirit gives, preaching the good news that the Kingdom of God was about to come. So, preaching both in the country and in the towns, they appointed their first fruits, when they had tested them by the Spirit, to be Bishops and Deacons for the future believers. And this was no new thing they did, for indeed something had been written about Bishops and Deacons many years ago; for somewhere thus, says the Scripture: 'I will appoint their Bishops in righteousness and their Deacons in faith'*[719]*"*[720] *"Let us, therefore, serve as soldiers, brothers, with all earnestness under His faultless orders. Let us consider the soldiers who serve under our commanders, how precisely, how readily, how obediently they execute orders. Not all are prefects or tribunes or centurions or captains of fifty and so forth, but each in his own rank executes the orders given by the emperor and the commanders. The great cannot exist without the small, or the small without the great. There is a certain blending in everything, and therein lies the advantage. Let us take our body as an example. The head without the feet is nothing; likewise, the feet without the head are nothing. Even the smallest parts of our body are necessary and useful to the whole*

---

[718] St Clement of Rome, *1st Corinthians,* 41, 1-4, in Lightfoot, *Apostolic Fathers,* pp. 50-51.
[719] Cf. Is. 60:17
[720] St Clement of Rome, *1st Corinthians,* 42, 1-5, in Lightfoot, *Apostolic Fathers,* p. 51.

body, yet all the members work together and unite in mutual subjection, that the whole body may be saved."[721]

St. Ignatius of Antioch very clearly proclaimed that "*only that Eucharist which is under the authority of the Bishop (or whomever he himself designates) is to be considered valid. Wherever the Bishop appears, there let the congregation be; just as wherever Jesus Christ is, there is the catholic Church. It is not permissible either to Baptise or to hold a love feast* (the Divine Liturgy) *without the Bishop. But whatever he approves is also pleasing to God, in order that everything you do may be trustworthy and valid.*"[722] Elsewhere he stated that "*when you are subject to the Bishop as to Jesus Christ, it is evident to me that you are living, not in accordance with human standards, but in accordance with Jesus Christ Who died for us in order that by believing in His death you might escape death. It is essential, therefore, that you continue your current practice and do nothing without the Bishop, but be subject also to the Presbytery as to the Apostles of Jesus Christ, our Hope, in Whom we shall be found, if we so live. Furthermore, it is necessary that those who are Deacons of the "Sacraments" of Jesus Christ please everyone in every respect. For they are not merely 'Deacons' of food and drink, but ministers of God's Church. Therefore they must avoid criticism as though it were fire.*"[723] "*Similarly, let everyone respect the Deacons as Jesus Christ, just as they should respect the Bishop, who is a model of the Father, and the Presbyters as God's Council and as the band of Apostles. Without these no group can be called a church.*"[724] "*Take care, therefore, to practice in one Eucharist (for there is one Flesh of our Lord Jesus Christ, and one Cup which leads to unity through His Blood; there is one Altar, just as there is one Bishop, together with the Presbytery and the Deacons, my fellow servants), in order that whatever you do, you do in accordance with God.*"[725]

According to St. Justin the Philosopher and Martyr, "*to the presiding of the brothers*" was offered "*the Bread and the Cup mixed with water.*" The first gave thanks on behalf of "*all the people*" with

---

[721] Ibid, *1ˢᵗ Corinthians,* 37, 1-5, in Lightfoot, *Apostolic Fathers,* p. 49.

[722] St Ignatius, *To Smyrnaeans,* 8, 1-2, in Lightfoot, *Apostolic Fathers,* pp. 112-113.

[723] St Ignatius, *To Trallians,* 2, 1-3, in Lightfoot, *Apostolic Fathers,* pp. 97-98.

[724] Ibid, *ToTrallians,* 3, 1, in Lightfoot, *Apostolic Fathers,* p. 98.

[725] Ibid, *To Philadelphians,* 4, in Lightfoot, *Apostolic Fathers,* p. 107.

Eucharist and *"the Deacons gave to each of those who were present and brought to those who were absent."*[726]

St. Cyprian stressed that *"if Christ is the High Priest of the Father Who presented Himself and commanded this to be done in His remembrance, it is also certain, that each Priest is in the place of Christ, because he repeats whatever Christ did."*[727] St. Cyprian also informed us that the Deacons give the Cup.[728]

In the *Apostolic Orders* it is stated that *"the Deacon can neither offer a proper Sacrifice nor Baptise."* However, according to the giving of the Eucharist *"the Bishop allows him to give the offering by saying 'Body of Christ' and he who receives, let him say: 'Amen.' Let the Deacon hold the Cup of Life and giving, let him say: 'Blood of Christ', and he who drinks, let him say: 'Amen."*[729]

Laymen were forbidden to officiate the Holy Mystery of the Eucharist[730], whereas it was permitted for them to carry the precious Gifts on serious occasions.[731]

5. Partakers of the Holy Mystery

Those who are not Baptised are excluded from partaking of Holy Eucharist as well as those who have fallen into major sin and who, in order to become worthy, must purify themselves through pure repentance.[732] In addition the Holy Mystery is never offered to heretics[733] and all those who have separated themselves from the One, Holy, Catholic and Apostolic Eastern Orthodox Church.

St. Paul instructed each of us to *"examine himself, and so let him eat of the bread and drink of the Cup. For he who eats and drinks in an unworthy manner eats and drinks Judgement to himself, not discerning the Lord's Body."*[734] Those who approach unworthily not

---

[726] St Justin the Philosopher and Martyr, *1 Apology,* 65, in **B**, v. 3, p. 197.

[727] St Cyprian, *Epistola63,* 14, in migne, *P.L.,* 4, 397.

[728] Ibid, *De lapsis,* 25, in migne, *P.L.,* 4, 50.

[729] *Apostolic Orders,* VIII, 46, 11 and 13, 15, in **B**, v. 2, pp. 171 and 158.

[730] Tertullian, *De exhort. Cast,* VII, in migne, *P.L.,* 2, 971. Ibid, *De coron. militiae,* c. 3, in migne, *P.L.,* 2, 99.

[731] Eusebius, *Church History,* VI, 44, in Migne, *P.G.,* 20, 629.

[732] St Symeon, *Euriskomena,* Homily XLI, pp. 188-193.

[733] St John of Damascus, *Exposition. About the holy and glorious mysteries of the Lord,* IV, 86, 13, in Migne, *P.G.,* 94, 1153.

[734] 1 Corinth. 11:28-29.

only face spiritual consequences but also threats against their health and even their lives.[735]

Didache instructs that *"let no one eat or drink of your Eucharist except those who have been Baptised into the Name of the Lord, for the Lord has also spoken concerning this: 'Do not give what is Holy to dogs.*[736]*"*[737] Furthermore, *Didache* urges those who are Baptised to break the Bread on the Lord 's Day *"having first confessed your sins, so that your Sacrifice may be pure."*[738]

Similarly, and according to St. Justin the Philosopher and Martyr, it was required from all those who would partake of the Holy Mystery to believe in the Christian Teaching and to promise that they would live in full agreement and obedience to it. Thus, those who were accepted in Baptism were presented in the gathering of the brothers and were accepted in the Holy Eucharist.[739]

St. Cyprian refers to the case of a mother and child who had unworthily approached the Holy Mystery resulting in their sickness and death.[740]

Origen repeatedly refers to the consequences when one does not prepare himself properly before approaching the Divine Mystery. Referring to the words of St. Paul, he asked the unworthy if they thought they could escape the Judgement of God by approaching the Eucharist without fear and ignoring that which was written: *"For this reason many are weak and sick among you, and many sleep.*[741]*"*[742] In other instances he used the example of Judas who took *"from Jesus bread similar to that which was given to the rest of the Apostles in the 'Take, eat,' but for them it was for Salvation, whereas for Judas it was for condemnation, as after the bread Satan entered in him"* because *"the benefit of the Lord's Bread is for the user, as long as he partakes of the Bread with a pure mind and clean conscience."*[743]

---

[735] 1 Corinth. 11:30.
[736] Matth. 7:6.
[737] *Didache*, 9, 5, in Lightfoot, *Apostolic Fathers,* p. 154.
[738] Ibid, 14, 1, in Lightfoot, *Apostolic Fathers,* p. 157.
[739] St Justin the Philosopher and Martyr, *1 Apology,* 66, in **B,** v. 3, p. 197.
[740] St Cyprian, *De lapsis,* 25 and 26, in migne, *P.L.,* 4.
[741] 1. Corinth. 11:30.
[742] Origen, *To Psalm* 37, Homily II, 6, in Migne, *P.G.,* 13, 138b. Ibid, in Migne, *P.G.,* 13, 901-904.
[743] Ibid, *To Matthew,* XI, § 14, in Migne, *P.G.,* 13, 950. Ibid, *To Ezekiel,* 7, in Migne, *P.G.,* 13, 793.

Finally, it became a custom that one should partake of the Holy Eucharist having fasted. Since infant Baptism is practised within the Orthodox Church, the infants and all those who are worthy must partake of the Heavenly Sacraments.[744]

III. INVISIBLE ASPECT OF DIVINE EUCHARIST
A REAL PRESENCE OF CHRIST

From the words of institution found in the New Testament, as well as from the Teachings of the Holy Fathers in the Tradition of the Orthodox Church, we are informed that in the Holy Mystery of Divine Eucharist we partake of the True Body and Blood of our Lord and Saviour Jesus Christ, the Son of God. The change that takes place in the bread and wine is beyond any human understanding. Externally the elements remain as they are. Christ is physically present, offering and being offered to the faithful. The results of this Supernatural change are that the bread and the wine of the Eucharist, because of the continuous Presence of the Lord, is always a vital part of our worship. The faithful partake of the whole Christ Who is distributed but not divided, being present in all the Holy Altars, the one and same Lord Who ascended into Heaven. When the faithful partake of this Heavenly and Divine Mystery, they become partakers of the same Body and Blood of Christ, partakers of the Divine Nature and become members of the one Bread and Body.[745] On the contrary, those who partake unworthily bring Judgement upon themselves.

1. The True Meaning of the Words of Christ

In the Holy Mystery of Divine Eucharist, through the Supernatural change of the elements of the Bread and Wine, the Orthodox Christians partake of the precious Body and Blood of our Lord and Saviour Jesus Christ, the Son of God. This is confirmed by the words of our Lord when He promised to deliver the Holy Mystery as well as when He characterised the Sanctified Bread and the Blessed Cup as being nourishment and drink for the faithful.

---

[744] Kritopoulos, *ch. 8*, in Karmeris, *The dogmatics,* v. II, p. 536. St Cyprian, in migne, *P.L.,* 20, 592.

[745] Dositheus of Jerusalem, *Confession,* ch. 17, part 7, pp. 65-66.

Our Lord and Saviour Jesus Christ assured us that He is " *the Living Bread which came down from Heaven. If anyone eats of this Bread, he will live forever; and the Bread that I shall give is My Flesh, which I shall give for the life of the world.*"[746] "*This is the Bread which came down from Heaven – not as your fathers ate the manna, and are dead. He who eats this Bread will live forever.*"[747] "*Whoever eats My Flesh and drinks My Blood has eternal Life, and I will raise him up at the last day.*"[748] "*For My Flesh is food indeed, and My Blood abides in Me, and I in him. He who eats My Flesh and drinks My Blood abides in Me, and I in him.*"[749] These words cannot be considered as having an allegoric meaning, for if anyone takes them as such, it would be scandalous as when those who, hearing Christ say them, took them literally and "*from that time many of His disciples went back and walked with Him no more.*"[750] Our Lord did not defend Himself by trying to explain what He had meant but instead He emphasised "*Most assuredly, I say to you, unless you eat the Flesh of the Son of Man and drink His Blood, you have no Life in you.*"[751] Seeing that some of His Disciples departed, He addressed the rest by asking them: "*Do you also want to go away?*"[752]

The Flesh that is offered by the Lord is truly the Body of God.[753] "*It is truly Body united to the Deity*" and "*the Bread and the Wine are changed into the Body and Blood of God.*"[754] This is the practice and Confession of Faith of the Orthodox Church that proclaims that the words of Christ are taken literally and that His Presence in the Holy Mystery is real and true.[755]

---

[746] John 6:51.
[747] John 6:58.
[748] John 6:54.
[749] John 6:55-56.
[750] John 6:66.
[751] John 6:53.
[752] John 6:67.
[753] St Ambrosius, *De mysteriis,* c. IX, § 58, in migne, *P.L.,* 16, 426.
[754] St John of Damascus, *Exposition. About the holy and glorious mysteries of the Lord,* IV, 86, 13, in Migne, *P.G.,* 94, 1145. St Cyril of Alexandria, *To John,* book IV, ch. 3, in Migne, *P.G.,* 73, 604. Ibid, *Against Nestorius,* book IV, ch. 5, in Migne, *P.G.,* 73, 192.
[755] Dositheus of Jerusalem, *Confession,* ch. 17, pp. 41-45. Georgopoulos, *Anthology,* p. 32.

2. The Teachings of the Holy Fathers of the Change and Real Presence

It is the common belief of all the Holy Fathers of the Orthodox Church that through the Supernatural change that occurs in the Divine Eucharist, the Presence of our Lord and Saviour Jesus Christ, the Son of God, is real and essential. In the Teachings of the Apostolic Fathers we have the first testimony clearly confirming this Doctrine.

St. Ignatius the Theophorus of Antioch, accusing the Docites *"who deny the good Gift of God"*[756] by not confessing that in the Eucharist the Flesh is that of our Saviour Jesus Christ Who suffered for our sins and rose from the dead. Elsewhere he advised the faithful *"to practice one Eucharist"* because *"there is one Flesh of our Lord Jesus Christ, and one Cup which leads to unity through His Blood."*[757]

St. Justin the Philosopher and Martyr, in his 1st Apology, described the way of celebrating the Divine Mystery during the 2nd century whereby *"the Eucharist is called Food; for we do not receive them as common bread nor as common drink."* He also proclaimed that *"we were taught that the Flesh and Blood of the Incarnated Jesus"* is Food. Furthermore he observed that there is a similarity between the Sanctification of the Eucharist to that of the Incarnation of our Lord *"Jesus Christ our Saviour Who was Incarnated and took up flesh and blood for our Salvation. Thus, the Word through prayer becomes Food."* He also commented that we were taught that this Flesh and Blood is of the Incarnated Word and Son of God. St. Justin identified that the Flesh and Blood of the historic and Incarnated Christ is the exact same Blood and Flesh of Christ in the Eucharist. The result of the Incarnation as well as that of the Sanctification of the Eucharist is one and the same. In other words it is the Body and Blood of Jesus Christ.[758]

Scheeben, in his work *"Les Mystères,"* observed that the Presence of Christ in the Eucharist is some kind of reproduction and extension of His Incarnation. The change of the Bread into His Body through the Power of the Holy Spirit is some kind of Regeneration of the admirable action by which Christ formed His Body in the womb of the Virgin through the Power of the same Spirit. In the Incarnation He

---

[756] St Ignatius, *To Smyrnaeans,* 7, 1, in Lightfoot, *Apostolic Fathers,* p. 112.
[757] Ibid, *To Philadelphians,* 4, 1, in Lightfoot, *Apostolic Fathers,* p. 107.
[758] St Justin the Philosopher and Martyr, *1 Apology,* 65, **B**, v. 3, p. 197.

appeared for the first time to the world, whereas in the Eucharist He multiplies His real Presence through time and space. This Presence is multiplied in order that the Body of Christ increases and extends through the members who are joined to Him and to one another. The Body of Christ is reproduced through the Sanctification, in order to be united with men through the Communion and to become one Body with Him, in order that He might be Incarnated again in each man, taking up the human nature of each person and uniting it to His.[759]

St. Irenaeus constantly spoke of the Mystery of the Eucharist by declaring that *"the mixed Cup and Bread, receiving the Word of God becomes the Eucharist which is the Body ."* and *"the Blood of Christ."* He presented the Eucharist as the New Sacrifice and offering that the Church received from the Apostles and which is offered to God by the entire world. He emphasised the benefits of the communion, reassuring us that from the Eucharist *"the hypostasis of our flesh grows and is composed"* and *"from the Body and Blood of the Lord it is nourished and becomes its member." "Thus, our bodies receiving the Eucharist are no longer mortal, having the hope of the Eternal Resurrection."*[760]

Tertullian spoke of Christ as our Bread because He is Life and the Bread is Life.[761] For this reason, His Body is contained within the Bread according His statement: *"This is My Body."*[762] Hence, the flesh of the Orthodox Christian is nourished by the Flesh and Blood of the Lord.[763] Taking into consideration that the Bread of the Lord at the Communion was placed on the palm of the faithful' s right hand, who then covered it with his left hand to signify the acceptance of the King and receiving of the Body of Christ, he would respond: *"Amen."*[764] Elsewhere, he cautioned us to be careful that nothing of the Sacred Body falls on the ground.[765]

St. Cyprian stressed that it is impossible when the wine is absent, to see His Blood, by Whom we were delivered and have received

---

[759] Scheeben, *Les Mystères*, p. 490.
[760] St Irenaeus, *Heresies,* book V, ch. 2, § 3; book IV, ch. 17, § 5 and ch. 18, §§ 1 and 5, in Migne, *P.G.,* 7, 1125-1127 and 1023-1024. Cf. Ibid, in Hadjephraimides, pp. 364, 297 and 297, 299-300.
[761] John 6:35, 48.
[762] Tertullian, *De oratione,* 6, in migne, *P.L.,* 1, 1262.
[763] Ibid, *De resurrection carne,* 8, in Migne, *P.G.,* 2, 852.
[764] St Cyril of Jerusalem, *Catechesis,* XXIV, *Mystagogia* V, § 21, in Migne, *P.G.,* 33, 1125.
[765] Tertullian, *De coron. militiae.*, in migne, *P.L.,* 2, 99.

Life.[766] When the wine is mixed with water in the Cup, it signifies that the people are united with Christ.[767] Concerning the request of the daily bread in the Eucharist, he declared that *"Christ is our Bread"* and whoever has communion with Him has Eternal Life. In addition, he taught that those who have fallen (*"lapsis"*) but were receiving Holy Eucharist without repentance and reconciliation with the Church, they were committing violence against the Body and Blood of Christ. Therefore they were sinning against Him through receiving Holy Communion unworthily, which was far more serious than when they had renounced Him. He spoke of penitence for those who unworthily received Communion. The shedding of blood of the Holy Martyrs was considered by him to have received great honour similar to that of the shedding of the Blood of Christ. [768]

The Alexandrian Holy Fathers and ecclesiastic writers are well known for their allegoric interpretation. Nevertheless, they also emphasised the real Presence of Christ in the Divine Eucharist.[769] Origen urged that the Divine Mystery of Eucharist should be carefully and with piety received and cautioned that no part should fall on the ground because this brings great guilt upon the conscious of the faithful.[770] He also referred to the seriousness and severe consequences that follow when one does not prepare and examine himself when approaching the Holy Sacraments. He used the example of Judas who unworthily received the bread from Christ, giving Satan the opportunity to enter into his heart.[771]

St. Athanasius the Great of Alexandria, writing to Maximus the Philosopher, verified that we are Deified through participation of the Body of the Word and not that of a mere mortal.[772]

St. Gregory of Nyssa observed that *"the Bread remains bread although it was common before, but once it is officiated in the Mystery, it becomes the actual Body of Christ."* Elsewhere he commented that *"we believe that the Bread which is Sanctified, is*

---

[766] St Cyprian, *Epistola*63, 2, in migne, *P.L.*, 4, 386.

[767] Ibid, *Epistola*63, 2, in migne, *P.L.*, 4, 386.

[768] St Cyprian, *De lapsis*, 16 and 25, in migne, *P.L.*, 4, 493 and 499-500. Ibid, *Epistola* 63, 15, in migne, *P.L.*, 4, 398.

[769] Clement the Alexandrian, *Pedagogus*, I, ch. 6, in *B*, v. 7, pp. 99 and 100. Ibid, *Pedagogus*, II, ch. 2, in *B*, v. 8, p. 409. Origen, *Against Celsus*, VIII, 33, in *B*, v. 10, p. 199. Ibid, *To Numbers*, Homily XIV, § 9, in Migne, *P.G.*, 12, 701.

[770] Origen, *To Exodus*, Homily XIII, in Migne, *P.G.*, 12, 391.

[771] John 13:26-27. Origen, *To John*, XXXII, § (16) 24, in Pros. Academy, p. 468.

[772] St Athanasius the Great, *To Maximus the Philosopher*, § 2, in Migne, *P.G.*, 26, 1087.

changed into the Body of God the Word" and that the Bread in the Eucharist "*is Sanctified by the Word of God and prayer, not through drinking and eating but immediately it is changed into the Body of the Word, as well as it is said by the Word, that 'This is My body.'*"[773]

St. Cyril of Jerusalem wondered who would dare to doubt the words of our Lord Who said "*This is My Blood.*" Therefore, who would dare to deny that this is not His Blood?[774] Elsewhere he confirmed that after the invocation "*the bread becomes the Body of Christ, the wine Blood of Christ.*"[775]

St. John Chrysostom recommended that when we see the Body in the Eucharist we must remember: "*This Body the sun saw and hid its radiance this is that Sanctified Body, which was pierced and from which the Saving Fountains sprang this is Body He gave us to have and to eat.*" Elsewhere, he wondered: "*How many say: I wanted to see Him, the prints of His Wound.*" He then explained: "*Behold, you are seeing Him, you are touching Him, and you are eating Him. He gives Himself not just to be seen but to be touched and to be eaten and to be received within.*"[776]

St. Cyril of Alexandria spoke of the Holy Mystery emphasising that "*the Lord was to be risen with His own flesh and to ascend to the Father. For us to have Salvation, He gave us His own Body and Blood, that through these the power of mortality might be abolished. He inhabits our souls through the Holy Spirit.*" Thus, "*Christ descends and is descended to all of us invisibly and visibly: invisibly as God and visibly in Body. He allows and offers His Holy Flesh but we do not eat the Deity in this Mystery but the Word's own Flesh, which becomes Life-giving Flesh because it belongs to Him Who lives with the Father.*"[777]

St. John of Damascus pointed out that in the Eucharist "*the bread and the wine are changed Supernaturally into the Body and Blood of God through the invocation and descent of the Holy Spirit.*" "*The*

---

[773] St Gregory of Nyssa, *To the baptism of Christ,* in Migne, *P.G.,* 46, 581. Ibid, *Catechesis,* 37, in Migne, *P.G.,* 45, 95-97.

[774] St Cyril of Jerusalem, *Catechesis,* XXII *Mystagogia* IV, § 1, in Migne, *P.G.,* 33, 1097.

[775] Ibid, *Catechesis,* XIX *Mystagogia* I, § 7, in Migne, *P.G.,* 33,1072.

[776] St John Chrysostom, *To 1 Corinthians,* Homily 24, §§ 2, 4-5, in Migne, *P.G.,* 61, 603. Ibid, *To Matthew,* Homily 82, §§ 4, 5. Ibid, *About repentance,* Homily 9, § 1, in Migne, *P.G.,* 61, 203, 58, 743, 49, 345.

[777] St Cyril of Alexandria, *To Matthew 26:26,* in Migne, *P.G.,* 72, 452. Ibid, *To John 20:27,* book XII, § 1, in Migne, *P.G.,* 74, 725. Ibid, *Against Nestorius,* IV, § 5, in Migne, *P.G.,* 76, 189.

bread is not the model of the Body and Blood of Christ. May God forbid! But it is the Deified Body of the Lord."[778]

St. Ambrosius of Mediolan reminded us that the word of Elijah was so powerful it was able to bring down fire from Heaven. Contemplating how the word of Christ Who brought forth everything from nothingness into being, could change the elements of bread and wine, explained that in this Mystery the elements are truly changed into the actual Body of Christ which was crucified, buried and resurrected.[779]

In the Divine Eucharist, we have the real and true Presence of our Lord and Saviour Jesus Christ, the Son of God, and not any symbolic or imaginary appearance. The change of the elements of bread and wine takes place by Supernatural means that surpasses all human understanding and which can only be understood through pure and undefiled faith.

3. The Permanency and Inextinguishable of the Change

If real change of the Sanctified elements (bread and wine) take place in the Divine Eucharist, the result of this change is that the Lord is Supernaturally present in the changed elements, not only during the time of the celebration of the Eucharist and the following Communion, but even after these in the remaining parts of the Sanctified elements or in the *"Artophorion"* (Tabernacle) which is preserved throughout the year for the use of the sick or extraordinary circumstances.

In the ancient Orthodox Church, the Sanctified Bread and Wine that were changed into the actual Body and Blood of our Lord and Saviour Jesus Christ, the Son of God, were sent to those who were absent from the Divine Liturgy, especially to those who were imprisoned due to the persecutions. It was customary for Orthodox Christians to have the precious Gifts in their homes, in order to receive Holy Communion daily.[780]

---

[778] St John of Damascus, *Exposition. About the holy and glorious mysteries of the Lord,* IV, 86, 13, in Migne, *P.G.,* 94, 1148.

[779] St Ambrosius, *De mysteriis,* c. IX, 52, in migne, *P.L.,* 16, 424.

[780] St Justin the Philosopher and Martyr, *1 Apology,* 65, in *B*, v. 3, p. 197. St Basil, the Great, *Epistle* 93 *to sister Caesaria,* in Migne, *P.G.,* 32, 485. Tertutllian, *De oratione* 19, in migne, *P.L.,* 1, 1286. St Cyprian, *De lapsis,* 26, in migne, *P.L.,* 4.

During the period of Great Lent a complete Divine Liturgy is allowed only on Saturdays and Sundays. The ancient tradition of the Presanctified Gifts was practised whereby the offered Gifts (the Body and Blood) of Christ were Sanctified during the previous Sunday's Liturgy and offered on Wednesdays and Fridays.

St. Cyril of Alexandria opposed the opinion that the remaining parts of the Eucharist lose their Sanctified Grace if they were to remain until the following day. He characterised this concept as madness, for Christ's is incorruptible. The power of the blessing and the Life-giving Grace is constant.[781]

The permanent, continuous and real Presence of our Lord and Saviour Jesus Christ, the Son of God, in the Eucharist obliges us to approach Holy Communion with fear *"as Isaiah was touched by one of the Seraphim with the burning ember."* We must *"receive the Sacred Body as though touching the Divine and Precious with our lips, likewise partaking of the saving Blood."*[782]

We are obliged even afterwards to accept the Body and Blood of God which is preserved in the *Artophorion* (Tabernacle) or which is transferred from it by the officiator (Bishop or Priest) to be given to the sick. We must respect it with the proper honour and worship as the Body and Blood of the Lord. The Sanctified elements of the Eucharist are preserved in the Orthodox Church as "the Holy things for the Holy people of God."

St. Cyril of Jerusalem instructed the faithful to kneel and recite the *"Amen"* in order to receive the Consecrated Bread during the Service with respect.[783]

St. Ambrosius of Mediolan observed that the use of the term *"footstool"* in Psalm 98:5 must be understood as being *"the flesh of Christ, which we worship to this day in the Sacraments."*[784]

St. Augustine giving the same interpretation for the term *"footstool,"* remarked that *"no one should eat that Flesh"* in the Mystery, *"if he does not previously worship it. Hence, one understands in which way he must worship this footstool of the Despot."*[785]

[781] St Cyril of Alexandria, *Epistle to Kalosorius,* in Migne, *P.G.,* 76, 1073.
[782] St John Chrysostom, *About repentance,* § 9, In Migne, *P.G.,* 49, 345.
[783] St Cyril of Jerusalem, *Catechesis Mystagogia* V, 22, in Migne, *P.G.,* 1125.
[784] St Ambrosius, *De Spiritu Sancto,* III, II, 79, in migne, *P.L.,* 16, 742.
[785] St Augustine, *Enarratio in Psalm* 98, 9, in migne, *P.L.,* 37, 1264.

"The honour which must be given to these frightening Sacraments, must be as that which is offered to Christ Himself for such reason when we worship each one we must say:: I believe, Lord, and confess, that You are truly the Christ."[786] *"This Body and Blood of the Lord in the Mystery of Eucharist we are obliged to honour with great respect and to worship; for one is the worship of the only Begotten Son and of His Body and Blood."*[787] *"We do not offer this Holy Mystery for the town square, but only when it is presented to a house of one who is ill; for it is not given to us to be transferred in the town square, but to partake of it with piety for the forgiveness of sins, according to the Despotic words."*[788]

This honouring worship is required because through the change of the Eucharistic elements and the real and essential Presence of Christ, we have in them *"the same Body of the Lord Deified"*[789] and *"not simple bread, but united with the Deity"* without the two Natures in Christ being confused as one. They remain *"one, that of the Body, which is united in Him and the other is the Deity; so that together are not one Nature, but two."* We have Christ present as He lives glorified in Heaven and *"whosoever partakes of the Body, partakes of the Blood that which sits in the Heavenly places and which is worshipped by the Angels, that which is close to the Power, this we eat."*[790] As Orthodox Christians we believe that *"the Eucharistic Bread is not united hypostatically with the Deity of the Word, but is truly changed into the real Body of the Lord, which was born in Bethlehem from the Ever-virgin Mary, the Theotokos, was Baptised in the Jordan, suffered, buried, raised, ascended, seated on the Right Hand of God the Father and will come again on the clouds of Heaven. The wine is changed to the same true Blood of the Lord, which when hanging on the cross was shed for the Life of the world."*[791]

---

[786] Mogilas, *A' 107,* in Karmeris, *The dogmatics,* v. II, p. 639.

[787] Dositheus of Jerusalem of Jerusalem, *Confession,* Term 17, in Karmeris, *The dogmatics,* v. II, p. 762.

[788] Kritopoulos, *ch. 9,* in Karmeris, *The dogmatics,* v. II, p. 537.

[789] Jeremias, *2nd Answer,* in Karmeris, *The dogmatics,* v. II, p. 460.

[790] St John of Damascus, *Exposition. About the holy and glorious mysteries of the Lord,* IV, 86, 13, in Migne, *P.L.,* 94, 1148-1149. St John Chrysostom, *To Ephesians 3,* § 3, in Montfaucon, v. 11, p. 24.

[791] Dositheus of Jerusalem, *Confession,* Term 17, in Karmeris, *The dogmatics,* v. II, p. 761.

One can understand why the Lord in the Gospel of St. John spoke of Himself as *"the Bread which came down from Heaven"*[792] and the Holy Fathers referred to this Heavenly Bread as spiritual food.

St. Ambrosius observed that in the Mystery of the Eucharist, Christ is present, because it is the Body of Christ, not material food, but spiritual Food. The Apostle spoke of the type that prefigured this Mystery, saying: *"All ate the same spiritual food, and all drank the same spiritual drink."*[793] This Holy Father expressed this opinion because Christ is Spirit.[794]

St. Athanasius of Alexandria verified that the Flesh of the Lord *"and His Blood are given as spiritual Food, in order that through them Resurrection and Eternal Life is given."* Referring to the words of Christ: *"It is the Spirit Who gives Life whereas the flesh profits nothing.'*[795] He observed that: *"the mentioned Flesh is Food from Above, spiritual and not material."*[796]

The Lord is not simply flesh. Neither does He urge us towards *"flesh eating"* or cannibalism for this Flesh is not sold in the butcher's shop but is received in the Divine Eucharist wherein He invites us to eat His Body.[797] This Bread is not like other food that *"enters the mouth, goes into the stomach and is eliminated"*[798] nor is it *"consumed, or perishable."* It is *"Life-giving Spirit because it was conceived from the Life-giving Spirit. This is said without refuting the Nature of the Body"* but manifests *"the Life-giving and Divine Body."*[799]

Surely, the Body of Christ is truly body and not spirit. As St. Paul assured us: *"There is a natural body, and there is a spiritual body."*[800] *"So, this corruptible has put on incorruptibility, and this mortal has put on immortality."*[801] *"The first man was of the earth, made of dust; the second Man is the Lord from Heaven. As was the*

---

[792] John 6:41.

[793] 1 Corinth. 10:3-4.

[794] St Ambrosius, *De mysteriis,* Cap. IX, § 58, in migne, *P.L.,* 16, 426.

[795] John 6:62-63.

[796] St Athanasius the Great, *To Serapion Epistle* 4, § 19, in Migne, *P.G.,* 26, 665.

[797] St Cyril of Jerusalem, *Catechesis Mystagogia* IV, § 4, in Migne, *P.G.,* 33, 1100.

[798] Matth. 15:17.

[799] St John of Damascus, *Exposition. About the holy and glorious mysteries of the Lord,* IV, 86, 13, in Migne, *P.G.,* 94, 1152.

[800] 1 Corinth. 15:44.

[801] 1 Corinth. 15:54.

man of dust, so also are those who are made of dust; and as is the Heavenly Man, so also are those who are Heavenly."[802]

4. The Benefits of the Holy Mystery of Eucharist

The first benefit that the faithful receive from their communion with the Divine Eucharist is their union with Christ and the growth in the Newness of Life.[803] The Lord declared His flesh *"is true food"* and His Blood *"is truly drink."* *"As the bread is suitable"* for preserving and strengthening human life, *"likewise the Word is suitable for the soul."* The *"Heavenly Bread and the saving Cup Sanctify the soul and body, our whole nature."* As without bread the preservation of bodily life is impossible, likewise *"he who does not eat"* the Heavenly Bread and *"does not drink the Blood of the Lord, does not have Life in him."* Without the Flesh of the Lord *"it is impossible to live."*[804]

Those who worthily partake of the Divine Gifts of the Eucharist become noble because *"they are Sanctified in soul and body."*[805] The Divine Eucharist as Heavenly and Supernatural Food preserves and strengthens the life of Grace, which is transmitted through the Holy Mystery of Baptism. Although day by day the old man and his remaining relics of sin (*"concupiscentia"*) pass away, his will is simultaneously strengthened to resist any temptation and he progresses *"until we all come to the unity of the faith and of the knowledge of the Son of God, to a perfect man, to the measure of the stature of the fullness of Christ."*[806]

It is understandable that *"he who eats the Sacred Flesh of Christ"* is strengthened and progresses in the Newness of Life in Christ since *"the Flesh has in itself the Word which is according to its Nature real Life"* and *"our Lord Jesus Christ through His own Flesh implants this Life within us as a seed of immortality, abolishing all mortality in us."*[807] Through the Eucharist, the faithful *"eat and drink the Life."*

---

[802] 1 Corinth. 15:47-48. Cf. Androutsos, *Dogmatique,* p. 359.

[803] Cf. Frangopoulos, *Christian Faith,* pp. 204-208.

[804] St Cyril of Jerusalem, *Catechesis Mystagogia* IV, § 5; and V, § 12, in Migne, *P.G.,* 33, 1100. St John Chrysostom, *To John,* holimy 47, § 2, in Migne, *P.G.,* 59, 265.

[805] Clement the Alexandrian, *Pedagogus,* I, 6, in *B*, v. 7, p.139.

[806] Ephes. 4:13.

[807] St Cyril of Alexandria, *To John,* book VI, in Migne, *P.G.,* 73, 581. Ibid, *To John,* book VI, ch. 2, in Migne, *P.G.,* 73, 565. St John Chrysostom, *To 1 Corinthians,* Homily 24, in Migne, *P.G.,* 61, 201.

St. Augustine urged the faithful: *"Eat the Life, drink the Life; you will have the Life"* which is offered through the Mystery.[808]

St. Basil the Great concluded that *"to have Communion every day and to partake of the Holy Body and Blood of Christ is good and beneficial."*[809]

Taking into consideration that we who partake with worthiness in the Divine Eucharist progress in Sanctification and in the Newness of Life in Christ, gradually becoming free of all tendencies towards evil and the falls of human weakness. St. John of Damascus characterised this Divine Food of the Eucharist as *"the purification from all stain"* through which *"when we become clean we are united to the Body of the Lord in His Spirit and we become Body of Christ."*[810] In the transmission of the Divine Sacraments the officiator reminds us of the forgiveness of sins by reciting aloud the words: *"The servant of God is receiving the precious Body and Blood of our Lord and Saviour Jesus Christ for forgiveness of sins and Eternal Life."*[811] The *"for the forgiveness of sins"* refers to our daily sins that do not *"lead to death"* and not to the mortal and serious sins. St. Paul reminds each faithful to: *"let a man examine himself, and so let him eat of the Bread and drink of the Cup. For he who eats and drinks in an unworthy manner eats and drinks Judgement to himself, not discerning the Lord's Body. For this reason, many are weak and sick among you, and many sleep."*[812] Those who approach with an evil and unclean conscience, not only do not receive forgiveness of sins, but become worthy of Judgement and Condemnation, for they do not discern the Holiness and Divinity of the Holy Mystery, but through their ungodliness they desecrate the Holy of all Holies.

The putting to death of the old man and the progress of the Life of Grace is perfected through our union with Christ in such a way that when we eat with worthiness, the Flesh of the Son of Man and drink His Blood, we have Him within our hearts, dwelling and living, because we are united as one with Him.[813] Through the Eucharist we are related to Christ and become even more closer to Him than to our

---

[808] St Augustine, *Sermo* CXXXI, 1, in migne, *P.L.*, 38, 729.
[809] St Basil the Great, *Epistle* 93 to patricia Caesaria, in Migne, *P.G.*, 32, 484.
[810] St John of Damascus, *Exposition. About the holy and glorious mysteries of the Lord,* IV, 86, 13, in Migne, *P.G.*, 94, 1152.
[811] Liturgy of St John Chrysostom.
[812] 1 Corinth. 11:28-30.
[813] Cf. Evdokimov, *Orthodoxia,* pp. 358-369.

closest relatives. In the Divine Eucharist our union with Christ is continuously renewed and always strengthened. Through the Eucharist we do not only live through Christ, but in Christ and for Christ.[814] This main fruit of the union with Christ was strongly proclaimed by the Holy Greek Fathers of the Orthodox Church, especially by St. Cyril of Jerusalem,[815] St. John Chrysostom,[816] St. Gregory of Nyssa,[817] St. Cyril of Alexandria[818] and St. John of Damascus.[819]

If every Orthodox Christian is united with Christ through the Divine Eucharist, it is obvious that through Christ everyone is united to one another. St. Paul accentuated the unity of all through the participation in the one Eucharistic Bread by declaring: " *we, though many, are one Bread and one Body, for we all partake of that one Bread*".[820]

Didache, in the prayers of the breaking of the bread and the Cup, calls upon the Heavenly Father with the following words:

"First, concerning the Cup:

We give you thanks, our Father,
For the Holy vine of David your servant,
which you have made known to us
through Jesus, your servant;
to you be the glory forever.

And concerning the broken bread:

We give you thanks, our Father,
For the life and knowledge

---

[814] Scheeben, *Les Mystères*, p. 498. St Dionysius, *About Ecclesiastic Hierarchy*, 3, 12, in Migne, *P.G.,* 3, 469.

[815] St Cyril of Jerusalem, *Catechesis Mystagogia* IV, § 33, 1100.

[816] St John Chrysostom, *To Matthew*, Homily 82, in Migne, *P.G.,* 58, 744. Ibid, *To John,* Homily 46, § 3, in Migne, *P.G.,* 59, 260. Ibid, *To 1 Corinthians,* Homily 24, § 2, in Migne, *P.G.,* 61, 200.

[817] St Gregory of Nyssa, *Catechesis 37,* in Migne, *P.G.,* 45, 93-97.

[818] St Cyril of Alexandria, *To Luke 22:20,* in Migne, *P.G.,* 72, 912. Ibid, *To Matthew 26:26,* in Migne, *P.G.,* 72, 452.

[819] St John of Damascus, *Exposition. About the holy and glorious mysteries of the Lord,* IV, 86, 13, in Migne, *P.G.,* 94, 1153.

[820] 1 Corinth. 10:17.

Which you have made known to us
Through Jesus, your servant;
To you be the glory forever.

Just as this broken bread was scattered
Upon the mountains and then was
Gathered together and became one,
So many your churches be gathered together
From the ends of the earth into your kingdom;
For yours is the glory and the power
Through Jesus Christ forever."[821]

St. Cyprian in his 63rd Epistle, referring to the mixing of the Wine with water in the Cup of the Eucharist, saw the sign of the unity of the people of God with Christ. As it is impossible to separate the wine and the water, likewise the Orthodox Church, based upon Christ, cannot be separated from Him.[822] He also pointed out that through the Mystery of Eucharist, the people appear to be united as one and as the grains of wheat are many but are gathered into one harvest, likewise in Christ Who is the Heavenly Bread, we know that our number is united into one Body.[823]

St. John Chrysostom, interpreting the abovementioned verse of St. Paul commented: *"For what is the Bread?* (It is the) *Body of Christ. What happens to those who participate?* (They become) *not many bodies, but one Body. For as the bread is composed of many grains that are unseen because of* their blending together, *likewise we are united to Christ and to one another. For you are not from another body, but everyone from the same Body."*[824]

St. Augustine agreed with the aforementioned belief, exalting the Eucharist as the sign of the unity and the bond of Love. He emphasised our incorporation in the Mystical Body of Christ as the fruit of the Divine Communion.[825]

St. John of Damascus stated that the Divine Eucharist is called *"Communion"* "*because we have communion and are united through it to one another. Because we all participate from the one Bread, we*

---

[821] *Didache,* 9, 2-4, in Lightfoot, *Apostolic Fathers,* p. 154.
[822] St Cyprian, *Epistola*63, 13, in migne, *P.L.,* 4, 395.
[823] Ibid, *Epistola*63 *ad Ceacil. De lapsis,* 13, in migne, *P.L.,* 4, 395.
[824] St John Chrysostom, *To 1 Corinthians,* Homily 24, § 2, in Migne, *P.G.,* 61, 200.
[825] St Augustine, *In Johannis evangelium, Tractatus* XXVI, 13, in migne, *P.L.,* 35, 1613.

become the one Body and one Blood of Christ and members of one another, being of the same Body of Christ."[826] Due to this sacred bond and the unity between one another, St. John warned us that it is forbidden for any Orthodox Christian to partake of the communion of the heretics.

The Holy Fathers of the Orthodox Church stressed that the Bread of the Eucharist "*is Medicine of Immortality and the Antidote against death so as to live in Jesus Christ forever.*" The unity of our Life with Christ begins in this world, fades away at the separation of the soul from the body at the time of our bodily death but continues in the After Life. Thus, the Bread is truly "*the Medicine of Immortality*" and "*the Antidote that we take in order not to die but to live forever in Jesus Christ.*"[827]

St. Irenaeus proclaimed that "*our bodies, receiving the Eucharist, are no longer mortal because they have the hope of the Resurrection.*"[828]

In other words, although those who partake of the Deified Body of our Lord and Saviour Jesus Christ, the Son of God, will taste the common Cup of death, the Supernatural Life that is transmitted to them by the Lord, will continue. And as the Lord was gloriously Risen, we too will not merely be Regenerated but will receive an immortal body similar to the Body of our Risen Lord. The glorious and blessed Immortality of the soul and body will only be for those who are proved to be worthy. They will enjoy Immortality for ever and ever whereas those who are proved to be unworthy servants, will suffer for all Eternity. "*And these (the ungodly) will go away into Everlasting Punishment, but the righteous into Eternal Life.*"[829]

IV. THE DIVINE EUCHARIST AS A SACRIFICE AND ITS FRUITS

The invisible aspect of the Divine Eucharist is that of a Sacrifice in which the High Priest is offered to God as the Sacrificial Lamb.[830]

---

[826] St John of Damascus, *Exposition. About the holy and glorious mysteries of the Lord,* IV, 86, 13, in Migne, *P.G.,* 94, 1153.

[827] St Ignatius, *To Ephesians,* 20, 2, in Lightfoot, *Apostolic Fathers,* p. 93.

[828] St Irenaeus, *Heresies,* book IV, ch. 18, § 5, in Migne, *P.G.,* 7, 1029. Cf. Ibid, in Hadjephraimides, p. 300.

[829] Matth. 25:46.

[830] Evdokimov, *Orthodoxia,* pp. 335-336.

The Sacrificial character of the Divine Eucharist, prefigured in the Old Testament, is testified to by the many prayers of Sanctification of the Eucharistic elements of bread and wine during the institution of the Holy Mystery. The Holy Fathers, concerning the words of the Lord Jesus Christ, assured us that the Blood and the character of the Divine Eucharist is characterised as the Blood of the New Testament. This Sacrifice is identical to the one, absolute and *"once and for all"* Sacrifice of the Cross. It is the Sacrifice without the shedding of blood, which receives its Power completely based upon the fruits of the Salvation of the entire world (General Salvation) and for every individual personally (personal Salvation). As a Sacrifice, the Eucharist is not only a Eucharistic Sacrifice as well as the glory and worship of God but the real re-enactment of the Sacrifice of the Lord on the Cross. It is the Atonement Sacrifice and the Sacrifice of Redemption whereby, presenting the Sacrificial Lamb on the Cross, we beseech the forgiveness of our sins. The Redeeming character of the Divine Eucharist is based upon the offering of this Sacrifice and for those who have fallen asleep for whom we pray that the Lord will grant rest.

1.   Sacrifice and Mystery

The Mystery of the Divine Eucharist according to its other aspect as the only true Sacrifice replaced the typical, shadowy sacrifices of the Old Testament because that which is offered is not an irrational animal or fruit of the earth but our Lord and Saviour Jesus Christ, the Son of God. Although the Divine Eucharist as a Mystery and as a Sacrifice is simultaneously perfected by the same Sanctification, it keeps the two inseparable features of the Mystery and the Sacrifice that differ according to their nature. Because the Eucharist as a Mystery is offered as the Heavenly Food to the faithful, uniting them to Christ and to one another while nourishing their souls to the hope of Resurrection of Eternal Life, it is moreover a Sacrifice offered to God, offering Christ as the Redeeming Sacrificial offering to Him. As a Mystery and as a Sacrifice the Divine Eucharist differs according to its goal. The Sacrifice is offered to God while the Mystery is received by us as Heavenly Food. The Sacrifice is an Act of worship that is offered by the entire Orthodox Church to the glory and thanksgiving of God. The Mystery is received for Sanctification and is the Gift of

Grace that is offered to each individual faithful. Finally, the Eucharist as a Mystery is a permanent reality since once the offerings are Sanctified, they continuously remain the Body and Blood of Christ. The Sacrifice of the Eucharist is extended only within the boundaries of time, when it is offered to God as an act of worship and an offering of the entire community to God. Once the Sacrifice is offered, it ceases while the Sanctified Gifts remain forever.

The Eucharist is the manifestation of the Church as the New Age. In the Divine Liturgy the Presence of our Risen Lord is a reality and we participate in the Heavenly Kingdom. It is not a repetition of His Coming into the world but the elevation of the Church into His Presence and the participation of the Church in His Heavenly Glory.[831]

2. The Prophetic Prefigurations of the Eucharist

St. Cyprian regarded the prophetic prefigurations of Holy Scripture that predicted the Divine Eucharist as the only True Sacrifice such as that of the Sacrifice of Melchizedek.[832] It was the prefiguration of the Mystery of the Lord's Sacrifice because Christ offered a Sacrifice to God the Father as had Melchizedek. In other words, He offered Bread and Wine which were His Body and Blood.[833]

St. John of Damascus believed *"that table pre-figured this mystical table, in the same manner as that Priest was the type and pre-figuration of the true High Priest, Christ."*[834]

All the Sacrifices of the Old Testament were considered as types, not only of the Sacrifice of the Lamb of God on the Cross, but also as the Sacrifice of the Eucharist

St. Justin the Philosopher and Martyr felt that *"the offering of semolina was a type of the Bread of the Eucharist, which is offered in remembrance of the Passion, which our Lord Jesus Christ suffered for the cleansing of the souls of men from all evilness."*[835]

---

[831] Schmemann, *The Church Praying,* p. 96.
[832] Gen. 14:18.
[833] St Cyprian, *Epistola*63, 4, in migne, *P.L.,* 4, 387.
[834] St John of Damascus, *Exposition. About the holy and glorious mysteries of the Lord,* IV, 86, 13, in Migne, *P.G.,* 94, 1149.
[835] St Justin the Philosopher and Martyr, *Dialogue,* 41, § 1, in *B*, v. 3, p. 244.

St Augustine, referring to the reason why Christ wanted to be a daily Sacrifice of the Orthodox Church, commented that this true Sacrifice had many and various signs such as the Sacrifices of the Old Testament Saints. [836]

The *Didache* considered the words of the Prophet Malachi as being a prophetic announcement of the Sacrifice of the Eucharist,[837] as did St Justin[838] and Irenaeus:[839] *"because even among you the doors shall be shut, and one will not kindle the fire of Mine Altar for nothing, I have no pleasure in you, says the Lord Almighty, and I will not accept a Sacrifice at your hands. For from the rising of the sun even to the going down thereof My Name has been glorified among the Gentiles; and in every place incense is offered to My Name, and a pure offering: for My Name is great among the Gentiles, says the Lord Almighty."*[840]

In reference to this prophecy St. John Chrysostom asked the Jews: *"When did these take place? When in all places was incense offered to God? When a pure Sacrifice?"* Then he pointed out: *"You have no other time except now after the appearance of Christ."*[841]

St. Cyril of Alexandria, referring to the same prophecy, said: *" so the Church is everywhere and Divine Altars on which the Lamb is Sacrificed by the Holy officiators and by Indians and Ethiopians, and this is the way which was clearly said by the Prophet."*[842]

Truly the offered sacrifices of the pagans before the Coming of Christ were regarded as unclean and an abomination, whereas those of the Jews were not pure, nor were they offered in all places except in Jerusalem. However, the one absolute Sacrifice that was offered once and for all humanity, was offered in one place. Therefore the Holy fathers applied the abovementioned prophecy of Malachi to the Divine Eucharist.

---

[836] St Augustine, *De civitate Dei,* X, c.20, in migne, *P.L.,* 41, 298.
[837] *Didache,* 14, 3, in Lightfoot, *Apostolic Fathers,* p. 157.
[838] St Justin the Philosopher and Martyr, *Dialogue,* 41, § 3, in *B,* v. 3, p. 244.
[839] St Irenaeus, *Heresies,* book IV, ch. 17, § 5 and ch. 18, § 1 in Migne, *P.G.,* 7, 1023 and 1024. Cf. Ibid, in Hadjephraimides, p. 297.
[840] Mal. 1:10-11.
[841] St John Chrysostom, *Against Jewss,* Homily 5, § 12, in Migne, *P.G.,* 48, 902.
[842] St Cyril of Alexandria, *To Zephaniah 3:10,* in Migne, *P.G.,* 71, 1008.

3. The New Testament Proof Concerning the Eucharist as a Sacrifice

The Tradition concerning the separate Sanctification of the two elements within the Eucharist was correctly accentuated. The separate elements of Bread and Wine, belonging to the one and same Body, symbolically represents the separation of the Blood of Christ from His Body when the Sacrifice on the Cross was offered.

The words of institution of the Holy Mystery testify to the Sacrificial nature of the Divine Eucharist. Truly, the Lord gave the bread to His Disciples and proclaimed that *"this is My Body which is given for you"*[843] thereby indicating that His Body is delivered as a Sacrificial Victim for His Disciples who represented all Faithful. Likewise, at the offering of the Cup He said: *"This is My Blood which is shed for you and for many for the remission of sins."*[844]

In addition, in all four accounts of the institution of the Holy Mystery, the Blood in the Cup is characterised by our Lord and Saviour Jesus Christ, the Son of God, as *"the Cup of the New Covenant"*[845] compared to the Old Testament blood, which was the blood of sacrifice. Truly, the Covenant with Abraham, like that with Israel[846] and Moses, was sealed with a Sacrifice.[847] In the Epistle to the Hebrews it is evident that *"neither the first"* Covenant *"without blood, was inaugurated"*[848] but Moses *"taking the blood of bulls and goats with water"* sprinkled *"the Book of the Covenant and upon the people saying. 'Behold the blood of the Covenant, which the Lord has made with you concerning all these words."*[849] So Christ offers His Blood to His Disciples to drink as *"the Blood of the New Covenant"*[850] and as the Blood of Sacrifice.

Christ added the instruction: *"Do this in remembrance of Me."*[851] The Lord instructed His Holy Apostles to renew and repeat whatever He taught them that night, in remembrance of Him. St. Paul assured us that this is real remembrance of His Death *"for as often as you eat*

---

[843] Luke 22:19
[844] Matth. 26:28.
[845] Matth. 26:28.
[846] Gen. 28:13-22.
[847] Gen. 15:9-18.
[848] Heb. 10:18-20.
[849] Ex. 24:5-8.
[850] Luke 22:20.
[851] Luke 22:19.

this Bread and drink this Cup, you proclaim the Lord's death until He comes."[852]

On the other hand, St. Paul in 1st Corinthians emphasised: *"The Cup of blessing which we bless, is the communion of the Blood of Christ. The Bread which we break, is the communion of the Body of Christ For we, though many, are one Bread and one Body; for we all partake of that one Bread. Observe Israel after the flesh: Are not those who eat of the sacrifice partakers of the altar? What am I saying then? That an idol is anything, or what is offered to idols is anything? Rather, that the things which the Gentiles sacrifice they sacrifice to demons and not to God, and I do not want you to have fellowship with demons. You cannot drink the Cup of the Lord and the cup of demons; you cannot partake of the Lord's Table and of the table of demons."*[853] The Orthodox Christians have a Mystical Table that gathers them together. On this Table *"the Bread, which we break, is the Communion of the Body of Christ"* and *"the Cup, which we bless, is the Communion of the Blood of Christ."* As the sacrifices and the participation in them brought the Israelites in communion with God and the idolaters in communion with demons, likewise the Body and Blood of Christ in the Eucharist places us in communion with our Lord and Saviour Jesus Christ, the Son of God, and consequently they are a Sacrifice to God. In Hebrews, it is proclaimed that *"we have an Altar from which those who serve the tabernacle have no right to eat."*[854]

4. The Teachings of the Holy Fathers of the Holy Mystery of Eucharist as a Sacrifice

Didache notes: *"On the Lord's own day gather together and break bread and give thanks, having first confessed your sins so that your Sacrifice may be pure. But let no one who has a quarrel with a companion join you until they have been reconciled, so that your Sacrifice may not be defiled. For this is the Sacrifice concerning that which the Lord said, "In every place and time offer Me a pure*

---

[852] 1 Corinth. 11:26.
[853] 1 Corinth. 10:16-21.
[854] Heb. 13:10.

Sacrifice, for I Am a great King, says the Lord, and My Name is marvellous among the nations.[855]"[856]

St. Ignatius the Theophorus of Antioch accused the Docites *"who deny the good Gift of God"*[857] of not confessing the truth that in the Eucharist, the Flesh is that of our Saviour Jesus Christ, which suffered for our sins and has risen from the dead. Elsewhere, he sternly warned the faithful to *"take care, therefore, to practice in one Eucharist (for there is one Flesh of our Lord Jesus Christ, and one Cup which leads to unity through His Blood; there is one Altar, just as there is one Bishop, together with the Presbytery and the Deacons, my fellow servants), in order that whatever you do, you do in accordance with God."*[858]

St. Justin the Philosopher and Martyr, found in *"the offering of semolina"* the *"type of the Bread of the Eucharist, which is offered in remembrance of the Passion, which our Lord Jesus Christ suffered for the cleansing of the souls of men from all evilness"*[859] and referred to the prophecy of the Prophet Malachi.

St. Irenaeus, proclaiming that God has no need of Sacrifices, believed that in the Old Testament He would not have asked for Sacrifices of blood and burnt offerings, but through them He announced the true meaning of Sacrifice, which found its perfection in faith, obedience and righteousness. Continuing, he described how the Lord instructed the Apostles to offer the Sacrifice by taking bread and giving thanks and saying: *"This is My Body"* and with the Cup saying: *"This is My Blood."* Thus, He taught the new Sacrifice of the New Testament, which the Church received from the Apostles and constantly offers it throughout the entire world thereby fulfilling the prophecy of Malachi.[860]

According to Irenaeus, the Divine Eucharist is the Sacrifice of the New Testament foretold by the Prophet Malachi, which was instituted by Christ Who delivered it to His Holy Apostles from whom the Church received it.

---

[855] Mal. 1:14.

[856] *Didache*, 14, 1-3, in Lightfoot, *Apostolic Fathers,* p. 157.

[857] St Ignatius, *To Smyrnaeans,* 7, 1, in Lightfoot, *Apostolic Fathers,* p. 112.

[858] Ibid, *To Philadelphians,* 4, 1, in Lightfoot, *Apostolic Fathers,* p. 107.

[859] St Justin the Philosopher and Martyr, *Dialogue,* 41, § 1, in *B*, v. 3, p. 244.

[860] St Irenaeus, *Heresies,* book IV, ch. 17, § 4, in Migne, *P.G.,* 7, 1023. Cf. Ibid, in Hadjephraimides, p. 296.

St. Cyprian stated that the Priest offers the Divine Eucharist exactly in the imitation of Christ. It is a true and complete Sacrifice.[861] Therefore, if the wine be excluded from the Cup then likewise the Blood of Christ would be excluded. Consequently it would not be the Sacrifice that our Lord offered.[862]

Furthermore, St. Cyril of Jerusalem,[863] St. John Chrysostom,[864] St. Cyril of Alexandria[865] and, generally speaking, all the Greek Fathers, used different terms to signify the Sacrificial Nature of the Divine Eucharist.

5. The Essence of the Divine Eucharist as a Sacrifice

We are taught that the essence of the Divine Eucharist as a Sacrifice is according to the exact words of our Lord and Saviour Jesus Christ, the Son of God, who said: *"Do this in My remembrance"*[866] whereas, according to the explanation of St. Paul who instructed us to *"do often, as you drink it in remembrance of (Christ). For as often as you eat this Bread and drink this Cup, you proclaim the Lord's death until He comes."*[867] It is obvious, therefore, that the Divine Eucharist is regarded as a Sacrifice that is directly related to the Sacrifice on the Cross and which was offered by our Lord. Furthermore, we offer that same Sacrifice in the Divine Eucharist and, although it is offered in many places, it always remains one and the same Sacrifice, not many, separate Sacrifices. Christ is simultaneously in the Divine Eucharist as He Who offers and as He Who is being offered. He is both the High Priest and the Sacrificial Victim.[868]

The Jews did not sacrifice Jesus Christ on the Cross. They were merely the instruments whereby the Lord Himself Sacrificed His own

---

[861] St Cyprian, *Epistola*63, § 14, in migne, *P.L.*, 4, 398.
[862] Ibid.
[863] St Cyril of Jerusalem, *Catechesis Mystagogia*, 5, §§ 8, 10, in Migne, *P.G.*, 33, 1117.
[864] St John Chrysostom, *About Priesthood*, 3, §§ 4 and 6, in Migne, *P.G.*, 48, 682. Ibid, *To the Holy Pentecost,* Homily 1, § 4, in Migne, *P.G.*, 50, 458-459. Ibid, *To Hebrews*, Homily 17, § 3, in Migne, *P.G.*, 63, 131.
[865] St Cyril of Alexandria, *To Zephaniah 3:10 and to Habakkuk 3:7,* in Migne, *P.G.*, 71, 1008 and 916.
[866] Luke 22:19.
[867] 1 Corinth. 11:25-26.
[868] St John Chrysostom, *To Hebrews,* Homily 17, § 3, in Migne, *P.G.*, 63, 131. Ibid, *To the betrayal of Judas*, § 6, in Migne, *P.G.*, 49, 380.

Life, as He alone has the Power to do: "*I lay down My Life that I may take it again. No one takes it from Me, but I lay it down of Myself. I have Power to lay it down, and I have Power to take it again. This Command I have received from My Father.*"[869] On the Cross He was not only the Sacrificial Victim but also, He Who offered the Sacrifice. Thus, the Divine Eucharist is nothing more than His Sacrifice on the Cross.

When we say "*in remembrance,*" we must understand that the Divine Eucharist is not simply a remembrance of the Sacrifice on the Cross, but a real, true and effective remembrance because we have before us the same Body of Christ that was crucified and the same Blood of Christ that was shed on the Cross.

The Sacrifice on the Cross was offered "*once and for all.*"[870] It can never be repeated with blood because its validity is beyond any value and is sufficient for the Salvation of the entire world. In addition, because Christ has "*been raised from the dead, He dies no more. Death no longer has dominion over Him.*"[871] This historic Sacrifice, which was offered "*once and for all*" is Mysteriously repeated through the Divine Eucharist, which as a Sacrifice bring forth all the fruits of that Sacrifice on the Cross and offers us the same Body and the same Blood that was crucified on Golgotha.

It is true, that the re-enactment presents Christ, in reality covered under the elements of the bread and wine. It is a real remembrance of Christ because in the Eucharist the Lord on the Cross is essentially and in reality present. The Gifts and benefits for the whole human race derived from the Sacrifice on the Cross. The Sacrifice in the Eucharist does not intend to fulfil the Sacrifice of the Cross because the Lord, "*after He had offered one Sacrifice for sins forever by one offering He has perfected those who are being Sanctified.*"[872] The Divine Eucharist is for the purpose of our benefit and the good things that result from the Sacrifice of the Cross, making these familiar to the faithful, who refer to and partake of God.

The difference between the two Sacrifices is in that:

---

[869] John 10:17-18.
[870] Rom. 6:10.
[871] Rom. 6:9.
[872] Heb. 10:12, 14.

1.   Christ on the Cross offered Himself as a Sacrifice to God the Father, without any mediator Priest, whereas in the Eucharist He offers Himself using the officiator as an instrument. He offers Himself, not only because He is invisibly present, uniting the faithful, but also, because He provides the Sacrificial Victim to the Church, He has the authority to offer the Sacrifice.

2.   Only the Sacrifice on the Cross shed Blood, whereas the Divine Eucharist is a bloodless Sacrifice. The High Priest, Christ, *"having been raised from the dead, dies no more. Death no longer has dominion over Him."*[873] Consequently it pleases Christ to have a true Sacrifice within His Church, without the shedding of blood and which is able to offer to the faithful the Gifts that arose from it.

3.   In the Sacrifice on the Cross, which was offered once and for all, *"God was in Christ, reconciling the world to Himself."*[874] That Sacrifice was a Sacrifice of Christ to the Father by means of which He reconciled the world to Him. The Sacrifice of the Eucharist is a Sacrifice that the reconciled Church offers not once, as that Sacrifice was offered once and for all, but is offered continuously *"until He comes"*[875] again.

Regardless of these differences, we cannot speak of two Sacrifices, independent of one another because the Sacrifice of the Eucharist depends directly upon the Sacrifice of the Cross, which is an absolute Sacrifice, whereas the Sacrifice of the Eucharist is a relative Sacrifice. The Sacrifice of the Cross does not depend on any other Sacrifice but is independent as its absolute Power being completely sufficient and perfect, is self-contained. On the contrary, the Divine Eucharist completely relies upon the Sacrifice on the Cross from which it receives the Victim, this being the remembrance, re-enactment and transmission of the Gifts to the faithful.

In the Divine Liturgy we distinguish three main parts: the Preparation, the Sanctification and the Holy Communion. The Preparation is obviously not the essential part of the Holy Eucharist as a Sacrifice because during this part of the Divine Liturgy, the Gifts are offered by the faithful. At this point, the bread and wine are ordinary elements that are prepared for the Sacrifice. Neither can Holy

---

[873] Rom. 6:9.
[874] 2 Corinth. 5:19.
[875] 1 Corinth. 11:26.

Communion, which is the central point of the Holy Eucharist as a Mystery, be considered the essential act of the Sacrifice. Holy Communion presupposes the Sacrifice and is not its critical point. The only remaining part of the Divine Liturgy is that of the Sanctification, during which the presented Gifts (bread and wine) are changed into the real Body and Blood of our Lord and Saviour Jesus Christ, the Son of God. Through the double blessing, one on each Gift, the Mysterious re-enactment, that of the symbolic and real separation of the shed Blood from the Body of the Lord, takes place. The Sacrifice, therefore, occurs during the Sanctification when *"through word, the Word is called"* by the officiator and without the shedding of blood, He separately Sanctifies the elements of the Body and Blood.

6. The Fruits of the Divine Eucharist as a Sacrifice

We recognise the results or fruits of the Divine Eucharist as a Sacrifice when we consider that it is a Sacrifice of worship and thanksgiving as well as a Sacrifice of imploring and mediating. Furthermore, we must remember that the nature of the Sacrifice as worship and thanksgiving is due to the Lord, at the institution of the Holy Mystery, giving thanks to the Father before the blessing after which He broke the bread and gave it to His Disciples. With thanksgiving, He again blessed the Cup.[876] In addition, according to St. Paul, when we celebrate the Divine Eucharist, we proclaim the Death of the Lord.[877] This Death is of the greatest of all the benefits of God towards mankind. It is the perfect expression of worship, devotion and the logical Sacrifice of Christ to His Father. It is the highest recognition of the Justice, Dominion and Majesty of God as well as being the most pleasing Sacrifice to God.

It is obviously evident that the Orthodox Church, by offering this Sacrifice to God through the Divine Eucharist, expresses her gratitude to Him and confesses her infinite obligation to His Goodness and to the Reconciliatory Justice. It also offers the Holiest and most God-pleasing Gift of the spotless and absolute Holy Sacrifice.[878]

Even the word *"Eucharist"* reveals the thanksgiving nature of the Holy Mystery as a Sacrifice. Furthermore, since the beginning, before

---

[876] Matth. 26:26, 27. Mark 14:22, 23. Luke 22:17, 19. 1 Corinth. 11:24, 25.
[877] 1 Corinth. 11:26.
[878] Jeremias, *Answer 1,* in Karmeris, *The dogmatics,* v. I, p. 404

the blessing and Sanctification of the offering Gifts, a thanksgiving was offered to God for all that He has done for mankind and for our redemption from the evil one.[879]

The imploring and meditating nature of the Sacrifice of the Divine Eucharist is testified to by the imploring part of the Divine Liturgy, in which we address petitions to God: for all Orthodox Churches, for the rulers and all civil authorities, for the people who travel by land, sea and air, for the soldiers, for the Bishop and all the Orthodox people, for the sick, and all those who need the help of God, for those suffering affliction, in danger and necessity, for those in prison and generally, for all those who are under any kind of suppression as well as for the Salvation of all humanity. [880] This form of petition developed according to the instructions of our Lord Who promised us: *"if two of you agree on earth concerning anything that they ask, it will be done for them by My Father in Heaven. For where two or three are gathered in My Name, I Am there in the midst of them."*[881]

St. Justin believed that the propitiatory nature of the Sacrifice of the Eucharist of *"the offering of semolina"* for the healing of the leper was considered as *"a type of the Bread of the Eucharist, which is offered in remembrance of the Passion, which our Lord Jesus Christ suffered for the cleansing of the souls of men from all evilness."*[882] Through the Eucharist souls are cleansed from all human wickedness because our Lord and Saviour Jesus Christ, the Son of God, guaranteed us that His Body and Blood are for the forgiveness of sins.

St. Cyril of Jerusalem characterised the Eucharist as *"a Sacrifice of propitiation."*[883]

St. John Chrysostom, referring to the Sacrifice of Propitiation that was mentioned in the Epistle to the Hebrews, commented that *"this Sacrifice is a type of (propitiation) for we offer Him always, not a different lamb now and tomorrow another, but always the same."*

---

[879] St Justin the Philosopher and Martyr, *Dialogue,* 41, in *B*, v. 3, p. 244.
[880] St Cyril of Jerusalem, *Catechesis Mystagogia* V, § 8, in Migne, *P.G.,* 33, 1116.
[881] Matth. 18:19-20.
[882] St Justin the Philosopher and Martyr, *Dialogue,* 41, § 1, in *B*, v. 3, p. 244.
[883] St Cyril of Jerusalem, *Catechesis Mystagogia* V, § 8, in Migne, *P.G.,* 33, 1116.

Elsewhere he compared the Holy Eucharist to the sacrificial lamb of the Old Testament Passover.[884]

The propitiatory nature of the Sacrifice of the Eucharist is also evident in the offering for those who have reposed.

Tertullian mentioned the offerings for those who have fallen asleep at the annual celebration of their departure.[885]

St. Cyril of Jerusalem characterised the Eucharist more strongly as "*a Sacrifice of Propitiation*" stating that it is offered for those Holy Fathers who have fallen asleep as well as for all faithful, believing that it is a great help for the souls for whom the prayers of the Sacred and awesome Sacrifice are offered.[886] In addition, the *Apostolic Orders* instruct the faithful to "*gather in the cemeteries*" and to offer the Divine Eucharist.[887]

St. Cyril of Jerusalem mentioned that on the spiritual propitiation Sacrifice "*we commemorate those who have fallen asleep; first Patriarchs, Prophets, Apostles and Martyrs.*"[888]

In the Divine Liturgy of St. John Chrysostom after the Sanctification, the officiator, addressing God, says: "*Again we offer to You this logical Sacrifice, without the shedding of blood, for those who have fallen asleep in the faith: Fathers, Patriarchs, Prophets, Martyrs, Confessors, and all spirits of the just who were perfected in faith, especially for our Blessed, Glorious Lady and Ever-Virgin Mary, the Theotokos, for the Holy Glorious Prophet, Forerunner and Baptist John, for the Holy Glorious and All-lauded Apostles.*"[889]

This custom of commemorating the Saints in the Divine Liturgy is an ancient one.[890] It is mentioned in *"The Martyrdom of (St) Polycarp:"* "*There gathering together, as we are able, with joy and gladness, the Lord will permit us to celebrate the birthday of his Martyrdom in commemoration of those who have already fought in*

---

[884] St John Chrysostom, *To Hebrews,* Homily 17, § 3, in Migne, *P.G.,* 63, 131. Ibid, *To Matthew,* Homily 82, § 1, in Migne, *P.G.,* 58, 739. Ibid, *To the Cross,* § 3, in Migne, *P.G.,* 49, 398. Ibid, *About Priesthood,* in Migne, *P.G.,* 48, 642.

[885] Tertullian, *De monogamia* 10, in migne, *P.L.,* 2, 992. Ibid, *De exhort Cast,* 11, in migne, *P.L.,* 2, 975.

[886] St Cyril of Jerusalem, *Catechesis Mystagogia* V, §§ 9 and 10, in Migne, *P.G.,* 33, 1116-1117.

[887] *Apostolic Orders,* VI, 30, 2, in ***B,*** v. 2, p. 115.

[888] St Cyril of Jerusalem, *Catechesis Mystagogia* V, § 9, in Migne, *P.G.,* 33, 1116.

[889] Divine Liturgy of St John Chrysostom.

[890] St Cyprian, *Epistola*XXXVII, 2 AND XXXIV, 3, in migne, *P.L.,* 4, 337 and 331. Origen, *About prayer,* 31, 5, in ***B,*** v. 10, p. 304.

155

the contest, and for the training and preparation of those who will do so in the future."[891]

It is obvious that the Sacrifice of the Divine Eucharist is not offered to the Saints or in the name of the Saints, but to God Who crowns them and exalts them within His Orthodox Church as "*the first-fruits of the faith*" and as Victors through His Grace.

The commemoration of the Saints is triumphantly offered and with gratitude for their Grace and Glory. The Orthodox Church exalts them as soldiers of Christ and as the Victorious Army of God.

The Power and results of Divine Eucharist as a Sacrifice in the Divine Liturgy acts regardless of the moral status, virtue, worthiness or unworthiness of the officiator. It is a pure and Holy Sacrifice, which cannot be influenced by the unworthiness or sinfulness of the officiator. Again the Church acts "*ex opere operato,*" because the Church is the Bride of Christ Who "*gave Himself for her, that He might Sanctify and cleanse her with the washing of water by the Word, that He might present her to Himself a glorious Church, not having spot or wrinkle or any such thing, but that she should be Holy and without blemish.*"[892]

As a Sacrifice of the Orthodox Church, which is offered by the Bishop or Priest and all those who participate in the Divine Mystery, it acts "*ex opera operantis,*" according to the level of dedication, virtue, internal intentions and proper preparation of each individual. Androutsos noted that the imploring Sacrifice is determined by the Will of the Divine Wisdom and Love, which does not always grant the requested good things, even to those who are worthy because they would not benefit from them.[893]

7. The Sacrament of Sacraments: The Great Communion[894]

In the lives of the great Saints, the bonds that confined fallen nature were already to some extent broken. But more than this, in the Church's whole Life of Grace, especially in the Sacraments, there is a glorification of earthly existence through the penetration of the Divine Actuality. And the consummation of this blending of two worlds is the

---

[891] *The Martyrdom of Polycarp,* 18, 3, in Lightfoot, *Apostolic Fathers,* p. 142.
[892] Ephes. 5:25-27.
[893] Androutsos, *Dogmatique,* p. 376.
[894] Arseniev, *Mysticism,* pp.55-61.

Sacrament of Sacraments, the Lord's Supper. The founders of the Church had already experienced the Presence of the Glorified Lord at the Lord's Supper. A Succession of appearances of the Risen Christ to His Disciples are connected with the taking of food. He was recognised by His Disciples at Emmaus *"while He broke bread."* The earliest Eucharistic prayer that has come down to us (in the *Didache*) cries in Aramaic: *"Come, O Lord!"* So, too, in the Liturgies of the Eastern Church – the Lord appears to the faithful and they receive Him with joy: *"Hosanna to the Son of David! Blessed be He that cometh in the Name of the Lord!"* *"Today the invisible Heavenly Powers serve with us, for lo! the King of Glory enters; behold the Mysterious Sacrifice; it is accomplished and is carried in pomp."* *"Let all mankind keep silence and stand in fear and trembling and think upon no earthly thing, for the King of Kings, the Lord of Lord's cometh to be Sacrificed and to offer Himself for the nourishment of them that believe."*

It is the sphere of exalted reality into which the faithful are admitted, between fear and joy. Thrilled and trembling with awe the invisible Hosts of Heaven stand around the Altar upon which the Sacrifice of Golgotha is re-enacted. This is, however, not only the suffering, but - to emphasize this once more - at the same time the Glorified, the Living Lord. Therefore, to receive His Body and Blood is to receive Eternal Life. Thus, St. Irenaeus and the early Fathers believed that this is the spirit of the prayers and praises of the Liturgy. And here, again, we are not dealing with an outward, mechanically assumed life; it must be a life morally fruitful and only in a spirit of moral purity and holiness may the Sacrament be approached. *"The Holy to the Holy ones!"* This warning is pronounced by the Priest before Holy Communion to which the congregation replies, trembling: *"One only is Holy, one only is Lord, Jesus Christ in the glory of God the Father."* Hence, this fervent appeal, this continuous, unceasing prayer from the congregation, this ardent wrestling with God, this humble appeal of the unworthy sinner for meekness and cleansing of the heart, which flows like a mighty stream through the whole Liturgy.

Only to the contrite, only to him who in his innermost heart prostrates himself before God's Grace and Mercy, only to him who in spirit bends the knee in fear and trembling before the Holiness of the Sacrament, only to him who trusts in God's Mercy, only to him who knocks and seeks and prays, and who realizing his own unworthiness, throws himself penitent, trembling but hopeful, upon God's Grace; only to such as say, not only with the lips but from the depths of the heart: *"I believe, Lord, and I acknowledge Thee to be the Son of God, Who came into the world to save sinners, of whom I am the most sinful"* – only to such who attain this spiritual state does the Sacrament bring Blessing, Redemption of soul and body, *"deliverance from the burden of many sins" "entry into Thy Kingdom"* and Eternal Life. This effect of the Sacrament – physical as well as spiritual - of which the earliest Fathers spoke, beginning with St. Ignatius, Tertullian and St. Irenaeus, as well as the earliest Liturgical prayers that have come down to us (since the 3rd century), is frequently reflected in the Communion prayers of the Eastern Church. I will quote one that Simeon Metaphrastes of the 10th century (which is the third of the thanksgiving prayers following the Communion): *"Thou Who hast willingly given Thy Flesh for my nourishment, Thou Fire that consumes the unworthy, consume me not. O my Creator! Rather penetrate my limbs, my bones, my innermost being, my heart! Burn up the thorns of my misdeeds; cleanse my soul and sanctify my spirit and strengthen my joints and bones. Nail me wholly to fear of Thee! Protect me always, shield and guard me from all deeds or words that destroy the soul. Cleanse, wash, and adorn me, make me better, and teach and enlighten me, that, having become as a partaker of Thy Sacrament, Thy dwelling, all sin and passion may flee from me like fire."* In another prayer: *"O awful Mystery, O Mercy of God! How can I, even I – unclean that I am, receive the Sacred Body and Blood and become incorruptible!"*

It is not only for the individual that the Sacrament of the Lord's Supper has a central, living and Mystic meaning, but for the whole Church, yes, for all mankind. For here the Divine mingles with the human, the terrestrial; here in the Holy Eucharist praise and Sacrifice are offered to the Lord for the whole world and by the whole world (*"offering Thine to Thee from Thine, for all men and all things"*), and the entire Universe is hereby potentially ennobled and Sanctified in that earthly elements of wine and bread become the Glorified Body and Blood of the Son of God. That is why the idea of all Creation assembled in spirit around the Eucharistic Altar so constantly recurs in the old Liturgies of the East. For through Him, through His Death and through the Glorification of His Risen Body, here Mystically represented, Creation partakes of the glory of the Redemption. *"Verily Heaven and earth are filled with Thy Glory through the Coming of our Lord and God and Saviour, Jesus Christ"* declares the old Egyptian Liturgy of St Mark. Not only the Presence but also the Power of the Living Lord is experienced here as well as the approach of the all-embracing Kingdom of His Glory. In the Lord's Supper we have a particularly powerful expression of the fundamental, all-pervading idea of the great totality, the Mystic Communion, of the all-embracing, Mystical Body of Christ.

We find a similar concept in Roman Catholicism. Perhaps some differences appear between the two ecclesiastical traditions concerning the fundamental idea – nay, rather, experience – of the great Mystical Communion. We point this out, not in a spirit of controversy, but merely with a view to defining the characteristics of the Eastern Orthodox Church that focuses upon God and the individual soul. For the Orthodox Church the individual soul and her relationship to God constitutes the most precious and essential sacredness of religion. But this communion of the soul with God is not a dialogue but a mighty harmony of many tones, a great organism, a powerful Kingdom, a comprehensive Brotherhood, a Church of God into which the individual is caught up as a member of the whole Body and which expands and grows into the infinite until it embraces not only all mankind but the whole of Creation, the whole Cosmos, in a Kingdom of Eternal Life. It is a cosmic, ecumenical concept.

I cannot refrain from quoting at this point the wonderful words of perhaps the greatest Russian Theologian (not a professional Theologian!) and *"Church philosopher,"* Alexei Khomiakov, (from his little tract on the Church):

"We know that when one of us falls, he falls alone, but no man is Saved alone. He who is Saved is Saved within the Church, as a member of the Church, in union with the other members. Does he believe? – Then he is in the Communion of Faith. Does he love? – Then he is in the Communion of Love. Does he pray? – Then he is in the Communion of Prayer. Do not ask: 'What prayer can I spare for the living or the dead, since my prayer does not suffice for myself?' For if you do not understand how to pray, of what avail is prayer for yourself? But it is the Spirit of Love Who prays also within you. Nor say: 'Why should another need my prayer, when he prays himself and Christ Himself intercedes for him'? When you pray, the Spirit of Love

prays within you. Nor say: 'God's Judgement is irrevocable' – for your prayers lie in God's path and He has foreseen them. If you are a member of the Church, your prayers are required for all the members of the Church. For if the hand were to say that it had no need of the blood nor of the rest of the body and that it would not give its blood to the rest of the body, the hand would wither. In the same way you are necessary to the Church so long as you are of the Church; but if you renounce the Brotherhood of the Church, you will die and cease to be a member. The prayer of the Church is a prayer one for the other and her breath is praise of the Lord."

The great unity of the Church is not, however, regarded as something formally authoritative, something capable of expression in a juridical formula. The Eastern Orthodox Church recognizes no formal, juridical authority. For her, Christ, the Apostles and the Church Councils are not *"authority."* There is no question of authority but an infinite stream of the Life of Grace, which has its source in Christ and within each individual. We do not have to deal with an external, authoritative power but with the essential principle of the Life of God within His Church and within ourselves. This way of life, the Life of Grace, raises us above our petty, individual selves on condition that we have not cut ourselves off from the whole Body of Christ. The Eastern Orthodox Church believes that this mighty stream of Grace shall sweep along with it and absorb all things, all brethren, all mankind, all creatures that long for deliverance from the bonds of corruption and death and for the *"glorious freedom of the children of God."* And this explains, as we have seen, that strong eschatological bias, that yearning, fervent cry of the Church, that joyous expectation of the coming Consummation: *"Arise, O God, for Thou shall inherit all nations!" "Arise, O God, judge the earth, for Thou reigned in eternity!"* Nor is this mere expectation, mere eschatology; it is joyful consciousness of the possession now, already, of Eternal Life: *"Christ is Risen!" "Truly He is Risen!" "From death to life and from the earth to Heaven Christ hath led us, who sing our song of triumph!"*

CHAPTER EIGHT
THE HOLY MYSTERY OF REPENTANCE

I. DEFINITION, IMPORTANCE AND NAMES

Repentance is the God-instituted Mystery, in which the officiator (Bishop or Priest), in the Name of the Lord, forgives the sins of the faithful that were committed after Holy Baptism and who, with sincere intention, decide to change their sinful ways and follow a virtuous life.[895] The importance and necessity of this Holy Mystery are obvious when one recalls the weakness of human nature and that man easily tends towards evil from his youth. After his Regeneration, man is not immediately raised to the Perfection of Christ but gradually and through constant struggle, abolishes the remaining sinful tendencies and desires. Repentance cleanses the faithful from all stain of sin committed after Baptism. It is the Holy Mystery that was instituted by God's Kindness and *Philanthropia* as He does not want the death of a sinner but rather that he repents and lives.

1. Repentance as a Virtue in the Old Testament and as a Holy Mystery of the New Testament

Our Lord and Saviour Jesus Christ, the Son of God, instituted the Holy Mystery of Repentance and Confession, making it a living Virtue that brings forth fruits. Repentance was always considered a necessary obligation by all men before Christ, who realised their need, not only those who worshipped the One and True God but many pagans as well. St. Paul proclaimed " *as many as have sinned without law will also perish without law, and as many as have sinned in the law will be judged by the law (for not the hearers of the law are just in the sight of God, but the doers of the law will be justified; for when Gentiles, who do not have the law, by nature do the things in the law, these, although not having the law, are a law to themselves, who show the work of the law written in their hearts, their conscience also*

---

[895] Cf. Plato of Moscow, *Orthodox Teaching,* pp. 155-157. Evdokimov, *Orthodoxia,* pp. 388-394. Kefalas, *Catechesis,* pp. 186-187. Frangopoulos, *Christian Faith,* pp. 208-210. Mitsopoulos, *Themata,* p. 320. Labadarios, *Sermons,* v. 1, pp. 115-123. Sophrony, *His Life,* pp. 71-76. Meyendorff, *Theology,* pp. 195-196. Georgopoulos, *Anthology,* pp. 69-76. For more detail on this Holy Mystery see: Galanopoulos, *System,* Athens, 1960.

bearing witness, and between themselves their thoughts accusing or else excusing them)."[896]

Not only did the Jews recognise the necessity for Reconciliation with the Divine but so did the Gentiles. All nations worshipping their gods, offered sacrifices to calm their anger and to secure their favour. The Gentiles too, acknowledged their guilt, which was a form of confession of sins, seeking reconciliation with the Divine. Besides these common practises amongst the pagans, the True Teaching of Repentance by those who were sent by the One and only True God, especially by the Prophets, was heard by them such as: "*I will judge you, O house of Israel, says the Lord, each one according to his way: be converted, and turn from all your ungodliness and it shall not become to you the punishment of iniquity. Cast away from yourselves all your ungodliness wherein you have sinned against Me; and make to yourselves a new heart and a new spirit: for why should you die, O house of Israel? For I desire not the death of him that dies, says the Lord*"[897] and "*Thus said the Lord; as I live, I desire not the death of the ungodly, as that the ungodly should turn from his way and live: turn you heartily from your way; for why will you die O house of Israel.*"[898] In the Book of Job we read: "*And when they saw him from a distance they did not know him; and they cried with a loud voice, and wept, and rent everyone his garment, and sprinkled dust upon their heads, and they sat down beside him seven days and seven nights, and no one of them spoke; for they saw that his affliction was dreadful and very great.*"[899] King David cried out: "*Blot out my transgressions. Wash me thoroughly from my iniquity, and cleanse me from my sin*[900] *Do not cast me away from Thy Presence, and do not take Thy Holy Spirit from me.*"[901]

Although in the Old Testament repentance was preached by God's delegates and included all the elements of true Repentance acceptable to God, it did not give the fruits nor did it have the Power and Strength that was received as a Mystery instituted by Christ and granted to the Church for the use of the faithful after the Sacrifice of the Lord. In the Old Testament the repentant did not become the

---

[896] Rom. 2:12-15.
[897] Ez. 18:30-32.
[898] Ez. 33:11.
[899] Job 2:12-13.
[900] Psalm 50(51):2.
[901] Psalm 50(51): 11.

Regenerated sons of God nor Co-heirs with Christ. They were not freed from the tyranny of death but were released only from the punishments of Divine Wrath, receiving the favour and Protection of God. Repentance as the Mystery that forgives sin and restores the repentant completely in the Rites of Baptism, which ensured Divine Grace upon the newly chosen people of God, did not exist before the Coming of the Messiah, our Lord and Saviour Jesus Christ, the Son of God.

2. The Establishment of the Holy Mystery of Repentance by the Lord

When certain Scribes heard our Lord Jesus Christ forgiving the sins of the paralytic, they were scandalised and speculated: *"Why does this Man speak blasphemies like this? Who can forgive sins but God alone?"*[902] They were grossly mistaken because they did not recognise the Divine Authority of the Divine Power of Jesus Christ due to their Spiritual blindness and envy. Although their opinion that only God can forgive sins was correct, they did not recognise the Truth despite personally witnessing so much Supernatural evidence proving that our Lord was not merely Man, but God. As Incarnated God, our Saviour proclaimed the Gospel to the world, preaching the forgiveness of sins, clearly explaining that the Son of Man came to *"seek and save that which was lost"*[903] and rightly claiming the Power *"on earth to forgive sins."*[904] Upon this Authority, He granted forgiveness to the paralytic[905] and to the sinful woman.[906] According to His Mission, the Messiah proclaimed *"liberty to the captives and recovery of sight to the blind."*[907] He constantly seeks that which was lost among *"tax-collectors and sinners"*[908] and therefore, He was accused of being *"friend"* to these social outcasts by *"eating and drinking"*[909] with them. To the Pharisees and Scribes who criticised Him and His Disciples for associating *"with tax collectors and*

---

[902] Mark 2:7.
[903] Luke 19:10.
[904] Mark 2:10.
[905] Mark 2:5.
[906] Luke 7:48.
[907] Luke 4:18.
[908] Matth. 11:19.
[909] Luke 7:34.

sinners"[910] He responded: "*I have not come to call the righteous, but sinners, to repentance.*"[911] Quite the opposite are those who approach Christ with faith for they enjoy His Divine Gifts. He grants them the peace of their consciences by telling them with Divine Authority: "*Go in peace.*"[912] Christ, wanting to pass down this Authority to His Church, instructed us to ask the Heavenly Father, in prayer, to forgive our daily sins.

Our Lord responded to the needs of the faithful by instituting Repentance as a Mystery within the Church[913] because He knew that for us "*it is impossible to cut off the love toward sinful passions.*"[914] As a result, every Christian continuously experiences Spiritual falls throughout his life even after his Regeneration that occurred at Holy Baptism. Therefore, without Repentance, which is the "*Medicine of offences, Consumer of unlawfulness, Weapon against the devil, Knife that cuts his head, Saving Hope, Refutation of despair*"[915] all Christians face the direct danger of being completely alienated from the Divine Gifts received at Holy Baptism and Chrismation. Without Repentance we become unworthy of participating in the Divine Eucharist and finally, most tragically, we will be excluded from the Salvation that is offered through Christ. However, even from the beginning, Christ as most Merciful God and foreknowing the hearts of men and their flexibility as well as knowing the wickedness of the devil who ceaselessly attempts to accuse God's servants of sins so that they may fall with him, granted a second Repentance, after Holy Baptism, to sinners. This is for the forgiveness of all who are tempted into sin and who have repented. Thus, "*all those who want to repent can receive the Mercy of God*" because "*God's Mercy, Philanthropia, and countless richness have the repentant as just and sinless.*"[916]

The ease with which mankind so easily falls into sin and the Power of the Divine Mercy within the Holy Mystery of Repentance provoked St. John Chrysostom to remark: "*If you have sins, do not despair. If you sin daily, then daily repent*" for we must do as "*we do to the old houses, when they are crumbling. We remove the rotten*

---

[910] Luke 5:30.
[911] Luke 5:32.
[912] Luke 7:50.
[913] Frangopoulos, *Christian Faith,* pp. 210-212. Mitsopoulos, *Themata,* pp. 320-321.
[914] Clement the Alexandrian, *Who is the saved rich man,* § 40, in *B*, v. 8, p. 371.
[915] St John Chrysostom, *About repentance,* Homily 8, § 1, in Migne, *P.G.,* 49, 337.
[916] Clement the Alexandrian, *Stromata,* II, § 13, in *B*, v. 7, p. 328.

parts from them and repair them. You have become old today because of sin. Renew yourself through Repentance." Repentance has so much Power from the *Philanthropia* of the Master that "*you would achieve the forgiveness of your sins.*" However, already "*with repentance are mixed God's Philanthropia, for God's Love for mankind has no limit, neither can His Kindness be interpreted.*" Furthermore, although man's wickedness "*is limited the medicine has no limits*" because "*God's Philanthropia is indescribable and infinite.*" To make this more understandable, St. John Chrysostom used the example of a spark: "*Think of a spark falling into the ocean. Can it exist or be seen? As a spark is compared to the ocean, thus is evil compared to God's Philanthropia. Not as such, but even greater. For the ocean, although large, has its limits but God's Philanthropia is infinite.*"[917]

3. The Names of the Holy Mystery

The names ascribed to the Holy Mystery of Repentance reveal either the essential part of the Mystery or the results that it brings. Thus the Holy Mystery was called: "*Repentance*" because of the change in the way of feeling, thinking and will of the repentant, "*Confession*" because the repentant confesses his sins before the officiator, "*Second Baptism,*" "*washing of tears,*" "*washing,*" "*absolution,*" "*purification of sins,*" "*reconciliation,*" "(life-saving) board of Salvation after the wreck.*"

II. THE DIVINE INSTITUTION OF THE HOLY MYSTERY AND ITS POWER

Our Lord and Saviour Jesus Christ, the Son of God, received the Authority to forgive sins as God and as the Son of Man[918] because of the hypostasis of His two Natures. He initially promised this Authority to St. Peter[919] and later to all His Holy Apostles.[920] On the day of His glorious Resurrection, He breathed upon the faces of the Holy Apostles, giving them the Holy Spirit and the Authority to

---

[917] St John Chrysostom, *About repentance,* Homily 8, § 1, in Migne, *P.G.,* 49, 337.
[918] Matth. 9:6. Mark 2:10. Luke 5:24; 7:47-48.
[919] Matth. 16:19.
[920] Matth. 18:18.

forgive or not to forgive the sins of the people.[921] Thus the Orthodox Church, through the Holy Apostles, received the Divine Authority to forgive not only those sins committed before Baptism but even those committed afterwards and this Authority is practised through her Bishops and Presbyters. This was the practice of the One, Holy, Catholic, Apostolic and undivided Eastern Orthodox Church as witnessed not only in the New Testament, but in the writings of all ecclesiastic writers and Holy Fathers who proclaimed the Saving Act of the God-instituted Mystery by means of which all sins of those who truly repent are forgiven. Those who do not repent, prevent the Grace of the Holy Spirit from descending and forgiving their sins, thereby simultaneously committing the sin of blasphemy against the Holy Spirit, which our Lord and Saviour Jesus Christ warned us shall not be forgiven in this world or in the world to come![922]

1. The Institution of the Holy Mystery By Our Lord

After the confession of St Peter that our Lord Jesus is *"the Christ, the Son of the living God"*[923] which was revealed according to Divine Revelation, our Lord and Saviour Jesus Christ, the Son of God, promised to give him *" the keys of the Kingdom of Heaven, and whatever you bind on earth will be bound in Heaven, and whatever you loose on earth will be loosed in Heaven."*[924] With these words, the Lord granted St Peter the Authority to permit entrance into the Kingdom of Heaven to the worthy, while preventing the unworthy from entering. *"To bring in or to prevent the entrance is the work of the key-holder."* Being entrusted with the keeping of the keys confirms St. Peter as having the undoubted right and authority according to the promise of the Lord that he is not simply a door-keeper of the Kingdom of Heaven but a steward, vested with Despotic Authority of Him Who entrusted and gave him the keys of Heaven. It is a full authority and in a measure infinite, which allows St. Peter to bring in or to exclude. This Authority was mainly so that *"whatever sin which will not be forgiven on earth shall not be forgiven in Heaven by God; and whatever will be forgiven here, will be forgiven there."*[925]

---

[921] John 20:22-23.
[922] Matth. 12:31-32. Mark 3:28-29.
[923] Matth. 16:16.
[924] Matth. 16:19.
[925] Zigabinos, *To Matthew 16:19,* in Migne, *P.G.,* 129, 468.

This Authority is infinite in that it refers to forgiving whatever sin, either big or small, according to the just judgement of the officiator. He who unjustly judges and binds on earth and not according to the Word of God or forgives not according to the Will of God, the gates of Hades prevail. The Gates of Hades are not obliged to prevail over him who wants to bind or lose because he who, with pride, misuses this Authority *"not knowing the Will of the Scriptures, has fallen in the sin of the devil"* unjustly and not according to the Will of God and judging *"in vain, he binds and loses."*[926]

Whatever the Lord promised in Caesarea to St. Peter who was first to confess that our Lord Jesus is *"the Christ, the Son of the living God"*[927] He also later promised to the other Holy Apostles as representatives at that time of the entire Church. Furthermore, Christ warned that he who refuses to obey the Church *"let him be to you like a heathen and a tax collector."*[928] Furthermore, *"what we decide on earth, God seals in Heaven. For those who are not healed* (through Repentance) *you cut off from the Church and those who repent, you receive later."*[929]

This Sacred Promise was fulfilled on the first day of Christ's glorious Resurrection when His Disciples were gathered together and He appeared in the midst of them, greeting them with the words: *"Peace to you! As the Father has sent Me, I also send you."*[930] With words the Lord gave the same Mission to the Apostles and made them His successors, reassuring them that He would send them *"as the Father has sent Me"* simultaneously revealing the rank of authority given to them.[931] In other words, as our Lord was sent by the Father to *"seek and save the lost"*[932] likewise were they sent by the Risen Lord to continue His Work, seeking as had Christ for the lost sheep and co-operating with God for their Salvation. In order for them to achieve this, they had to be vested with the Authority to forgive and bind sins, similar to the Authority which our Lord had. Therefore, immediately as the Lord pronounced these words, *"He breathed on*

---

[926] Origen, *To Matthew,* XII, 14, In Migne, *P.G.,* 13, 1013.
[927] Matth. 16:16.
[928] Matth. 18:17.
[929] Zigabinos, *To Matthew 16:19,* in Migne, *P.G.,* 129, 468.
[930] John 20:21.
[931] St Cyril of Alexandria, *To Matthew 16:19,* in Migne, *P.G.,* 72, 424 and 709. Zigabinos, *To Matthew 16:19,* in Migne, *P.G.,* 129, 1485.
[932] Luke 19:10.

them and said to them: 'Receive the Holy Spirit. If you forgive the sins of any, they are forgiven them; if you retain the sins of any, they are retained.'"[933]

To forgive the sins or iniquities means that the sins are "*abolished*" and they are "*erased.*" It also means that the sins are "*covered*" completely in such a way that they no longer appear and they are "*washed*" away so that no trace or spot can be found.

This Authority was given to the Holy Apostles and Disciples, not as a personal *Charisma* but as a permanent institution that was passed down through them to the Church and remains effective until the end of the ages.

2. The Transmitting of the Authority to Forgive

The transmission of the Authority to forgive the sins to the Church, presupposes and suggests *The Didache*, which addresses the commandment to each faithful: "*In church you shall confess your transgressions, and you shall not approach your prayer with an evil conscience. This is the way of life*"[934] and urging everyone "*on the Lord's own day* (to) *gather together and break bread and give thanks, having first confessed your sins so that your sacrifice may be pure.*"[935]

Taking into consideration that the life of the Christians at that time was very strict, their confession was done in public and before the officiators of the Church with all the other faithful present.

Similar advice is found in the epistle of St. Ignatius the Theophorus of Antioch to the Philadelphians: "*the Lord, however, forgives all who repent, if in repenting they return to the unity of God and the council of the Bishop*"[936] and "*for all those who belong to God and Jesus Christ are with the Bishop, and all those who repent and enter into the unity of the Church will belong to God, that they may be living in accordance with Jesus Christ.*"[937]

St. Clement of Rome recommended that those "*who laid the foundation of the revolt*" submit themselves "*to the Presbyters and*

---

[933] John 20:22-23.
[934] *Didache,* IV, 14, in Lightfoot, *Apostolic Fathers,* p. 152.
[935] *Didache,* XIV, 1, in Lightfoot, *Apostolic Fathers,* p. 157.
[936] St Ignatius, *To Philadelphians,* VIII, 1, in Lightfoot, *Apostolic Fathers,* p. 108.
[937] Ibid, *To Philadelphians,* III, 2, in Lightfoot, *Apostolic Fathers,* p. 107.

accept discipline leading to repentance, bending the knees of their hearts."[938]

St. Polycarp of Smyrna advised the *"Presbyters (to) be compassionate, merciful to all, turning back those who have gone astray, visiting all the sick, not neglecting a widow, orphan or poor person, but 'always aiming at what is honourable in the sight of God and of men,'[939] avoiding all anger, partiality, unjust judgement, staying far away from all love of money, not quick to believe things spoken against anyone, nor harsh in judgement, knowing that we are all in debt with respect to sin. Therefore, if we ask the Lord to forgive us, then we ourselves ought to forgive, for we are in full view of the eyes of the Lord and God, and we must 'all stand before the Judgement Seat of Christ' and 'each one must give an account of himself.'[940]"[941]*

The Authority to forgive or to bind the sins by the Bishops or Presbyters was evident during the period of persecutions. Thus St. Cyprian addressed those who during persecution had renounced their faith and, without repentance and confession, approached Holy Communion. He pointed out to them that others of the faithful were under repentance for minor sins but came to Confession with the laying on of the hands of the Bishop and the clergy, thereby receiving the right to Communion.[942] He also praised those who had neither sacrificed to any idol nor were bound by any unholy *"libelli"* but because they had thought about it and even consented within their hearts, they approached the Priests of God with deep contrition, confessing by revealing the depths of their souls. St. Cyprian exhorted all to confess their misdoings until they received the forgiveness of the Lord through His Priests. [943] In another letter the Hieromartyr Bishop, having received letters of recommendation by Confessors of the Faith regarding the fallen, permitted those who were in danger of death, not to wait for his arrival to forgive them as the Authorised Bishop but to request any Presbyter to do so. In their absence a Deacon could receive death-bed confessions and grant them

---

[938] St Clement of Rome, *1st Corinthians,* 57, 1, in Lightfoot, *Apostolic Fathers,* p. 60.

[939] Prov. 3:4. 2 Corinth. 8:21.

[940] Rom. 14:10, 12. 2 Corinth. 5:10.

[941] St Polycarp, *To the Philippians,* VI, 1-2, in Lightfoot, *Apostolic Fathers,* p. 126.

[942] St Cyprian, *Epistola*9, § 2, in migne, *P.L.,* 4, 257.

[943] Ibid, *De lapsis,* 28, 29, in migne, *P.L.,* 4, 503.

the forgiveness through the laying on of hands so that they may depart in peace to the Lord.[944]

Origen, interpreting the belief of the Alexandrian Church, assured that the officiators and Priests of the Church take up the sins of the people and imitating the Teacher, grant forgiveness of sins.[945] Elsewhere he numbered the ways of forgiveness of sins according to the Gospel.[946] Interpreting the promise given by the Lord to St Peter, he believed that *"those who desire the position of the Bishop need to receive the words of the Lord and the keys of the Kingdom of Heaven as Peter, and they teach that whatever they bind are bound in Heaven and those which are loosened, in other words have received forgiveness, are loosened in Heaven."*[947]

St. Athanasius the Great of Alexandria commented that *"as a man is Baptised by a Priest and is Enlightened by the Grace of the Holy Spirit, likewise he who confesses with repentance through the Priest receives the forgiveness through the Grace of Christ."*[948]

St. Basil the Great warned us that it is *"necessary to confess the sins to those who were entrusted with the Economia of the Sacraments of God"* in other words to the Presbyters and Bishops. Justifying this instruction, the Holy Father reminded us that *"in such a manner those who repented practised. For it is written in the Gospel that they confessed their sins to John the Baptist; and in Acts (19:18) to the Apostles, by whom all were Baptised."* For the Confession of virgins who have been dedicated into Sisterhoods (Nuns), it is not permissible for them to confess to the Abbess but instead they may confess in the presence of an older sister to the Presbyter who is able to give the proper medicine. [949]

St. John Chrysostom observed that the Priest as *"Judge is sitting on earth and the Despot follows the servant and whatever he considers, that He confirms from Above."*[950]

St. Leo, the Great Pope of Rome, in one of his letters, proclaimed that the Mediator of God and men, the Man Jesus Christ, gave the Authority to the Elders of the Church to impose Repentance on those

---

[944] St Cyprian, *Epistola*12, 1, in migne, *P.L.,* 4, 265.
[945] Origen, *In Leviticus,* homily V, 3, in Migne, *P.G.,* 12, 451.
[946] Ibid, *In Leviticus,* homily II, 4, in Migne, *P.G.,* 12, 418.
[947] Ibid, *To Matthew*, XII, 14, in Migne, *P.G.,* 13, 1012-1013.
[948] St Athanasius the Great, in Migne, *P.G.,* 26, 1315.
[949] St Basil the Great, in Migne, *P.G.,* 31, 1284-1285, 1157.
[950] St John Chrysostom, *About priesthood,* III, § 5, in Migne, *P.G.,* 56, 130.

who confess and cleanse themselves through the Saving punishments. Afterwards they were to receive them in the Communion of the Sacraments through the door of Reconciliation.[951]

3. The Relatively Infinity of the Authority

That our Lord and Saviour Jesus Christ, the Son of God, entrusted the authority to His Church to forgive sins without any restriction is evident from His words: *"whatever you bind"* and *"whatever you loose"*[952] as well as *"if you forgive the sins of any"* and *"if you retain the sins of any."*[953] No matter how many sins are forgiven or bound, those who received the Authority from the Lord, the Apostles and through them the Church, have the right to grant the forgiveness of sins. Besides that, the Lord gave this Mission to the Church: *"As the Father has sent Me, even so I send you."*[954] This Mission includes the absolute and infinite Authority to forgive sins. St. John Chrysostom believed that *"all the Judgement which the Father has committed to the Son*[955] *is committed to all"* the Apostles and Priests.[956] The Lord using this Authority which He committed to His Church, forgave serious sins, as that of the adulteress,[957] that of the sinful woman,[958] that of the thief on the Cross[959] and that of St. Peter.[960] On the other hand St. Paul accepted to forgive the one who had fallen and whom the Church of Corinth would forgive. *"Now whom you forgive anything, I also forgive. For if indeed I have forgiven anything, I have forgiven that one for your sakes in the presence of Christ, lest Satan should take advantage of us; for we are not ignorant of his devices."*[961] Also in his 1st Letter to the Corinthians, he wrote: *"It is actually reported that there is sexual immorality among you, and such sexual immorality as is not even named among the Gentiles – that a man has his father's wife! And*

---

[951] St Leo of Rome, the Great, *Epistola*108 *ad Theodorum*, § 2, in migne, *P.L.,* 54, 1011.
[952] Matth. 18:18.
[953] John 20:23.
[954] John 20:21.
[955] John 5:22.
[956] St John Chrysostom, *About priesthood,* III, § 5, in Migne, *P.G.,* 48, 643.
[957] John 8:3-11.
[958] Luke 7:36-50.
[959] Luke 23:43.
[960] John 21:15-19.
[961] 2 Corinth. 2:10-11.

you are puffed up, and have not rather mourned, that he who has done this deed might be taken away from among you. For I indeed, as absent in body but present in spirit, have already judged (as though I were present) him who has so done this deed. In the Name of our Lord Jesus Christ, when you are gathered together, along with my spirit, with the Power of our Lord Jesus Christ, deliver such a one to Satan for the destruction of the flesh, that his spirit may be Saved in the day of the Lord Jesus."[962]

Concerning the teachings of the Apostolic Fathers, the *Shepherd of Hermas* noted, that "*when I recovered myself and remembered the Glory of God and took heart, I knelt down and once more confessed my sins to the Lord, as I had done before. And she came with six young men, whom I had seen before, and she stood by me and listened attentively as I prayed and confessed my sins to the Lord.*"[963]

In Africa some Bishops wanted to exclude those who committed adultery and fornication from Repentance but because their fellow Bishops in the Synod prevailed, they also followed their opinion and did not disrupt the unity of the Church.[964]

Clement the Alexandrian spoke of the one Repentance after Baptism, which he characterised as "*second Baptism*" and demanded that repentance should be sincere and without returning to the old sinful way of life. He quoted the Epistle to the Hebrews: "*For it is impossible for those who were once enlightened, and have tasted the Heavenly Gift, and have become partakers of the Holy Spirit, and have tasted the good word of God and the powers of the age to come, if they fall away, to renew them again to repentance, since they crucify again for themselves the Son of God, and put Him to an open shame.*"[965] The hardening of the heart into which one can fall makes him unreceptive to sincere repentance. However, for those who with all their heart turn back to God with sincere repentance, the doors are open.[966]

Origen mentioned Christians who had fallen and who the other faithful mourned "*as though they were lost and dead for God*" but who were "*raised from the dead, if they accepted change.*" Origen

---

[962] 1 Corinth. 5:1-5.
[963] *Shepherd of Hermas,* Vision 3, 5-6, in Lightfoot, *Apostolic Fathers,* p. 200.
[964] St Cyprian, *Epistola*52, 21, in migne, *P.L.,* 3, 811.
[965] Heb. 6:4-6.
[966] Clement the Alexandrian, *Stromata,* II, 13, in *B*, v. 7, p. 329. Ibid, *Who is the saved rich man,* 42, 40, 39, in *B*, v. 8, pp. 373, 371, 370.

believed that for serious sins there can be only one true repentance, whereas daily sins can be forgiven without the intervention of others.[967] When he spoke of one repentance for serious sins, he meant that if anyone falls more than once, he may be forgiven but under the condition that he will not fall in the same sins again. [968]

The *Apostolic Orders* repeatedly address the admonition that the Bishop should act with compassion to those who have sinned and not to consider them detestable. *"The one who has fallen once and twice in the same mistake the Lord did not give up, but ate with the publicans and sinners."* If one of the sinners *"returns and shows fruits of repentance"* then the Bishop is obliged to receive him *"as the lost son, the prodigal, who consumed the fatherly fortune with sinful women, who became shepherd of swine and ate with them."*[969]

Parallel to the 52nd Canon of the Apostles that demands that if any Bishop or Presbyter refuses to receive anyone who has repented, he shall be deposed from his position because *"he has saddened Christ Who said that there is joy in Heaven when a sinner turns with repentance."*[970]

St. John Chrysostom believed that Repentance *"has much power on him who is Baptised to make* (himself) *greater, if he wishes. She* (Repentance) *is able to take away the heaviness of sins and to secure the one who is in danger, even if he has come down to the bottom of sin."* Elsewhere, encouraging the repentant, he advised that *"whenever you fall in the market, so many times you must stand. Thus as many times as you sin, repent for your sin; do not despair; even if you sin twice, twice repent. Even if you are in old age and you have sinned, enter; repent, for here is a hospital, which offers forgiveness of sins."*[971]

St. Cyril of Alexandria believed that *"there is no sin which God cannot forgive for those who sincerely repent."*[972]

St. Athanasius of Alexandria proclaimed that *"the remarkable repentance looses all sins."*[973]

---

[967] Origen, *Against Celsus,* III, 51, in *B*, v. 9, p. 213. Ibid, *In Leviticus* XV, 2, in Migne, *P.G.,* 12, 561.

[968] Ibid, *In Leviticus* XI, 2, in Migne, *P.G.,* 12, 533.

[969] *Apostolic Orders,* II, 40, 1, and 41, 1, in *B*, v. 2, p. 42.

[970] 52nd Canon of the Apostles.

[971] St John Chrysostom, *To Hebrews,* Homily 9, § 4, in Migne, *P.G.,* 63, 80. Ibid, *About repentance,* III, § 4, in Migne, *P.G.,* 49, 297.

[972] St Cyril of Alexandria, *To Matthew,* in Migne, *P.G.,* 72, 409.

[973] St Athanasius the Great, *Fragment to Matthew*, in Migne, *P.G.,* 27, 1388.

Jeremias observed that when the Lord promised St. Peter *"the keys of Heaven"*. Peter *"asked how many times he should forgive the sinners. Seven times? (By this Peter believed that he was achieving a great thing)* (until) *the Lord responded, not seven, but seventy times seven."*[974]

If some of the ecclesiastic writers and Holy Fathers of the early Orthodox Church hesitated to forgive mortal sins, this was because they were very concerned that if one repeatedly returned to these sins, he would become used to them and would face the danger of becoming insensitive and developing a condition that could not receive Repentance. This condition is that which our Lord referred to as the blasphemy against the Holy Spirit, which forever remains inexcusable and unforgiveable. It is called the callousness and hardening of the heart because he who reaches this stage reveals a stubborn resistance to the influence of the Holy Spirit Who urges him towards repentance and the change of the way of life. This resistance is due to the free will of the sinner.[975] *"He who willingly falls into sin and knowingly blasphemes God will not be forgiven."*[976] These sins, which were characterised as blasphemies against the Holy Spirit, are inexcusable not because of God or the Church but because of the sinner's unrepentance and stubbornness.[977] The blasphemy against the Holy Spirit is inexcusable, unforgiveable and eternal because it falsifies the nature of man and creates a permanent and unchangeable condition. The Eternal Punishment is the result of sin, which hardens the heart of the unrepentant sinner due to his own free will and which has become irreparable and incurable.[978]

III. COMPONENTS OF REPENTANCE

The power and effectiveness of repentance is manifested when it is true and sincere. It is absolutely necessary that sincere Godly sorrow and repentance are expressed before the absolution of sins is granted by the Bishop or Priest. The repentant must be steadfast in his decision not to return to his sinful way of life and to bear fruits worthy

---

[974] Jeremias, A', in Karmeris, *The dogmatics,* v. I, pp. 391 and 396.
[975] Clement the Alexandrian, *Stromata* II, 13, in **B**, v. 7, p. 329.
[976] Zigabinos, *To Matthew 12:32,* in Migne, *P.G.,* 129, 381.
[977] Androutsos, *Dogmatique,* p. 379.
[978] Trempelas, *Dogmatique,* v. III, p. 258.

174

of his repentance. The seal of this internal change of thoughts and decisions must follow the recognition and confession of the committed sins, not only in the repentant prayers but with humility revealing before the confessor Bishop or Priest his sins as one who reveals his illness to a doctor in order to receive the medicine for the healing of his Spiritual wounds. After Confession the absolution follows which consists of the remission of sins and the re-establishment in the condition of Grace.

1. Self-condemnation and Contrition as Pre-requirement Terms

Since repentance requires the renouncement and the turning away from sin beforehand as well as the change of the way of thinking and making decisions, it is obvious that the first step of repentance is to *"know the sins and to acknowledge the iniquities and to condemn oneself."*[979] Without this acknowledgement and self-condemnation, repentance is completely inconceivable. Justification of any sin or the passing of the responsibility to others dulls the centre of repentance and prevents the development of the humble and broken heart.

St. Basil the Great observed that: *"Repentance calls someone to live with the recognition of his guilt, followed by a contrite heart."*[980] It is not enough that he simply admits *"I have sinned"* but that he acknowledges his own sins through his sincere self-examination. *"The medicine of repentance is prepared at first from the knowing of our own sins."*[981]

Without the knowing and complete acknowledgement of one's guilt for committed sins, it is impossible to create a sincere contrite heart and the *"Godly sorrow,"* which comprise the first necessary and essential elements of true repentance. St. Paul taught that *"Godly sorrow produces repentance leading to Salvation, not to be regretted; but the sorrow of the world produces death."*[982]

St. Justin the Philosopher and Martyr, using King David as an example of repentance, observed that *"he was forgiven when he cried and mourned."* Consequently, *"if this great King, anointed one and*

---

[979] St John Chrysostom, *To 1 Corinthians,* Homily 28, § 2, in Migne, *P.G.,* 61, 234.
[980] St Basil the Great, *To Isaiah,* ch. 15, § 297; and ch. 1, § 34, in Migne, *P.G.,* 30, 640 and 185.
[981] St John Chrysostom, *To Hebrews,* Homily 9, § 4, in Migne, *P.G.,* 63, 80.
[982] 2 Corinth. 7:10.

Prophet, received the forgiveness, how can it be possible for 'the unclean' to be forgiven 'unless they cry and mourn. '"[983]

St. John Chrysostom accentuated the example of the Ninevites who *"put on their wounds"* and *"vested themselves with sack cloths and ashes and cried.*[984]*"* In another example King David *"cried about his sin with a broken heart, devoutness of soul, and remembered it continuously."* St. Peter repented and his *"tears cleansed his sin."*[985]

Hence right from the beginning the great importance of the contrite heart was proclaimed by Holy Tradition. This contrite heart makes the repentance sincere and effective.

The Shepherd of Hermas proclaimed: *"Listen, he said. Your sins are numerous, but not so numerous that you should be handed over to this Angel. But your family has committed great sins and iniquities, and the glorious Angel was incensed by their deeds, and for this reason he ordered that you should be afflicted for a while, in order that they too might repent and cleanse themselves from every desire of this world. So when they repent and are cleansed, then the Angel of punishment will leave."*[986] *"So, do you think that the sins of those who repent are forgiven immediately? Certainly not! But the one who repents must torment his own soul and be extremely humble in everything he does and be afflicted with a variety of afflictions; and if he endures the afflictions that come upon him, then assuredly the One Who created all things and endowed them with power will be moved with compassion and will give some healing."*[987]

Tertullian considered the humble heart as the primary element of repentance.[988]

Origen presented the one who committed a mortal sin as *"not being able to inhabit with the corps, but being tortured within his heart, not being able to drink or eat because of the pain of repentance, all day scowling and wearing out, yelling with groans from his heart, seeing his sin before him always accusing him, not for one day nor for one night, but for a long time being punished."*[989]

---

[983] St Justin the Philosopher and Martyr, *Dialogue,* 141, in **B,** v. 3, p. 338.
[984] Jonas 3:5-9.
[985] St John Chrysostom, *To 1 Corinthians,* Homily 4, §§ 5-6, in Migne, *P.G.,* 61, 425-426. Ibid, *To 1 Corinthians,* Homily 4, §§ 5-6, in Migne, *P.G.,* 49, 298.
[986] *Shepherd of Hermas,* Parable 7, § 2, in Lightfoot, *Apostolic Fathers,* p. 251.
[987] Ibid, Parable 7, § 4, in Lightfoot, *Apostolic Fathers,* p. 252.
[988] Tertullian, *De poenitentia,* IX, in migne, *P.L.,* 1, 1354.
[989] Origen, *To Jeremiah,* homily XIX, 9, in Migne, *P.G.,* 13, 521.

St. John Chrysostom presented the tears of contrition as *"uniting the repentant with God"* and as making the sinful woman *"more modest than the virgins."* He used the example of the rain, when after the storm peaceful weather follows. Likewise, the tears bring inner peace and abolishes the darkness caused by sins. He also emphasised that these tears should not be shed because of vainglory but for devoutness, without being watched by anyone and in our secret places, shed only for God. *"You must groan, when you have sinned"* not because *"you will be punished, for this is nothing, but because you have clashed with your Master Who loved you and gave His Son for you."*[990]

According to the above, the primary and main element of true and sincere repentance is the awareness of one's mistakes, recognising without justifying his sins before God with absolute humility, contrite heart and Godly sorrow. The reason and cause of this humility and Godly sorrow must be due to not only having disobeyed the Law of God and having fallen into the various offences but due to the fact that we have proved to be unworthy and ungrateful of God's Love and numerous benefits.

2. The Double Confession as Term of Repentance

Confession follows the contrite heart. When we speak of confession, we must remember that it has a double meaning:

1. Confession with a contrite heart, tears with prayers and petitions to God, and
2. Confession before the Spiritual father (Bishop or Priest).

Simultaneously, it is important to emphasise that confession before God expressed in our personal and private prayers does not replace or make the Confession before the Spiritual father (Bishop or Priest) unnecessary. The Holy Mystery of Confession seals and perfects our confessions particularly those concerning mortal sins. Only through the Holy Mystery of Confession can these sins be forgiven and through the pedagogic measures one achieves his healing and restoration.

---

[990] St John Chrysostom, *To Matthew,* Homily 6, § 5, in Migne, *P.G.,* 57, 68-69. Ibid, *To 2 Corinthians,* Homily 4, § 6, in Migne, *P.G.,* 61, 426.

It is natural that he who recognises his sins with a humble heart turn to God confessing his iniquities, asking for God's Mercy and Forgiveness. Confession without humility before God becomes completely typical and useless.

St. John Chrysostom, numbering the components of the Medicine of Repentance, initially placed awareness and confession of one's own sins before the Lord. Elsewhere, he stressed that Confession of sins wipes out iniquities. Accentuating the necessity of Confession, he observed that God seeks sinners' confessions so that we, learning the magnitude of His forgiveness of our debts, will offer constant thanksgiving and, by our striving to resist temptation, will become virtuous. [991]

This confession continues:

1.   As a natural reaction against the attacks of sinful thoughts, imagination and deeds;
2.   the renouncement and forgiveness of sin;
3.   the remaining of one's memories concerning his falls and
4.   a recognition and admission of our own weakness and the necessity of calling upon the Divine Mercy and Healing Grace of God.

St. Basil the Great reassured us that God "*wants to show mercy*" to the repentant sinner whose heart has become humbled and contrite through the sincere Confession of his secret sins, which were made unashamedly known in public. As the result of this God grants His abundant Mercy. After the public Confession it is characteristic for the Bishop or Priests to call upon the faithful to assist the repentant sinner with their prayers for the complete healing of his wounds.[992]

As the crowning necessity for receiving the forgiveness of sins by means of the Holy Mystery of Confession to God, the recognition and admission of sins must be combined with Confession to the Spiritual Father (Bishop or Priest) who uses the Authority of binding or loosing of sins. He then administers the necessary Medicine for the

---

[991] St John Chrysostom, *To Hebrews,* Homily 9, § 4, in Migne, *P.G.,* 63, 80. Ibid, *To Genesis,* Homily 20, § 3, in Migne, *P.G.,* 53, 170. Ibid, *To Lazarus,* Homily 4, § 4, in Migne, *P.G.,* 48, 1012.

[992] St Basil the Great, *To Psalm 32,* § 3, in Migne, *P.G.,* 29, 332. St Irenaeus, *Heresies,* book I, ch. 13, § 5, in Migne, *P.G.,* 7, 588. Cf. in Hadjephraimides, p. 71.

healing of the repentant sinner.[993] It must note that during the early years of the Church, when sins of the faithful did not cause scandals, they were confessed in public and in the presence of the officiators.

Origen advised that one should find an experienced doctor who, amongst other things, will guide and heal the sinner.[994]

3. Absolution by the Bishop or Priest

After the Confession of our sins, the Absolution or Forgiveness of the confessed sins by the officiator of the Holy Mystery follows. The Bishop or Priest has the Authority, should he find it necessary, to postpone the Forgiveness for a certain period. The officiator offers Absolution or Forgiveness of the confessed sins through prayer. These forgiven sins are completely erased and abolished by the Divine Grace of the Holy Spirit through tears of repentance and no longer exist as an obstacle to the return to the condition of Grace from which he had temporarily strayed because of sin.

Forgiveness is offered *"ex opere operato"* according to the Authority which was given by our Lord and Saviour Jesus Christ, the Son of God, to His Orthodox Church. And above all other Holy Sacraments the imploring prayer of the Priest is Justified. This imploring type of prayer in the Orthodox Church is: *"may the same God forgive you through me a sinner all in this life and in the Life to come."*[995] In the Roman Catholic Church the type of prayer is: *"I absolve you from your sins in the Name of the Father and of the Son and of the Holy Spirit."*[996]

The imploring type of forgiveness in the Mystery of Repentance is Justified not only because the real Officiator within the Holy Mystery is actually the High Priest Jesus Christ. This is due to the fact that forgiveness depends not only on the Absolution offered by the Bishop or Priest but on the sincere repentance of the one who has confessed.

Jesus Christ, the Son of God, is the only One Who is able to search the very depths of man's heart and soul. Men (Bishops and Priests) make mistakes in their judgement and those who confess their

---

[993] Cf. Plato of Moscow, *Orthodox Teaching,* pp. 156-157.
[994] Origen, *In Psalm* XXXVII, Homily II, 6, in Migne, *P.G.,* 12, 1386.
[995] Service of Confession, in Euchologion, ed. M. Saliberos, p. 164.
[996] St Augustine, *Sermo* 99, *in Luce* VII, 35, in migne, *P.L.,* 38, 599. Leo I, *Epistola*CLXVIII, 2, in migne, *P.L.,* 54, 1211. Ibid, *Epistola* CVIII, 2, in migne, *P.L.,* 54, 1011.

sins hide certain iniquities from the Confessor. Furthermore because of partiality or interest, the repentant sinner may mislead the officiator of the Holy Mystery into a wrong assessment that God does not confirm. However that does not decrease the *"ex opere operato"* Power of the Mystery, neither does the repentant sinner's Sanctification or Condemnation depend on the degree of his sincerity. Therefore, the Holy Mystery of Repentance acts *"ex opere operato"* only when the repentant sinner approaches with sincere repentance and a humble, contrite heart, confessing his sins to the best of his ability.

IV. THE ABSOLUTION AS AN ACT OF JUDGEMENT AND THE NATURE OF PENANCE

It is obvious that the use of the Authority to bind or to loose and the forgiveness or the postponement of the forgiveness of confessed sins is an act of judgement. The Bishop or Priest looses or not the bonds of sins of the repentant one and imposes pedagogic penances on him depending on the circumstances, with the Authority of Judgement, which *"the Father has given to the Son"*[997] and which the Son has given to His Orthodox Church.

One must never forget that the Bishop or Priest as judge, essentially differs from any other worldly judge, since his attribute as a Spiritual Father, Shepherd and Doctor overshadows that of Judge. For this reason, all his actions related to the Authority which he uses, must consider not only the Spiritual punishment of evil but rather the correction and re-establishment of the repentant sinner by means of paternal, compassionate care as well as the skill Enlightenment of a Spiritual Doctor.

The Spiritual Medicine and measurement of the paternal Love used by Spiritual Fathers are known as penances, which are obviously not punishments that satisfy the Divine Justice of God but which are the means and ways of correction, used according to their judgement. They may decide to increase or decrease the penances or even possibly lift them completely from the repentant sinner depending on relevant circumstances.

---

[997] John 5:22.

1. The Spiritual Father

The Spiritual Father officiating in the Holy Mystery of Repentance acts as a judge and this is understandable when we consider that all judgement has three prerequisites:

1. Judicial Authority.
2. That which is judge is according to pre-existing law.
3. The expressed decision.

It is evident that the Spiritual Father is vested with Judicial Authority from the words of institution of the Divine Mystery when our Lord and Saviour Jesus Christ, the Son of God, gave the Authority to bind or loose the sins through His Holy Apostles to His Holy Orthodox Church, as well as from the verification that *"the Father gave all the Authority to the Son."*[998] This means that the Father gave Authority to the Son to Judge by judging men *"not only as God Who knows their nature, but as Man Who has experienced (human nature)."* Dependent upon and derived from the Authority that Christ received from His Father and according to which, as the Son of Man, He will come again in all His Glory to Judge the living and the dead, is that same Authority that was transferred to Christ's Orthodox Church by His Holy Apostles. Upon this Authority that Christ received from His Father and according to which, as the Son of Man, He will come again in all His glory to Judge the living and the dead, depends and derives that which was transferred by the Holy Apostles to Christ's Orthodox Church[999]

Hence in the *Apostolic Orders* addressed to the Bishops are admonitions such as: *"Judge, O Bishop, with authority as God"* and *"sit in the Church teaching the Word as with authority to judge those who have sinned, because to you, the Bishops, is said: Whatever you will bind on earth will be bound in Heaven and whatever you will loose on earth will be loosed in Heaven"*[1000] *"You have the authority, O Bishop, to return and to send those who are crushed with forgiveness. For through you the Saviour said to him who came with*

---

[998] John 5:22.
[999] Zigabinos, *To John,* in Migne, *P.G.,* 129, 1220.
[1000] *Apostolic Orders,* II, 11, 12, in *B,* v. 2, p. 18.

sins: Your sins are forgiven, your faith has saved you, go in peace."[1001]

St. John Chrysostom observed that "*Heaven begins its judgement from the earth. Because the judge sits on earth, the Master follows the servant and whatever he judges below, the same He confirms Above.*"[1002]

Tertullian characterised the judgement of the Bishop or Priest on the sinner as supreme pre-judgement of the future Judgement.[1003]

In accordance to this Authority with which the Bishop or his representative is vested, he judges the confessed sin and expresses a just decision based upon the Justice and Law of God. Because the Lord, by proclaiming that the Father gave "*all Authority*" to Him, it "*does not exclude the Father from the Authority of Judging, but the Son Judges with the consent of the Father, co-operating with the Holy Spirit*" so that "*all the Judgement of the Son is not deprived of the Paternal Will.*"[1004] Consequently, the officiator of the Mystery of Confession judges the sin of the repentant with Judicial Authority and either positively grants forgiveness or negatively does not forgive.

More characteristically, the *Apostolic Orders* describe the practise of the Judicial Authority of the Bishop or the Presbyter who replaces him, as a judge who sees "*the sinner and commanding him to be thrown out. Brought out by the Deacons*" who with sadness hold him "*outside of the Church and entering*" they ask the Bishop about him. "*Then the Bishop commands them to bring him in and judging him, if he has repented and if he is worthy to be delivered completely to the Church*" he gives him the appropriate penance, addressing "*him, whatsoever is proper to him who has sinned, rebuking, teaching and advising*" him before releasing him. The form and the method are similar to that of worldly courts.[1005]

This Spiritual Authority differs in its nature and prerequisites. The essential and primary difference that separates one from the other, is that the judgement is a Judgement of Grace, Mercy and Compassion, whereas the worldly judicial is a judgement of justice and intolerant retaliation. Furthermore the aims of each have different goals. The Judicial Authority of the state aims primarily to punish the

---

[1001] Ibid, II, 20, in *B*, v. 2, p. 25.
[1002] St John Chrysostom, *To Isaiah,* Homily 5, § 1, in Migne, *P.G.,* 56, 131.
[1003] Tertullian, *Apology* 39, in migne, *P.L.,* 1, 532.
[1004] St Gregory of Nyssa, *That there is no three gods,* § 8, in Migne, *P.G.,* 45, 128.
[1005] *Apostolic Orders,* II, 16, in *B,* v. 2, p. 22.

guilty according to the unbending law and to protect other citizens and the community in general from criminals. In some cases, if required by law, it does not hesitate to execute the condemned criminal whereas, on the contrary, the only vital goal of the Authority of the Spiritual Father is to forgive the sinner, to raise him up and to restore him to good spiritual health in the midst of his Brethren in Christ. In addition, the Bishop or Priest does not condemn the sinner but may simply refuse to grant forgiveness and absolution. The only reason for the Bishop to excommunicate the ill person from the main body of the Church would be in the case of heresy or major moral sin that scandalized the public. Finally, it is essential that the judgement of Mercy and Compassion of the court of Repentance be freely accepted by the repentant whereas the decisions of the worldly court are compulsory.[1006]

The attribute of a compassionate and caring father is the primary role of the Spiritual Father. He must be *"as a compassionate doctor towards all sinners"* in order to cure *"not only by cutting and burning, but by binding and putting on sweet medicine which will heal the wounds and with proper words water them"* and not to *"demand the responsibility as in court"* changing the seat of Confession but *"as an inn granting the forgiveness of sins."* Hence, the Spiritual Father receives the repentant sinner with much compassion *"with mercy and pity judging"* them, encouraging them *"to have hope for Salvation and to turn with tears to God."* Furthermore the repentant sinner receives " *the remission* (of sin) *as from the Good Father* (God)." Under no circumstances it is allowed for the officiator of the Holy Mystery of Repentance to deal with the sinner as though he were an abomination by preventing him from Confessing or attending the teachings, since our Lord Himself had not *"resigned from eating and drinking with the tax collectors and sinners."*[1007]

2. The Nature of Penance

Penances that are imposed upon the repentant sinner by the Spiritual Father, under no circumstances must be regarded as

---

[1006] Balanos, *Crisis,* p. 37. Androutsos, *Dogmatique,* p. 383. St John Chrysostom, *To Genesis,* Homily 20, §§ 3-4, in Migne, *P.G.,* 53, 171. Ibid, *About Priesthood,* II, § 3, in Migne, *P.G.,* 48. Ibid, *To 2 Corinthians,* Homily 6, § 3, in Migne, *P.G.,* 61, 438.
[1007] *Apostolic Orders,* II, 12, 16, 40 and 41, in *B,* v. 2, pp. 2, 18, 21, 42 and 43. St John Chrysostom, *About repentance,* 3, § 4; and 1, § 4, in Migne, *P.G.,* 49, 297-298 and 283.

punishments to satisfy Divine Justice. They are pedagogic measures that are imposed by the Spiritual Father either before the Absolution of sins or after the Forgiveness of sins.[1008]

No man can offer anything in order to satisfy Divine Justice. This is clearly evident from the fact that the Son and Word of God had to become Man in order to Save mankind. The God-Man had to shed His Precious Blood on the Cross so as to reconcile sinful man to God the Father. And through the shedding of His Blood, we have been washed clean from all our sins and iniquities.

Penance has a pedagogic nature and is not a necessary component of Repentance[1009] without which forgiveness would not be granted. It can be increased, decreased or even be completely removed according to the good intention of the repentant sinner. [1010] Penance is considered healing medicine that is offered for the cure of the ill person, the sinner, who with humility seeks the forgiveness of his sins. Therefore, the Bishop does not easily excommunicate anyone but rather, with patience, love and compassion struggle for the sinner's correction. Nevertheless, it is also necessary for the sinner to produce fruits of repentance.[1011]

CHAPTER NINE
THE HOLY MYSTERY OF PRIESTHOOD

I. DEFINITION, NAMES, LEVELS AND DIVINE INSTITUTION

Priesthood is the Holy Mystery that was instituted by our Lord and Saviour Jesus Christ, the Son of God, by which, through the prayers with the laying on of the hands of a Bishop upon the head of an Ordained person, Divine Grace enabling him to practice the services of each level of Priesthood with authority is transmitted to him. [1012] The Priesthood comprises a special order within the Church

---

[1008] Mitsopoulos, *Themata,* p. 322.

[1009] Mesoloras, v. II, b, p. 308. Karmeris, *Synopsis,* p. 102.

[1010] St Basil the Great, in Migne, *P.G.,* 31, 205. Ibid, *Epistle* 217, § 74, in Migne, *P.G.,* 32, 804, 808. St John Chrysostom, *To 2 Corinthians,* Homily 4, § 4, in Montfaucon, v. 10, p. 536.

[1011] St Basil the Great, *The principal of morality. Term A',* ch. 4, in Migne, *P.G.,* 31, 701. Ibid, *To Isaiah 20:9,* § 230, in Migne, *P.G.,* 30, 521. St Symeon, *Euriskomena,* Homily LXIX, pp. 370-375.

[1012] Cf. Plato of Moscow, *Orthodox Teaching,* pp. 157-158. Kefalas, *Catechesis,* p. 187. Frangopoulos, *Christian Faith,* pp. 212-213. Mitsopoulos, *Themata,* p. 322.

distinguished by three different ranks or levels: Deacon, Presbyter and Bishop. The Divine institution of the Holy Mystery of Priesthood is witnessed by Holy Scripture, not only by the practice and Teachings of the Holy Apostles, but also by the election of the Holy Apostles by Christ.

1. Priesthood as *"Diakonia"*

The Officiator of all the Holy Sacraments is our Lord and Saviour Jesus Christ, the Son of God, Who is invisibly present in His Orthodox Church as the active High Priest. However, the Lord uses the officiators chosen from the main body of His Orthodox Church and sent for *diakonia* as His necessary instruments to perform the Heavenly Sacraments. They become worthy by the Grace of the Holy Spirit to receive the Mystery of Priesthood and although *"they are still from flesh and blood, yet they come close to the blessed and Divine Nature."* They serve for the Salvation of their brethren in the Church, *"working with Power,"* which *"does not raise them to the heights neither gives* [them] *civil power," "neither to the Angels nor Archangels God gave"* [Power] but to weak men *"who live on earth."*[1013] The necessity of this Holy Mystery of Priesthood is obvious, by means of which those who are elected and consecrated for this most high and Heavenly *diakonia* are raised in an Order in which they serve Heavenly things that not even the Angelic Hosts can look into, although they desire to do so.

Thus *"we all have received the same Spirit and we all have been called to adoption."* We all compose the royal Priesthood by means of which, through the union with Christ, we have communion with His threefold Offices. However, through Ordination candidates are placed in a special Order within the Church. They are able to perform the Sacraments and to serve before the Holy Altar, whereas those who have not received this special Grace of the Royal Priesthood, cannot serve. And although all Orthodox Christians partake of the general Priesthood and are members of the *"royal nation of God, as the same God testifies saying, that in all places the Gentiles will offer sacrifices pleasing to Him and pure offerings; and God does not accept by anyone else sacrifices, but only through His Priests."* All Orthodox

---

[1013] St John Chrysostom, *About Priesthood*, Homily 3, § 5, in Migne, *P.G.*, 46, 643. Ibid, *About anathema*, § 4, in Migne, *P.G.*, 48, 950.

Christians "*as Priests of God and healers*" pray for kings and soldiers.[1014]

St. Augustine speaks not only of the Bishops and the Presbyters who are called specially in the Church as Priests as it was said that "*they shall be Priests of God and of Christ*"[1015] but also for all those who are called anointed ones because of the mystical Chrismation and who are likewise called Priests because they are members of the One Priest, of Whom St. Paul spoke of as the "*holy nation, royal Priesthood.*"[1016] Thus St. Leon I, the Great Pope of Rome, adds that as the sign of the Cross makes all those who are Regenerated in Christ kings, likewise the Anointing of the Holy Spirit makes them Priests, so that besides the special Order of Ministry, every Orthodox Christian partakes of the royal nation and the rank of the general Priesthood.[1017]

We do not only have the titles of "*Bishop,*" "*Presbyter*" and "*Deacon*" in the Holy Book of Acts but also in the Holy Epistles. The titles of "*High Priest*" and "*Priest*" found in the Old Testament were quickly used within the Christian Faith, although at the beginning with some hesitation, because these terms were also used by the Gentiles. Thus the biblical terms "*Bishop,*" "*Presbyter*" and "*Deacon*" were preferred.

Tertullian first used the term "*Sacerdos*" ("*Priest*") to signify not only the Bishops, but also the Presbyters.

St. Cyprian refers the above term only to the Bishops without rejecting it, as well as to the Presbyters.[1018]

St Innocent I and St Leon I speak of the Presbyters as being second class Priests.[1019]

St. Augustine calls the faithful to a certain level "*Sacerdotes*" ("*Priests*"). He applies this term especially to the Bishops and Presbyters.[1020]

[1014] St Justin the Philosopher and Martyr, *Dialogue*, 116, § 3, in **B**, v. 3, p. 316. Tertullian, *Exhort. Cast. 7; De baptismo 17; De monogamia,* 7. St Irenaeus, *Heresies,* book IV, ch. 8, § 3, in Hadjephraimides, p. 277-278. Origen, *Against Celsus,* VIII, 73; and *About prayer,* 28,9 and *In Leveticus,* Homily IX, 9, in **B**, v. 10, pp. 230 and 291. Evdokimov, *Orthodoxia,* pp. 223-225.

[1015] Rev. 20:6.

[1016] St Augustine, *De civitate Dei,* XX, 10, in migne, *P.L.,* 41, 676.

[1017] St Leo I of Rome, the Great, *Sermo* IV, 1, in migne, *P.L.,* 54, 149.

[1018] St Cyprian, Epistola58, in migne, *P.L.,* 3, 1005.

[1019] St Innocent, *Epistolaad Decentium,* 3, in migne, *P.L.,* 30, 554.

[1020] St Augustine, *De civitate Dei,* XX, 10, in migne, *P.L.,* 4, 676.

The Greek term "*ιερεύς*" ("*Priest*") is ascribed during the first centuries mainly to the Bishop, because at that period he was the main officiator of the Holy Sacraments. From the 4th century "*Priests*" were also called "*Presbyters*" because with the growth of the Church, they also offered the Divine Eucharist, and henceforth the Bishop was entitled "*Archpriest*" or "*Hierarch.*"[1021]

The names ascribed to the ceremony of this Holy Mystery were formed either by the way of performance, such as "*Ordination*" or "*Laying on of hands,*"(in Latin "*Benediction Presbyteri,*" "*ordinatio*") either because of the result which it brought about such as "*hieratic perfection,*" "*Consecration,*" either from the total ceremony, such as "*sacramentum autistitis,*" "*Priesthood,*" "*ceremony.*"

Mogilas differentiates two types of Priesthood, the general Priesthood in which all Orthodox Christians partake and the Mysterious Priesthood. The latter "*is a Mystery and was instructed by Christ to the Apostles and through the laying on of their hands until this day is the Ordination performed, since the Bishops succeeded the Apostles to give out the Divine Sacraments and to serve the Salvation of men, as the Apostle said: 'Let a man so consider us as servants of Christ and stewards of the Sacraments of God.*[1022]*"*[1023]

Jeremias observes that through Priesthood "*all our ceremonies are perfected and we have no holy thing without a Priest.*"[1024] Elsewhere he observes that "*the Gospel is preached and read in public, and the Sacraments are spread by no one else, but rather by those who were dedicated for this service. For the Catholic (Orthodox) Church, those who are Sealed canonically and are called alone and are Ordained, as the ecclesiastic tradition requires, not holding any evil heresy, allows them to teach and to celebrate.*"[1025]

Kritopoulos observes that "*it is an ancient and Apostolic custom, which was delivered to the Church, that not all the Christians proceed for the diakonia of the Word and the celebration of the Sacraments, but they are elected among those who are great in virtue; afterwards by the laying on of the hands of those who were before them, they are*

[1021] *Apostolic Orders,* VIII, 11, in **B**, v. 2, p. 149. St Dionysius, *About the hieratic perfections,* ch. V, 2, in Migne, *P.G.,* 3, 509.
[1022] 1 Corinth. 4:1.
[1023] Mogilas, A' 108, in Karmeris, *The dogmatics,* v. II, 640.
[1024] Jeremias, *Answer* II, § 4, 4, in Karmeris, *The dogmatics,* v. II, p. 461.
[1025] Jeremias, Answer I, in Karmeris, *The dogmatics,* v. II, p. 406.

*placed for this service and through the common prayers of the Church
they are raised to this diakonia.*"[1026]

2. The Differentiation of the Three Levels of Priesthood

The Divine Grace that is transmitted to the person who is
Ordained, differs in each level, creating the three ranks of Priesthood:
that of Deacon, Presbyter and Bishop. The Ordained person gradually
moves from the lower level to the higher and through three different
Ordinations the one who was previously a simple Christian, passing
through the level of Deacon to that of Presbyter becomes at the end a
Bishop.[1027]

At the time of the Holy Apostles, only two ranks were
distinguished, that of Presbyters and Deacons. But when the Holy
Apostles passed away, the rank of Bishop was established into Church
life. Thus St. John the Apostle, Evangelist and Theologian, addressed
letters to the Angel-bishops of the seven churches in Asia Minor;[1028]
and his disciples, St. Ignatius of Antioch and St. Polycarp of Smyrna,
were Ordained Bishops by the Holy Apostle, both mentioning the
three ranks of Priesthood in their writings.

Besides these three levels, which compose the high level of
Priesthood, earlier the lower clergy was distinguished by the simple
laying on of hands which took place outside the Holy Altar. The one
being Ordained was simply blessed but as the sub-deacons, the
exorcists, the readers, the door-keepers, the chanters and the candle
holders[1029] he did not participate in the Mystery of Priesthood. The
ranks of sub-deacons, readers and chanters are still in use to this day.

The authority of each rank of the high Clergy is determined by
the *Apostolic Orders* as follows: "*To the Bishops we distributed those
things of the Archpriesthood, to the Presbyters the things of
Priesthood, to the Deacons the diakonia of both. For neither it is
permitted for a Deacon to offer a Sacrifice or to Baptize or to give a
small or great blessing. Neither is it permitted for a Presbyter to
perform an Ordination.*" The Bishop "*Ordains, lays on hands and*

[1026] Kritopoulos, ch. 11, in Karmeris, *The dogmatics,* v. II, p. 539.
[1027] Mitsopoulos, *Themata,* pp. 265-267, 322.
[1028] Rev. 2:1-3:22.
[1029] Cornelius to Phabius, in Eusebius, *Church History,* VI, 43, in Migne, *P.G.,* 20, 616.
Apostolic Orders, III, 11, 2, in *B*, v. 2, p. 64. Pseudo-Ignatius, *To Antiochians,* ch. 12, in *B*, v.
2, p. 328.

offers. We receive blessings from the Bishop, but nothing from the Presbyters." Likewise, *"the Bishops defrock all Clergy who are worthy of being defrocked, but a Bishop"* cannot be dethroned. The Presbyter *"receives blessings from the Bishop and a co-presbyter. Likewise, he gives blessings to a co-presbyter."* "He lays on hands, but does not Ordain, does not defrock and he excommunicates the lower ranks if they are accountable for such punishment." Elsewhere the *Apostolic Orders* forbid the Presbyters to Ordain Deacons or Deaconesses or Readers or servants or Chanters or door-keepers because only the Bishops may do so. The Deacon is not allowed to bless but may receive blessings from the Bishop and the Presbyter. The Bishop or the Presbyter gives blessings while he (the deacon) serves the faithful not as a Priest, but by serving the Priests.

Women Deaconesses were Ordained in the Altar like today's Deacons, during the Divine Liturgy when they received a Deacon's Stole (Orarion). They received not just the blessing of the laying on of hands, but a real Ordination in same manner as that of the Deacon. Deaconesses were ranked higher than the Sub-deacon and the rest of the lower Clergy. Hence *"the Deaconess does not bless, nor performs anything which the Presbyters or the Deacons do, but rather they keep the doors and serve the Presbyters in the Baptism of women for decency."*[1030]

3. Divine Institution

The Divine Institution of the Holy Mystery of Priesthood has its roots in the election by our Lord and Saviour Jesus Christ of the Twelve Apostles[1031] who comprised the close group of Disciples. The Lord called the Apostles for a special Mission, promising them that they would become *"fishers of men"*[1032] and *"named them Apostles;"*[1033] and *"to them it has been given to know the Sacraments of the Kingdom of Heaven."*[1034] Christ called the Holy Apostles for a special Mission *"that they might be with Him and that He might send them out to preach and to have power to heal sicknesses and to cast*

[1030] *Apostolic Orders,* VIII, 46 and 28, 2-4, 6; and III, 11, 2, in **B**, v. 2, pp. 171, 162 and 64.
[1031] Matth. 3:13-14; 4:18-22; 10:1-4. Mark 1:16-20; 3:13-19. Luke 5:1-11; 6:12-16. Cf. Frangopoulos, *Christian Faith,* pp. 213-215.
[1032] Matth. 4:19. Luke 5:10.
[1033] Luke 6:13.
[1034] Matth. 13:11.

out demons."[1035] After Christ's glorious Resurrection, "*He breathed on them*" and gave them the Holy Spirit,[1036] vesting them with Authority to "*forgive*" or to "*retain the sins.*"[1037] He transmitted the Mission to them, as the Father had sent Him, proclaiming them to be His successors of His work of Salvation.[1038] At the mountain of Galilee He instructed them to "*make disciples of all nations*"[1039] and promised them that He would be with them "*always, even to the end of the age.*"[1040] Through these instructions, Christ implied that after their deaths the Authority with which they were vested would be passed down to their successors and practised until the end of this age.

Concerning the question: "*Did the Lord, when giving this Authority, use any external ceremony?*" we can perceive that our Lord and Saviour Jesus Christ, the Son of God, being the Founder of the Holy Sacraments was not restricted to the use of any such things but as God, He brought upon His Disciples the desired results. Nevertheless, as in the case of the Sacraments of Holy Priesthood and Holy Confession He breathed upon the faces of the Holy Apostles in order to give them the Holy Spirit, or, in the case of Baptism, He inculcated the use of water. After the Lord's Ascension into Heaven, the Holy Apostles and the rest of the faithful had chosen Matthias to replace the "*Ministry and Apostleship*" from which Judas Iscariot "*by transgression fell.*"[1041]

Besides the Twelve Holy Apostles, the Lord had "*appointed seventy others also*" to whom He gave the Authority to go and preach "*into every city and place where He Himself was about to go,*"[1042] to "*heal the sick,*" to proclaim that "*the Kingdom of God has come*"[1043] and to cast out demons in His Name.[1044] Thus we have a second group who assisted the Lord although not on the same level as the group of the Twelve.

It is obvious and indisputable that our Lord and Saviour Jesus Christ, the Son of God, established within His Orthodox Church a

---

[1035] Mark 3:14-15.
[1036] John 20:22.
[1037] John 20:23.
[1038] John 20:21.
[1039] Matth. 28:19.
[1040] Matth. 28:20.
[1041] Acts 1:23-26.
[1042] Luke 10:1.
[1043] Luke 10:9.
[1044] Luke 10:17.

special Order that was distinguished from the rest of the faithful, in which some, such as the Twelve Apostles, were vested with all the Authority and the Mission of the Teacher, while others such as the Seventy Apostles, were vested with less Authority.

In the Book of Acts, besides the election of Matthias, we have a detailed description of the election and Ordination of the seven Deacons of whom the faithful *"chose Stephen, a man full of faith and the Holy Spirit, and Philip, Prochorus, Nicanor, Timon, Parmenas, and Nicolas, a proselyte from Antioch,"* and *"whom they set before the Apostles; and when they had prayed, they laid hands on them."*[1045]

St. John Chrysostom observed that *"the laying on of the hands is of man, but everything else God works and His Hand is touching the head of the one who is Ordained."*[1046]

The fact that the seven Deacons had the Authority to Baptise proves that they did not receive the rank of Deacon but instead that of a Presbyter, taking into consideration that there were no Bishops at that time, but only the Apostles.[1047]   St. Paul mentions the rank of Bishops and Deacons in his Epistles to the Philippians[1048] and to St Timothy.[1049]

In the Book of Acts we find the rank of Apostles and Elders[1050] who were not elderly in age but who had ecclesiastic authority. This is manifested in the Apostolic Synod that took place in Jerusalem (49 A.D.).[1051] *"And as they* (St. Paul and St Timothy) *went through the cities, they delivered to them the decrees to keep, which were determined by the Apostles and Elders at Jerusalem."*[1052] Afterwards the differentiation of the Presbyter appeared serving within the Church on a special level as mentioned by the Apostolic Synod and in the Epistle instructing all Christians to *"call for the Elders of the Church"* to *"pray"* over the sick, *"anointing them with oil in the Name of the Lord."*[1053]

It is obvious that the Presbyters comprised a special Order within the Orthodox Church who were highly ranked clergy, vested with

---

[1045] Acts 6:5-6.
[1046] St John Chrysostom, *To Acts,* Homily 14, § 3, in Migne, *P.G.,* 60, 116.
[1047] Ibid.
[1048] Phil. 1:1.
[1049] 1 Tim. 3:1-13.
[1050] Acts 15:6, 22, 23; 16:4
[1051] Acts 15:6-29.
[1052] Acts 16:4.
[1053] James 5:14.

Hieratic attributes. This is confirmed by the Book of Acts, according to which, during their First Apostolic Journey, St. Paul and St Barnabas strengthened *"the souls of the Disciples"* in Lystra, Iconium and Antioch where they *"appointed Elders in every church."*[1054] Such Presbyters or Elders or Overseers were Ordained by St. Paul in Ephesus and Miletus, having called them on his last trip from Jerusalem to Ephesus and having exhorted them to *"take heed"* to themselves *"and to all the flock, among which the Holy Spirit has made"* them *"overseers, to shepherd the Church of God which He purchased with His own Blood."*[1055] In his Pastoral Epistles St. Paul speaks of the Elders, referring to them as *"the Elders who rule well counted worthy of double honour, especially those who labour in the Word and Doctrine"*[1056] and that *"for this reason"* he left St Titus *"in Crete"* so that he *"should set in order the things that are lacking, and appoint Elders in every city."*[1057]

These *"Presbyters"* are referred to as *"Bishops"* in the Epistles since there were no Bishops as such *"but the Apostles alone."*[1058] The terms *"Presbyter"* and *"Bishop"* are identical according to the New Testament, not only from what St. Paul said to the Presbyters of Ephesus, characterising them as *"Overseers"* but from how he commemorates *"Bishops and Deacons"*[1059] in his Epistle to the Philippians as well as in his Epistle to St Titus concerning *"Elders"* whom he refers to as *"Bishops."*[1060]

Theodoretus of Cyrus, interpreting the verse *"a Bishop then must be"*[1061] wrote that they *"were also called at that time Presbyters and Bishops."*[1062]

We see St Timothy and St Titus vested not with Apostolic Authority but nevertheless with Authority greater than that of a Bishop-Presbyter because the Holy Apostles appointed Presbyters whom they Ordained, in each city. It is also manifested in the seven letters of the Book of Revelation that the Bishops are mentioned as

---

[1054] Acts 14:21, 22, 23.
[1055] Acts 20:17, 28.
[1056] 1 Tim. 5:17.
[1057] Tit. 1:5.
[1058] St John Chrysostom, *To Acts,* Homily 14, § 3, in Migne, *P.G.,* 60, 116.
[1059] Phil. 1:1.
[1060] Tit. 1:5.
[1061] 1 Tim. 3:2.
[1062] Theodoretus of Cyrus, *to 1 Timothy 3:2*, in Migne, *P.G.,* 82, 804.

"Angels" of the churches of Asia Minor.[1063] *"And He Himself gave some to be Apostles, some Prophets, some Evangelists, and some Pastors and Teachers, for the equipping of the Saints for the work of Ministry, for the edifying of the Body of Christ."*[1064]

4. The Church's Testimony About the Three Levels of Priesthood

The Tradition of the Orthodox Church, which followed the Apostolic era, bears witness of the Divine establishment of the ecclesiastic Hierarchy and the spiritual Authorities which are transmitted by Divine Grace to those who receive the three ranks of Priesthood that were distinguished clearly during the post-Apostolic era.[1065]

St. Clement of Rome very often referred to the Presbyters or Elders, condemning the rebellion against the Presbyters. *"It is disgraceful, dear friends, yes, utterly disgraceful and unworthy of your conduct in Christ, that it should be reported that the well-established and ancient church of the Corinthians, because of one or two persons, is rebelling against its Presbyters."*[1066] *"For this reason, therefore, having received complete foreknowledge, they appointed the officials mentioned earlier and afterwards they gave the offices a permanent character; that is, if they should die, other approved men should succeed to their Ministry. Those, therefore, who were appointed by them or, later on, by other reputable men with the consent of the whole Church, and who have ministered to the flock of Christ blamelessly, humbly, peaceably, and unselfishly, and for a long time have been well spoken of by all – these men we consider to be unjustly removed from their Ministry. For it will be no small sin for us, if we depose from the Bishop's Office those who have offered the Gifts blamelessly and in holiness. Blessed are those Presbyters who have gone on ahead, who took their departure at a mature and fruitful age, for they need no longer fear that someone might remove them from their established place."*[1067] *"Only let the flock of Christ be at peace with its duly appointed Presbyters."*[1068] *"You, therefore, who*

[1063] Rev. 2:1-3:22.
[1064] Ephes. 4:11-12.
[1065] Cf. Damalas, *Catechesis,* p. 67.
[1066] St Clement of Rome, *1st Corinthians,* 47, 6, in Lightfoot, *Apostolic Fathers,* p. 55.
[1067] St Clement of Rome, *1st Corinthians,* 44, 2-5, in Lightfoot, *Apostolic Fathers,* p. 52-53.
[1068] Ibid, *1st Corinthians,* 54, 2, in Lightfoot, *Apostolic Fathers,* p. 58.

laid the foundation of the revolt, must submit to the Presbyters and accept discipline leading to repentance, bending the knees of your heart."[1069]

In the *Didache*, we see that the *"Prophets and Teachers"* who had special charisma, had a main role in worship. *"On the Lord's own day gather together and break bread and give thanks, having first confessed your sins so that your sacrifice may be pure. But let no one who has a quarrel with a companion join you until they have been reconciled, so that your sacrifice may not be defiled. For this is the sacrifice concerning which the Lord said, 'In every place and time offer me a pure Sacrifice, for I Am a great King, says the Lord, and My Name is marvellous among the nations.' Therefore appoint for yourselves Bishops and Deacons worthy of the Lord, men who are humble and not avaricious and true and approved, for they too carry out for you the Ministry of the Prophets and Teachers. You must not, therefore, despite them, for they are your honoured men, along with the Prophets and Teachers."[1070]* *Didache* also urges the faithful to present their *"first fruits"* *"to the Prophets"* *"for they are your High Priests."[1071]* Elsewhere we read *"But permit the Prophets to give thanks however they wish."[1072]* *"Now concerning the Apostles and Prophets, deal with them as follows in accordance with the Rule of the Gospel. Let every Apostle who comes to you be welcome as if he were the Lord."[1073]* Furthermore, *Didache* distinguishes the real Prophets and Teachers from those who are false.[1074]

In the writings of St. Ignatius, the Theophorus of Antioch are mentioned clearly the three Offices of Priesthood. St. Ignatius seeks to unite the Christians around the Bishop, the Presbytery and the Deacons before the danger of heresies. *"Take care, therefore, to participate in the one Eucharist (for there is one Flesh of our Lord Jesus Christ, and one Cup which leads to unity through His Blood; there is one Altar, just as there is one Bishop, together with the Presbytery and the Deacons, my fellow servants), in order that whatever you do, you do in accordance with God."[1075]* Elsewhere, we

---

[1069] Ibid, *1ˢᵗ Corinthians*, 57, 1, in Lightfoot, *Apostolic Fathers*, p. 60.

[1070] *Didache*, 14-15, in Lightfoot, *Apostolic Fathers*, p. 157.

[1071] Ibid, 13, 3 and 6, in Lightfoot, *Apostolic Fathers*, p. 157.

[1072] Ibid, 10, 7, in Lightfoot, *Apostolic Fathers*, p. 155.

[1073] Ibid, 11, 3-4, in Lightfoot, *Apostolic Fathers*, p. 155.

[1074] Ibid, 11, 5-12 and 12, 1, in Lightfoot, *Apostolic Fathers*, pp. 155-156.

[1075] St Ignatius of Antioch, *To Philadelphians*, 4, in Lightfoot, *Apostolic Fathers*, p. 107.

read: *"Continue to gather together, each and every one of you, collectively and individually by name, in Grace, in one Faith and one Jesus Christ, Who physically was a descendant of David, Who is Son of Man and Son of God, in order that you may obey the Bishop and the Presbytery with an undisturbed mind, breaking one Bread, which is the Medicine of Immortality, the Antidote we take in order not to die but to live forever in Jesus Christ."*[1076] *"I have therefore taken the initiative to encourage you, so that you may run together in harmony with the Mind of God. For Jesus Christ, our inseparable Life is the Mind of the Father, just as the Bishops appointed throughout the world are in the Mind of Christ. Thus, it is proper for you to act together in harmony with the mind of the Bishop, as you are in fact doing. For your Presbytery, which is worthy of its name and worthy of God, is attuned to the Bishop as strings to a lyre."*[1077]

St. Justin the Philosopher and Martyr, addressing the Roman Emperor, described the Christian way of worship in his Apology and spoke of the *"first of the brethren"* who addresses prayers and gives glory and thanks to the Father of all, and who Consecrates the Mystery of the Eucharist and *"through words makes the admonition and invitation for the imitation of the good."*[1078]

Clement the Alexandrian[1079] and Origen literally referred to the three Offices of Priesthood. St. Gregory of Nyssa[1080] and St Augustine[1081] exalted the effectiveness of the Grace that is transmitted through the Holy Mystery of Priesthood.

II. RESPONSIBILITIES OF TRANSMITTING AND RECEIVING PRIESTHOOD

The only responsible Officiator of the Holy Mystery of Priesthood is the Bishop who holds the highest Office within the Orthodox Church and consequently uses the Spiritual Authority of the Holy Apostles to appoint the Elders in the Church according to the

---

[1076] Ibid, *To Ephesians,* 20, 2, in Lightfoot, *Apostolic Fathers,* pp. 92-93.
[1077] St Ignatius of Antioch, *To Ephesians,* 3, 2 – 4, 1, in Lightfoot, *Apostolic Fathers,* p. 87. Dositheus, *Confession,* ch. 10, pp. 32-35.
[1078] St Justin the Philosopher and Martyr, *1 Apology,* 65, 3 and 67, 4, in *B*, v. 3, pp. 197-198.
[1079] Clement the Alexandrian, *Pedagogus,* 3, in Migne, *P.G.,* 8, 677. Ibid, *Stromata,* III, 12, in Migne, *P.G.,* 8, 1180 and 1189. Ibid, *Stromata,* VI, 13, in Migne, *P.G.,* 9, 328.
[1080] St Gregory of Nyssa, *To the day of Lights,* in Migne, *P.G.,* 46, 581.
[1081] St Augustine, *Contra EpistolaParmeniani,* II, 13, 28, in migne, *P.L.,* 43, 70.

New Testament. Bishops lay their hands upon those who are Ordained and, in some cases, more than one Bishop may also lay hands upon an Ordained one, signifying the unanimous election and consent of the participants. It is a necessary requirement that the one who will receive the Holy Mystery of Priesthood not only be Baptised within the Orthodox Church and uphold the Orthodox Faith, but he must also be of the proper age of candidates for the Office of Bishop having passed through the first two Offices. In addition, he must lead a blameless life, although the Divine Grace of the Holy Spirit acts even through the unworthy. Nevertheless, it is required that the candidate approaches in person and with his own freewill, and in the case of Deacon or Presbyter, if married, with the consent of his wife.

1. The Responsible Officiator of the Holy Mystery According to the New Testament and the Tradition of the Orthodox Church

The only responsible Officiator of the Holy Mystery of Priesthood is the Bishop who holds the highest Office within the Orthodox Church and who is the steward of the Spiritual Authority that was transmitted by the Lord through the Holy Apostles to His Church.[1082] Thus the seven Deacons were Ordained by the Holy Apostles.[1083] St. Paul reminded St Timothy that *"the Gift of God,"*[1084] which appointed him as the highest Officiator in the Church, made him responsible for appointing Presbyters or Bishops[1085] in each city. That Holy Gift was transmitted to him *"through the laying on of his hands"*[1086] and he cautioned St Timothy therefore *"not to lay hands on anyone hastily."*[1087] The *"laying on of the hands of the Eldership"*[1088] mentioned in his First Epistle to St Timothy is simply the external consent of the Presbytery before the whole Church for that specific Ordination. St. Paul also wrote to St Titus: *"For this reason I left you in Crete, that you should set in order the things that are lacking, and appoint Elders in every city."*[1089] As it is apparent from the above, St

---

[1082] Cf. Damalas, *Catechesis,* pp. 65-67.
[1083] Acts 6:5-6.
[1084] 2 Tim. 1:6.
[1085] Cf. 1 Tim. 3:1-13.
[1086] 2 Tim. 1:6.
[1087] 1 Tim. 5:22.
[1088] 1 Tim. 4:14.
[1089] Tit. 1:5.

Titus and St Timothy were the responsible Officiators for the transmitting of the Divine Grace of Priesthood. Also, in the Book of Acts St. Paul and St Barnabas Ordained the Presbyters in Lystra, Iconium and Antioch.[1090]

The consent of the faithful was also required, whether the one who was to be Ordained was worthy or not.

St. John Chrysostom, interpreting the verse in 1 Timothy 4:14, observed that *"the Presbyters did not Ordain the Bishop"* and elsewhere he proclaimed that the Bishops *"are higher than the Presbyters in that they alone Ordain."*[1091]

St Hieronymus recognised that only the Bishop has the responsibility of Ordaining.[1092]

St. Athanasius the Great of Alexandria, with regard to the Priesthood of Aeschylos asked: *"From where did Aeschylos become a Presbyter? From Colluthos? But since Colluthos was a Presbyter and died and all his Ordinations are invalid all those who were appointed by him in his schism laymen are doubtful."*[1093]

According to the *Egyptian Order* (Apostolic Tradition of St Hippolytus) it is stated that *"when a Presbyter is Ordained, let the Bishop lay his hands on his head; the Presbyters, let them touch also."* But this laying on of the hands of the Presbytery does not have a Mystic nature and merely confirms the consent of the Presbyters to the Ordained one as being accounted amongst the body of the Presbyters.[1094]

Hence in the Ordination of a Bishop, the demand of the participation of two or three other Bishops[1095] does not imply that one Bishop alone cannot Ordain another Bishop if necessary. However the presence of more than one Bishop is required because, with the witness of two or three, the Proclamation that the Elected is worthy to be Ordained to the Office of Bishop is more assured. The laying on of the hands by the rest of the Bishops implies the consent of the Election.[1096] Additionally, the laying on of hands upon a Deacon's

---

[1090] Acts 14:23.

[1091] St John Chrysostom, *To 1 Timothy,* Homily 13, § 1 and 11, § 1, in Migne, *P.G.,* 62, 565 and 553.

[1092] St Hieronymus, *Epistola*146 *ad Evangel.,* in migne, *P.L.,* 22, 1194.

[1093] St Athanasius, the Great, *Apology against Arians,* § 12, in Migne, *P.G.,* 25, 269.

[1094] Achelis, *Die ältesten Quellen,* p. 43. Papadopoulos, *History,* p. 483.

[1095] *Apostolic Order,* III, XX, in *B*, v. 2, p. 68. 4th Canon of the 1st Ecumenical Council.

[1096] Papadopoulos, *History,* p. 433. Synesius of Ptolemais, *Epistolale* 62, in Migne, *P.G.,* 66, 1405. Theodoretus of Cyrus, *Church History,* V, 23, in Migne, *P.G.,* 82, 1248. *Apostolic*

head at the Gospel Reading or that at the end of the Holy Mystery of Confession upon the repentant's head, differs from that of Ordination.

2. Those who are Skilled for Receiving the Three Offices

Not all Faithful or Officers in the Clergy are responsible for transmitting the Holy Mystery of Priesthood. Similarly, not every Orthodox Christian can be considered as having the proper skills necessary for acceptance in the Holy Order of the Clergy.

In order for one to be considered an Orthodox Christian, it is necessary to have received the Canonical Baptism, because it is not sufficient that one confesses Jesus Christ correctly. Rather it is required that one be Baptised in the One, Holy, Catholic and Apostolic Eastern Orthodox Church. Consequently, Clergymen who belong to any heretical organisation, regardless of what rank they might have held, must be Baptised Canonically and according to the Tradition and Rites of the Orthodox Church because any previous Baptism is not recognised as being Canonical. If they are laymen, they must be tested as to whether they are worthy to enter the Clergy and be Ordained Canonically.

St. Paul recommends that he who is called to the Office of Bishop should not be "*a novice, lest being puffed up with pride he fall into the same condemnation as the devil.*"[1097] Hence, the Holy Councils determined the age limit of 25 years for Deacons, 30 years for Presbyters and 45 years of age for Bishops.

In addition to the above, in order to receive the third Office of Priesthood, it is necessary that he who is elevated has passed through the two previous Offices of Deacon and Presbyter.

According to the advice of St. Paul: "*Do not lay hands on anyone hastily, nor share in other people's sins; keep yourself pure.*"[1098] The Bishop "*must examine previously the life of the one who is to be Ordained and then call the Grace of the Holy Spirit upon him.*"[1099] In the Book of Acts St. Peter advised the faithful to "*seek among them seven men of good reputation, full of the Holy Spirit and Wisdom,*"[1100]

Orders and *Apostolic Order,* in Funk, *Didascalia et Constitutions apostolorum,* ed.27, v. 2, p. 98. *Covenant of the Lord,* in Rahmani, p. 27.
[1097] 1 Tim. 3:6.
[1098] 1 Tim. 5:22.
[1099] Theodoretus of Cyrus, *To 1 Timothy 5:22,* in Migne, *P.G.,* 82, 821.
[1100] Acts 6:3.

in order that they may Ordain them as Deacons. The skills that St. Paul described in his Pastoral Epistles presuppose investigation and test by the one who will Ordain in order to determine if the one who seeks Ordination is suitable of such high honour. St. Paul demands that he who shall be Ordained *"have a good testimony among those who are outside, lest he falls into reproach and the snare of the devil."*[1101]

According to the above, those who have fallen into mortal sins after their Baptism must be excluded from the Priesthood. Also those who have married twice must be excluded, according to the Teaching of St. Paul that *"the Bishop must be the husband of one wife."*[1102]

St. John Chrysostom observed that *"God does not Ordain all, but acts through all."*[1103] This means that God disapproves of those who receive Priesthood unworthily, although He works the Holy Sacraments through them for the sake of those faithful who are Sanctified.

To receive Priesthood, it is required that he who is Ordained accepts with his own free will, without any pressure, deceitful tricks or radical methods. One must examine himself very carefully before entering the great and most Holy Mystery of Priesthood.

Furthermore one must not forget the instruction of St. Paul who said: *"Let your women keep silent in the churches, for they are not permitted to speak; but they are to be submissive, as the law also says."*[1104] In the early Church there were charismatic women who were also Prophets, as was the daughter of St. Philip, yet they were never accepted into the higher levels of Priesthood, serving only as Deaconesses in order to assist the Bishops or Presbyters in the Baptism and Catechism of women.

The celibacy of Bishops became a administrative matter, enforced at first by the Emperor Justinian I, who, in his laws known as *"Nearas"* (Imperial Law, no. 6, 123 and 137), demanded that those who were elevated to the Office of Bishop must be elected from those who followed the Monastic way of life or from those Clergymen who willingly and with the consent of their wives, separated themselves from them. Afterwards the 6th Ecumenical Synod with her 12th

[1101] 1 Tim. 3:7.
[1102] 1 Tim. 3:2.
[1103] St John Chrysostom, *To 2 Timothy,* Homily 2, § 3, in Migne, *P.G.,* 62, 610.
[1104] 1 Corinth. 14:34.

Canon[1105] literally forbade married men from being Ordained Bishops while they lived with their wives.

In the practice of the Eastern Orthodox Church one is allowed to be married before his Ordination into the first Office of Priesthood - as a Deacon – on condition that it is by his free will and not by force. In addition, according to the 18th Canon[1106] of the 6th Ecumenical Synod, it is forbidden to separate the one who will be Ordained from his wife.

III. EXTERNAL SIDE OF THE HOLY MYSTERY OF PRIESTHOOD AND THE TRANSMITTED DIVINE GRACE

The laying on of the hands of the Bishop upon the head of the one who will receive the Gift of Priesthood, accompanied with a special prayer literally referring to the Priestly Office in which he has been accepted, consists of the external and visible aspect of the Holy Mystery of Priesthood. The invisible result, which affects the soul of the Ordained, is the transmission by the Holy Spirit of the Gift of Priesthood, which enables him to bring forth the work of his Office, assuring him of the necessary terms exalting him as a worthy servant of the Lord through the co-operation with the Divine Grace and additionally imprinting within him the inexhaustible Seal, which prevents the repetition of Ordination into the same Office.

1. The Laying on of the Hands with Prayer as the External Aspect of the Holy Mystery

The laying on of the hands accompanied with prayers that differ according to each Office to which the Ordained is elevated, consists of the external aspect of the Holy Mystery. The Apostolic roots of the laying on of the hands is witnessed not only in the Ordination of the seven Deacons[1107] and St Timothy,[1108] but also in those who were elected to be Ordained by St Timothy.[1109]

In the Tradition of the Orthodox Church one will find countless testimonies that witness to this Apostolic Tradition.

[1105] Pedalion, pp. 303-305.
[1106] Pedalion, pp. 446-447.
[1107] Acts 6:6.
[1108] 2 Tim. 1:6
[1109] 1 Tim. 5:22.

Thus in the *Apostolic Orders* we find the Commandment: *"When you Ordain a Presbyter, O Bishop, you yourself must lay your hand upon the head."*[1110] Concerning the Ordination of a Deacon, it is instructed: *"When you establish a deacon, O Bishop, place on him your hands."*[1111] In the rest of the Holy Canons we find the expressions: *"if any Bishop receives the laying on of hands of one Bishop this laying on of hands is invalid"* *"and through the laying on of their hands they had the spiritual charisma."*[1112] All the testimonies of the 4th Century literally commemorate or indicate the laying on of the hands during Ordination.[1113]

It is understandable that with the laying on of the hands the special prayer followed, by which the Bishop called the Divine Grace of God to descend upon the one being Ordained. This is testified to in the Book of Acts, concerning the Ordination of the seven Deacons, since the Holy Apostles *"when they had prayed, they laid hands on them,"*[1114] as well as in the case of the Ordination of the Elders in Lystra, Iconium and Antioch where *"they had appointed Elders in every church, and prayed with fasting they commended them to the Lord in Whom they had believed."*[1115] Furthermore, today's way of Ordination is derived from the ancient Tradition of the Orthodox Church as witnessed in the ancient writings.

At the time of Ordination the Bishop calls upon the Holy Spirit saying: *"The Divine Grace which heals all weaknesses elevates the devoted Sub-deacon to be a Deacon (or the Deacon to be a Presbyter, or the Presbyter to be a Bishop.)"* This invocation by the Bishop is considered to be the beginning of the Holy Mystery, since the Ordination follows. The most important moment of the Ordination is the prayer, with the laying on of the hands, addressed to the Holy Trinity, when the Bishop calls upon the Grace of the Holy Spirit to descend and rest upon the head of the one who is being Ordained, thereby elevating him from his previous Office to a higher one. At

---

[1110] *Apostolic Orders,* VIII, 16 in **B**, v. 2, p. 159.

[1111] Ibid, VIII, 17 in **B**, v. 2, p. 160.

[1112] Canon 9 of the 1st Ecumenical Synod, *Pedalion,* pp.177-179. Canon 17 of the Synod of Antioch, *Pedalion,* p. 544. Canon 6 of the Chalcedon. Canon 1 of St Basil the Great, *Pedalion,* pp. 773-789.

[1113] St John Chrysostom, *To Acts,* Homily 14, § 3, in Migne, *P.G.,* 60, 116. Cornelius of Rome to Phabius of Antioch in Eusebius, *Church History,* VI, 43, in Migne, *P.G.,* 20, 620. St Dionysius the Aeropagite, *About the hierarchal perfections,* ch. 5, § 2, in Migne, *P.G.,* 3, 509.

[1114] Acts 6:6.

[1115] Acts 14:23.

that moment Heaven and earth are joined together. The hands of the Bishop become like a fiery bridge that leads directly to God. For the Orthodox Church each Ordination, regardless of the level of Office, is a Day of Pentecost, especially at the Ordination of a Bishop.

2. The Gift that is Transmitted as the Invisible Aspect of the Holy Mystery

The invisible aspect of the Holy Mystery of Priesthood comprises of the Gift that is transmitted by Divine Grace to the one who is Ordained. This Divine Gift offers to the one who is Ordained the Spiritual Authority to perform the Work and the *Diakonia* of the Office in which he was elevated. The lives of those who receive this Gift worthily are Sanctified.

This Divine Gift needs to be renewed and one must not only rely on the receiving of the Spiritual Authority but one must struggle for his own spiritual growth in the newness of Life in Christ, becoming a living example for the faithful; a vessel through which God will be glorified. St. Paul gives us this example when he proclaimed: *"I discipline my body and bring it into subjection, lest, when I have preached to others, I myself should become disqualified."*[1116]

Clergymen receive the Authority to perform the Holy and Divine Sacraments through Ordination, regardless of their personal state of worthiness or unworthiness. However, the Divine Grace that Sanctifies them and which proves them to be worthy and enlightened servants, is offered only to those who are worthy. Hence one can understand the opinion of St. John Chrysostom that *"God does not Ordain all, but works through all."*[1117]

Examining this Gift concerning the Authority to perform the Work of each Office, it appears to be united, although it is received gradually. The Deacon receives a limited Authority, the Presbyter or Elder a higher level and the Bishop the fullness of this Authority. This differentiation of Authority in each Office does not take away the unity of the Holy Mystery. Instead, it indicates the growth of the given Gift in order to perform a higher level of work and this, altogether, composes the united Mystery of Priesthood. So in the

---

[1116] 1 Corinth. 9:27.
[1117] St John Chrysostom, *To 2 Timothy,* homily 2, § 3, in Migne, *P.G.,* 62, 610.

Orthodox Church we do not have three Holy Sacraments of Priesthood, but only one.

The Holy Mystery of Priesthood imprints on the soul an inexhaustible Seal that cannot be removed or repeated.[1118] As in the case of Baptism, one is forbidden to receive the Holy Sacrament twice, since once received Canonically, likewise with Ordination, it is forbidden to be repeated.[1119] Thus he who is Ordained Canonically in the Orthodox Church by a Canonically established Bishop, receives the Authority to perform the duties assigned to him with the same Power. Whether worthily or unworthily as he may be, sinner or holy, he performs them Canonically, either believing or not, as long as he does not alienate himself from the Canonical Body of the Orthodox Church. Invalid Ordinations of the three Offices are considered as being all those that were performed by heretics and schismatics.[1120]

CHAPTER TEN
THE MYSTERY OF MARRIAGE

I. DEFINITION AND DIVINE INSTITUTION

Marriage is the Holy Mystery in which, through the Blessing of the Church, the physical bond between man and woman is Sanctified.[1121] Husband and wife are joined for their lifetime in a Holy Communion of Life. Divine Grace restores the Blessing given to the first-formed and aims at the fulfilment of the Divine Plan as described in the Book of Genesis. Thus marriage is firstly the Divine

---

[1118] Androutsos, *Dogmatique,* p. 314. Ibid, *Symbolique,* p. 381. Trempelas, *Dogmatique,* v. III, p. 312. Mesoloras, p. 333. St Gregory of Nyssa, *To the day of Lights,* in Migne, *P.G.,* 45, 581. St Augustine, *Contra EpistolaParmeniani,* II, 13, 28, in migne, *P.L.,* 43, 70.

[1119] Canon 48 of the Synod ion Carthage, *Pedalion,* pp. 632-633.

[1120] Epistolale Cornelius of Rome to Phabius of Antioch, in Eusebius, *Church History,* VI, 43, in Migne, *P.G.,* 20, 620. Canon 16 of the 1st Ecumenical Synod, *Pedalion,* p. 189. Canon 13 of the Synod of Antioch, *Pedalion,* p. 542. Canon 76 of the Apostles, *Pedalion,* pp. 136-137. Canon 23 of the Synod of Antioch, *Pedalion,* p. 547. Canon 1 of St Basil the Great, *Pedalion,* pp. 773-777. Canons 1 and 68 of the Synod of Carthage, *Pedalion,* pp. 605, 645. Canon 8 of the Synod of Antioch, *Pedalion,* p. 539. St Basil the Great, *Epistle* 240, § 3 in Migne, *P.G.,* 32, 897. Ibid, *Epistle* 239, in Migne, *P.G.,* 32, 892. Ibid, *Epistle* 244, in Migne, *P.G.,* 32, 920. Dyobouniotes, *Dogmatique of Chr. Androutsos,* p. 52. Kotsonis, *The canonical,* p. 164. Androutsos, *Symbolique,* p. 384.

[1121] Cf. Plato of Moscow, *Orthodox Teaching,* pp. 158-159. Evdokimov, *Orthodoxia,* pp. 394-401. Kefalas, *Catechesis,* pp. 187-188. Frangopoulos, *Christian Faith,* pp. 215-216. Mitsopoulos, *Themata,* pp. 324-326. Labadarios, *Sermons,* v. 1, pp. 89-92. Meyendorff, *Theology,* pp. 196-199.

Institution commanded by the Creator for the assistance of the one to the other of the first couple and the granting of the Divine Blessing for the multiplication of the human race for the filling of the earth. Marriage was instituted as a Mystery by our Lord and Saviour Jesus Christ, the Son of God, in the New Testament. The physical union of husband and wife was raised to the Image of the Mysterious Union of Christ with His Church in an insoluble and Holy Union, which secures Divine Grace given to those who enter into the Community of Marriage in order to achieve its high and sacred goals.

1. The Physical Institution of Marriage Raised into a Divine Mystery

Marriage is the Divine Institution, which was established by the Creator Himself, Who Blessed the first couple at the Creation. This is manifested by the fact that God formed two different sexes, *"male and female,"*[1122] right from the beginning implanting in their nature the instinct of multiplication. This is witnessed literally by the narration of the Creation of the first couple in the Old Testament, which presents God as Blessing the first couple and instructing them to *"increase and multiply, and fill the earth."*[1123]

The physical bond that is created is closer than any other bond. The woman is made of the same flesh, living and sharing in everything together with her husband, who in the same way is combined in flesh and spirit to his lawful wife. This bond was indicated by the creation of Eve from the side of Adam who, when seeing her and being Enlightened by God, said: *"This now is bone of my bones, and flesh of my flesh; she shall be called woman, because she was taken out of her husband. Therefore, shall a man leave his father and mother and shall cleave to his wife, and the two shall be one flesh."*[1124] These words, although uttered by the mouth of Adam, were ascribed by the Lord to be of God.[1125]

The closeness of this relationship is manifested not only because the natural bond between parents and children is overruled, (*"therefore shall a man leave his father and mother"*) but also because

---

[1122] Gen. 1:27. Matth. 19:4.
[1123] Gen. 1:28.
[1124] Gen. 2:23-24.
[1125] Matth. 19:5.

the man *"shall cleave to his wife, and the two shall be one flesh."* According to these words, God did not Command the man to simply come to the woman, but that he was to '*to cleave to his wife,*' expressing the inseparability of the bond.[1126]

After the Fall the first couple multiplied but their descendants were overwhelmed by evil and wickedness; and the Wrath of God prevented them from filling the earth even more, for God said: *"I will blot out man whom I have made from the face of the earth," "for I Am grieved that I have made them."*[1127] And God destroyed the wicked generation of mankind through the Cataclysm. *"And all things which have the breath of life, and whatever were on the dry land, died. And God blotted out every offspring which was upon the face of the earth, both man and beast, and reptiles, and birds of the sky, and they were blotted out from the earth."*[1128] However, God in His Kindness and Love for man-made provision for a new generation of mankind to come forth through the Righteous Noah and his family. Thus He Commanded Noah to build an Ark so that he, his sons and their wives, together with pairs of every species of animal, were saved from the worldwide catastrophe. After the Flood, God repeated His Blessings to Noah saying: *"Increase and multiply, and fill the earth and have dominion over it."*[1129] Nonetheless, because of the invasion of sin into man's nature, these repetitions of God's Blessings did not secure either the monogamy or inseparability of marriage proclaimed by the God-inspired words of Adam. Consequently, it was necessary not only to re-establish the Institution but also to renew the Grace given to those who are united in Christ, strengthening them in order to achieve the high goals of marriage.

According to the New Testament there is, on one hand, the renewal and assurance of the words addressed to the first-formed couple by our Lord and Saviour Jesus Christ, the Son of God, referring to the God-established Institution as well as the renewal of the Blessing of Marriage. On the other hand, there is the invisible Grace that strengthens the couple, working together with God's Grace to achieve the ideal of Marriage predetermined by the Creator. Hence

---

[1126] St Cyril of Alexandria, *To Malachi 2:14,* in Migne, *P.G.,* 72, 324. Zigabinos, *To Matthew 19:5,* in Migne, *P.G.,* 129, 516. St John Chrysostom, *To Matthew 19:5,* in Migne, *P.G.,* 58, 597.
[1127] Gen. 6:8.
[1128] Gen. 7:22-23.
[1129] Gen. 9:1.

Marriage according to the New Testament was raised to a God-established Mystery. Furthermore, the renewal of God's Words by means of which the Divine establishment of the natural Institution of Marriage and its indissolubility was proclaimed by our Lord when He was asked by the Pharisees: *"Is it lawful for a man to divorce his wife for just any reason?"*[1130] Then the Lord answered: *"Have you not read that He Who made them at the beginning made them 'male and female,' and said, 'For this reason a man shall leave his father and mother and be joined to his wife, and the two shall become one flesh'? So then, they are no longer two but one flesh. Therefore, what God has joined together, let no man separate."*[1131] By these Words the Lord confirmed that they were Words of God and consequently vested with indestructible Authority by proclaiming that *"He Who made them at the beginning made them 'male and female."*[1132] *"In other words, one male and one female, that he may have one (woman)."*[1133]

Thus, the interpretation of the Divine Will of God gives the Law of monogamy and the insolubility of Marriage. Truly, if God wanted man to have more than one wife, then at the beginning He would have created many more females. But because He did not create more women than were necessary, His Will is for men not to divorce their wives and that one man is joined to one woman. In addition to the above, the Lord added: *"Therefore what God has joined together, let no man separate"*[1134] and the proof of this is that it is *"abnormal and against the Law"* to divorce. Divorce is *"abnormal"* because the one flesh in which the couple are united as one, is divided; and *"against the Law"* because *"God united them and commanded them not to separate."*[1135] Thus Marriage is elevated by the Lord above its first value, since polygamy is absolutely forbidden as well as divorce, since he or she who divorces commits adultery. *"But I say to you that whoever divorces his wife for a reason except sexual immorality causes her to commit adultery; and whoever marries a woman who is divorced commits adultery."*[1136]

1130 Matth. 19:3.
1131 Matth. 19:4-6.
1132 Matth. 19:3.
1133 Zigabinos, *To Matthew 19:3,* in Migne, *P.G.,* 129, 513.
1134 Matth. 19:4-6.
1135 Zigabinos, *To Matthew 19:3,* in Migne, *P.G.,* 129, 513.
1136 Matth. 5:32.

In addition, our Lord and Saviour Jesus Christ, the Son of God, Blessed the Marriage in Cana of Galilee. In order to honour the decency of Marriage with a God-given Sign, He performed the first Miracle thereby Blessing the Marriage, not just with His presence alone but by *"honouring it with a Gift,"* having *"changed the water into unmixed wine"* and *"offering to the wedding the greatest Gift of all."* Thus, by means of His Holy support and participation in the joy of Marriage, *"He Sanctified the beginning of man's birth."* He went there (to Cana), He Who is *"the desire and joy of all, to draw away the ancient gloom of childbirth"* that was the curse of women:[1137] *"I will greatly multiply thy pains and thy groanings; in pain shall thou shall bring forth children, and thy submission shall be to thy husband and he shall rule over thee."*[1138]

The mysterious nature of Marriage is clarified by St. Paul who commands that it should be joined *"only in the Lord,"*[1139] proclaiming Marriage as an Institution inseparable, Sacred and above that which was in the Garden of Eden because the Christian is a member of the Mystical Body of the God-Man to Whom he belongs in spirit and body. When two Christians are united through Marriage, they are not just two human beings or two souls gifted with Grace but two Sanctified Members of the Mystical Body of Christ who are united in order to expand this Body by childbirth and predestined to be incorporated into the Body of Christ. Those Christians who are joined in the Community of Marriage act only in the Lord, in the Name of the Divine Head to Whom they belong, for Whom they work as Its members. They cannot multiply except with the consent and in the spirit of Christ, for their bodies are no longer their flesh but the Flesh of Christ. They cannot join with one another unless their union is based on Christ.[1140]

St. Paul declared that, on the one hand, *"the woman who has a husband is bound by the Law to her husband as long as he lives. But if the husband dies, she is released from the Law of her husband. So then if, while her husband lives, she marries another man, she will be called an adulteress; but if her husband dies, she is free from that Law, so that she is no longer an adulteress, though she has married*

[1137] St John Chrysostom, in Migne, *P.G.,* 51, 210. St Epiphanius, *Pananrion Heresy* 67, 6. St Cyril of Alexandria, *To John 2:1,* in Migne, *P.G.,* 73, 225.
[1138] Gen. 3:17.
[1139] 1 Corinth. 7:39.
[1140] Scheeben, *Les Mystères,* p. 602.

another husband."[1141]   On the other hand he exhorted " *the married*" by Command of the Lord that "*a wife is not to depart from her husband*" "*.and a husband is not to divorce his wife.*"[1142]   St. Paul, forbidding the dissolution of Marriage of the husband to the wife, expressed the opinion that not only the woman becomes an adulteress if she marries another man as long as her first husband lives, but the man, too, becomes an adulterer under the same circumstances.[1143]

Finally, St. Paul sees the union of husband and wife through Marriage as the Image of the Mysterious and Confidential Union of Christ with His Church.[1144]   When the Apostle stated that Marriage must be according to the Lord, he meant "*not in fornication or adultery, not in stealing Marriage, but lawful, in frankness*"[1145] "*with wisdom, with decency.*"[1146]   Christ left His Father and came down to His Bride and became one Spirit with Her. This is a Union of Grace, since the Union of Christ with His Church becomes through her members, a Fountain of Divine Grace and a Communion of Holiness and Divine Prosperity.[1147]   "*This is a great Mystery, but I speak concerning Christ and the Church.*"[1148]   Since Marriage is a type of Mystery of Christ and the Church, it remains as "*pure with him*" as he who has recently ascended from the Baptismal Font and who has been Regenerated.[1149] For "*Marriage is honourable among all, and the bed undefiled.*"[1150] It becomes a means of transmitting Sanctification since "*the unbelieving husband is sanctified by the wife, and the unbelieving wife is sanctified by the husband*" and as a result, the children from this union "*are holy.*"[1151]   This presupposes Divine Grace within the Marriage, which is transmitted through the Holy Sacraments.

The meaning of Marriage as a great Mystery obviously depends on the way one relates to Christ and the Church. This relationship can be considered as merely symbolic or as a Reality. The Apostle, at

---

[1141] Rom. 7:2-3.

[1142] 1 Corinth. 7:10, 11.

[1143] Rom. 7:3.

[1144] Ephes. 5:22-33.

[1145] St Epiphanius, *Pnanrion, Heresy 59, § 6*, in Migne, *P.G.,* 41, 1028.

[1146] St John Chrysostom, *To 1 Corinthians 7:39*, in Migne, *P.G.,* 61, 160.

[1147] Ibid, *To Ephesians,* Homily 20, § 4, in Migne, *P.G.,* 62, 140.

[1148] Ephes. 5:32.

[1149] St John of Damascus, *To Ephesians,* in Migne, *P.G.,* 95, 852. Theodorus Mopsuestias, in Migne, *P.G.,* 66, 920. St Gregory of Nazianzus, *Homily 40 to the holy Baptism,* § 18, in Migne, *P.G.,* 36, 381.

[1150] Heb. 13:4.

[1151] 1 Corinth. 7:14.

first, presented Marriage in its natural essence as the symbol of the supernatural union of Christ and His Church. Marriage would not simply have been a Mystery but only the image of a Mystery of the union of Christ with His Church, being alien to it. In reality this is the Marriage among non-Christians and this was the Marriage everywhere before Christ, even in Israel being considered as a Divine Institution. Nonetheless, the Christian Marriage is realised in a true, essential and internal relationship with the Mystery of the union of Christ and the Church. It is joined upon this Mystery and it is organically united with Him, participating in His Divine and Mysterious Nature. Christian Marriage is not merely symbolic but also an imitation derived from the union of Christ with the Church, being ruled and inspired by Her. Therefore, in this manner the Apostle considered Marriage. He wanted every Christian to gather the nature and the responsibilities of Marriage with a Christian woman from the union of Christ and His Church as its ideal and source.[1152]

2. Marriage According to the Tradition of the Orthodox Church

In the Tradition of the Orthodox Church we find testimonies that witness to the Holy Mystery of Marriage: in some circumstances as an ecclesiastic ceremony performed and blessed by the Officiators while in others literally characterised as a Mystery.

St. Ignatius the Theophorus of Antioch proclaimed that *"it is proper for men and women who marry to be united with the consent of the Bishop that the Marriage may be in accordance with the Lord and not due to lustful passions."*[1153] He also advised the wives *"to love the Lord and to be content with their husbands physically and spiritually. In the same way command, my brothers in the Name of Jesus Christ to love their wives, as the Lord loves the Church.*[1154] *If anyone is able to remain chaste to honour of the Flesh of the Lord, let him so remain without boasting. If he boasts, he is lost; and if it is made known to anyone other than the Bishop, he is ruined."*[1155]

Tertullian confirmed that among the Christians illegal and secret unions not made known before the Church, are considered as adultery

---

[1152] Scheeben, *Les Mystères*, pp. 604-605.
[1153] St Ignatius, *To Polycarp,* 5, 2, in Lightfoot, *Apostolic Fathers,* p. 117.
[1154] Cf. Ephes. 5:25, 29.
[1155] St Ignatius, *To Polycarp,* 5, 1-2, in Lightfoot, *Apostolic Fathers,* p. 116.

and fornication.[1156]   On the contrary, however, he exalted the Marriage that is Blessed and Sealed by the Church, which the Angels announce and the Father Confirms.[1157]   Elsewhere he drew the attention of the Christian to the attempts of Satan who constantly struggles to humiliate the Holy Sacraments of the Church by imitating them and falsifying them in the ceremonies of the idolaters. Thus Satan does not only imitate the Baptism and the Eucharist but also imprints his seal on the foreheads of his soldiers, even calling the high Priest to bless the Marriage of the pagans.[1158] Thus Tertullian relates Marriage to the Christian Baptism, Divine Eucharist and Chrismation, ascribing to it the title "*Mystery*."

St. Basil the Great calls Marriage a "*bond through the Blessing*."[1159]

St. Gregory of Nazianzus informs us that at Marriages "*the golden Olympics, were present in the group of Bishops*."[1160]

St. John Chrysostom advises us "*to call a Priest*" to the weddings "*and through Prayers and Blessings to unite the oneness of mind of the match.*" He strictly condemned improper music that fills the bride's ears and the fruitless procession that casts away the modesty of Marriage.[1161]

St. Augustine literally spoke of Marriage as "*Sacramenti Nuptiarum*" assuring us that in Christian Marriage the Holiness of the Mystery has greater Power than the fertility of the mother. He proclaimed that Marriage is not only a Marital Bond but an insoluble Mystery.[1162]

The opinion of St Hippolytus is even more remarkable. He accused Pope Callistus of allowing elderly women belonging to a higher society to enter in the Community of Marriage with men not equal to their social level "*to have one who they desire as a husband, either a slave or a free man.*" He characterised such secret weddings

---

[1156] Tertullian, *De pudicitia* 4, in migne, *P.L.*, 2, 1038.

[1157] Ibid, *Adversus uxorem,* II, 9, in migne, *P.L.*, 1, 1415.

[1158] Tertullian, *De praescriptione haereticorum,* c. 40, in migne, *P.L.*, 2, 66.

[1159] St Basil the Great, *Hexaemerus,* Homily VII, § 5, in Migne, *P.G.*, 29, 160.

[1160] St Gregory of Nazianzus, *Epistle* 193 *to Procopius,* in Migne, *P.G.*, 37, 316.

[1161] St John Chrysostom, *To Genesis,* Homily 48, § 6, in Migne, *P.G.*, 54, 443. Ibid, in Migne, *P.G.*, 51, 211. Ibid, in Montfaucon, v. 3, p. 260. Ibid, *To Genesis,* Homily 56, § 1, in Montfaucon, v. 4, p. 625.

[1162] St Augustine, *De Nupt. Et concup.,* I, c. 10, § 11, in migne, *P.L.*, 44, 419. Ibid, *De bono conjugal,* c. 18, § 21, in migne, *P.L.*, 40, 387. Ibid, *De Genesis ad litter.,* IX, 7, in migne, *P.L.*, 34, 397.

as not only illegal but also pointing out that we must " *see to what ungodliness came the illegal teaching adultery.*"[1163]

Kritopoulos determined Marriage as "*the legal union of man and woman*" and that "*it is called a Mystery by the Apostle, not because it contributes to the Eternal Life*" but because it is considered "*as the other two Sacraments*" of Baptism and Eucharist. It is called a Mystery, because "*it is assimilated to Christ and the Church. As it is said that 'Christ loved the Church, likewise the husbands must love their own wives;'*[1164] even more '*Great is the Mystery, but I speak concerning Christ and the Church.'*[1165] Marriage is considered to be honourable, and the bed spotless and undefiled, according to Apostolic Teaching.[1166]

3. The High Objectives of Marriage

The high objectives of marriage, according to the Lord, are: "*wisdom and self-control, childbirth, and the dominion over the house for which the woman was given.*"[1167] When the Creator of all wanted to create Eve, He said: "*It is not good that the man should be alone; let us make for him a help suitable to him.*"[1168] As a bond Marriage makes the couple helpers of one another in life, exercising and urging them to tolerate one another, to bring to harmony to their different characters, to love and serve one another, to suffer and to enjoy together, to help one another in sicknesses and different needs, carrying together the burden of life and the responsibilities of the family. The help for which Eve was given to Adam does not refer simply to physical needs. It is also an exercise of patience and tolerance that makes the woman, through her obedience to her husband "*of the same body*" and "*somehow mixed in flesh and spirit with the man*" through the cultivation of the sameness of mind and love, with which Christ loved the Church and gave Himself for Her.[1169],[1170] The expression "*let us make for him a help suitable to*

[1163] St Hippolytus, *Heresies,* IX, 12, in ***B***, v. 5, p. 352.
[1164] Ephes. 5:25.
[1165] Ephes. 5:32.
[1166] Kritopoulos, ch. 12, in Karmeris, *The dogmatics,* v. II, p. 542.
[1167] Clement the Alexandrian, *Stromata,* III, § 12, in ***B***, v. 8, p. 38.
[1168] Gen. 2:18.
[1169] Ephes. 5:25.
[1170] St Gregory of Nazianzus, *Homily* 37, § 9, in Migne, *P.G.,* 36, 293.

him"[1171] applies to the man as well because he is obliged to offer help to his wife and it expresses the struggle of each step in life that brings forth the fruit of moral progress and perfection of the couple.

The wisdom and self-control are one aspect of this moral progress and perfection of the couple. St. Paul categorically and without any hesitation expressed the admonition: *"Nevertheless, because of sexual immorality, let each man have his own wife, and let each woman have her own husband."*[1172]

Finally, childbearing crowns the objectives of Marriage although this is not the primary objective of Marriage since we have Marriages that are unfruitful with regard to childbearing. Furthermore St. Paul stressed that *"because of sexual immorality, let each man have his own wife"*[1173] not only for childbearing because he instructed: *"Do not deprive one another except with consent for a time that you may give yourselves to Fasting and Prayer; and come together again"* not to become fathers of children but *"so that Satan does not tempt you because of your lack of self-control."*[1174] [1175]

It is obvious that childbearing and the raising of children according to God's Will are high objectives of Marriage. For this reason, St. Paul proclaimed that the woman *"will be saved in childbearing, if she continues in faith, love and Holiness, with self-control."*[1176]

4. Monogamy as a fundamental requirement

Monogamy was the main characteristic of Marriage right from the beginning in the Garden of Eden. Our Lord and Saviour Jesus Christ, the Son of God, proclaimed that God from the beginning made *"male and female"* and that they are to be *"one flesh."*[1177] Since God made one male and not many, and gave him one woman whom He took from the male's side in order that the two shall be one flesh, it is obvious that the Creator excluded polygamy as being alien to His Divine Plan of Creation. Without any doubt, polygamy contradicts

---

[1171] Gen. 2:18.
[1172] 1 Corinth. 7:2.
[1173] 1 Corinth. 7:2.
[1174] 1 Corinth. 7:5.
[1175] St John Chrysostom, *About virginity,* ch. 19, in Migne, *P.G.,* 48, 547.
[1176] 1 Tim. 2:15.
[1177] Matth. 19:5.

the first form of Marriage as the Creator had instituted it, for it dissolves the family, putting obstacles in the path of natural gestation and normal childbirth, thereby creating differences between the half-siblings. Polygamy is incompatible to the idea of a true family and to the morality of couples by encouraging sexual immorality of the man as well as jealousy and division between his many wives, even though it may contribute to the multiplication of the human race. Polygamy is an act of rebellion against God's Divine Plan, a "dis-Grace" for the human race and an instrument of sinful sexual desires.

In the Old Testament we see Lamech taking two wives[1178] as a result of his sins, for he had "*slain a man*" to his "*sorrow and a youth to*" his "*grief.*"[1179] This sin continued even among the Patriarchs Abraham[1180] and Jacob.[1181]. Hence, Moses placed Laws concerning children born from polygamous relationships.[1182] Polygamy was also practised during the time of the Judges[1183] and Kings[1184] as in the case of King Solomon. "*And it came to pass in the time of the old age of Solomon, that his heart was not perfect with the Lord his God, as was the heart of David his father. And the strange women turned away his heart after their gods. Then Solomon built a high place to Chamos the idol of Moab, and to their king the idol of the children of Ammon, and to Astarte the abomination of the Sidonians. And thus he acted towards all his strange wives, who burnt incense and sacrificed to their idols.*"[1185]

Although this regime was tolerated in the Old Testament, in the New Testament our Lord and Saviour Jesus Christ, the Son of God, renounced it by proclaiming that the Creator "*at the beginning made male and female*" and that "*the two shall become one flesh. So then, they are no longer two but one flesh.*"[1186]

St. Paul also assures that "*the woman who has a husband is bound by the Law to her husband as long as he lives*" and only "*if the husband dies,*" is she "*released from the Law of her husband.*"[1187] St.

[1178] Gen. 4:19.
[1179] Gen. 4:23.
[1180] Gen. 16:3.
[1181] Gen. 29:23, 28; 30:4, 9.
[1182] Deut. 21:15.
[1183] Judges 8:30.
[1184] I Samuel (I Kings) 18:7; 25:42, 43. 2 Samuel (2 Kings) 3:2, 7.
[1185] I Kings (3 Kings) 11:1, 4.
[1186] Matth. 19:4, 5-6.
[1187] Rom. 7:2.

Paul renounced the miserable regime of polygamy since elsewhere he also proclaimed that *"because of sexual immorality, let each man have his own wife"*[1188] and referring to the words of the institution of natural Marriage, explained: *'For this reason a man shall leave his father and mother and be joined to his wife, and the two shall become one flesh.'*[1189]

Hence the Apologists stressed that monogamy is practised by the Orthodox Christians. Athenagoras observed that the second marriage, after the death of the first wife, is considered as *"a noble adultery,"*[1190] whereas Theophilus stated that among the Orthodox Christians *"self-control is practiced, monogamy is observed, chastity is kept."*[1191]

Clement the Alexandrian observed: *"the Lord renewing the old did not forgive polygamy, for then the time requested, when it was necessary to increase and multiply, He introduced monogamy."*[1192]

St. Epiphanius repeatedly proclaimed that *"the Church honours the noble marriage and the monogamy,"* thereby placing noble marriage and monogamy immediately after virginity and being widowed.[1193]

The Eastern Orthodox Church insists on monogamy, revealed by Her opinion of second and third Marriage. According to the *Shepherd of Hermas,* he who enters into a second Marriage after the death of his first wife *"does not sin,"* although, *"if the survivor remains single, one gains for oneself greater honour and great glory with the Lord"* as well as reassuring us that *"even if one does remarry, one does not sin."*[1194]

St. Cyril of Jerusalem urged those who had conducted a first Marriage, not to disregard *"those who entered in a second Marriage"* observing that *"chastity is good and admirable"* although it is forgiven for one to enter into a second Marriage, in order that *"the weak not commit fornication."*[1195]

[1188] 1 Corinth. 7:2.

[1189] Gen. 2:24. Ephes. 5:31. 1 Corinth. 6:16.

[1190] Athenagoras, *Deputation* 33, in *B*, v. 4, p. 308.

[1191] Theophilus of Antioch, *Autolycus* III, 15, *B*, v. 5, p. 58.

[1192] Clement the Alexandrian, *Stromata*, III, 12, *B*, v. 8, p. 38.

[1193] St Epiphanius, *Panarion, Heresy* 48, § 9, in Migne, *P.G.,* 41, 868. Ibid, *Brief true homily about faith,* § 21, in Migne, *P.G.,* 42, 824.

[1194] *Shepherd of Hermas,* Mandate 4, 32, 2, in Lightfoot, *Apostolic Fathers,* p. 219. Methodius, *Symposium,* Homily 3, 12, in Migne, *P.G.,* 18, 80-81. St Epiphanius, *Panarion, Heresy* 48, § 9, in Migne, *P.G.,* 41, 869.

[1195] St Cyril of Jerusalem, *Catechesis,* IV, § 26, in Migne, *P.G.,* 33, 488.

5. The Insolubility of the Sacred Bond of Marriage

The insolubility of Marriage is combined with its monogamy. The testimonies of Holy Scripture concerning monogamy simultaneously prove the insolubility of this Holy Bond. The fact that the institution of Marriage was proclaimed in the beginning by Adam and that the one man shall leave his father and mother and shall cleave to his one wife, becoming one flesh with her, implies that Marriage is composed of two people of different genders. The union *"in one flesh"* makes Marriage inseparable and insoluble[1196] and, according to the words of Christ *"what God has joined together, let not man separate,"*[1197] shows that divorce, by means of which the unity of one flesh is divided, is *"abnormal and against the Law; abnormal because it divides one flesh;, against the Law because God United and Commanded not to separate"* through divorce.

Simultaneously, the Lord recognises one reason for divorce: if one of the two commits adultery. *"But I say to you that whoever divorces his wife for any reason except sexual immorality, causes her to commit adultery; and whoever marries a woman who is divorced, commits adultery."*[1198] Obviously according to these Words of the Lord the right of the person who suffered injustice is recognised and thereby allows a divorce as well as permitting entry into a new Marriage without sinning.

Concerning inter-faith Marriages, it is understandable that since the Holy Sacraments are for those who are members of the Mystical Body of Christ, they should not be given to unbelievers, heretics, schismatics, Jews and Muslims because these, being non-Orthodox Christians, may disregard and mock them, as the Lord very clearly stated: *"Do not give what is Holy to the dogs; nor cast your pearls before swine, lest they trample them under their feet, and turn and tear you in pieces."*[1199]

[1196] St John Chrysostom, *To Matthew 19:5,* in Migne, *P.G.,* 58, 597.
[1197] Matth. 19:6.
[1198] Matth. 5:32.
[1199] Matth. 7:6.

6. Mixed Marriages

It is true that in the first centuries, one of a couple might have been drawn to the Faith. Concerning these couples, St. Paul advised that they should not separate since *"the unbelieving husband is Sanctified by the wife, and the unbelieving wife is Sanctified by the husband"* and that the children of such Marriages *"are Holy."*[1200] In addition, because of the persecutions and the difficulties of the times, some married Jews or idolaters. These marriages were regarded by the Orthodox Church as unholy; sodomite matches and those who conducted such marriages were considered worthy of Excommunication from the Church because to enter into the Community of Marriage with an unbeliever was considered equal to delivering the members of Christ to fornication.[1201]

The gravity with which the Orthodox Church considered marriage with any non-Christian can be understood as having been unacceptable considering that it was strictly forbidden to give any Orthodox member into the Community of Marriage to a heretic or schismatic.

Today Orthodox families are advised to raise and maintain their children in the True Faith. Should the other member of the married couple not be Orthodox Christian, then they should strive through pure love to bring the non-Orthodox into the True Christian Faith. This must only be done without force and according to the free will of the non-Orthodox.

II. EXTERNAL ASPECT OF THE HOLY MYSTERY

The external aspect of the Holy Mystery of Marriage as the natural bond consisting of the common consent of the couple that is expressed according to their free will. As a Mystery, it is a ceremony celebrated by the Officiator (Bishop or Priest) of the Orthodox Church. Thus, for the composition of the Christian Marriage the couple are not the main Officiators through their common consent to be joined in the Community of Marriage. The physical bond of Marriage is Sanctified by Christ through the Officiator Bishop or

---

[1200] 1 Corinth. 7:14.
[1201] Tertullian, *Adversus uxorum,* II, 3, in migne, *P.L.,*1, 1405. St Cyprian, *De lapsis,* 6, in migne, *P.L.,* 4, 483.

Priest who joins the hands of the newlywed couple and through Prayers calls upon them the Grace and Blessings of the Holy Spirit. This invisible Divine Grace contributes to the growth of the Holiness of the couple, making them worthy of co-operating with God in order *"that each of you should know how to possess his own vessel in Sanctification and honour, not in passion of lust."*[1202] Consequently Marriage remains *"honourable among all, and the bed undefiled."*[1203] The couple is united in one flesh through the harmony of their wills and desires, and their whole life to the Will of our Lord Jesus Christ. From the moment they have children, they must raise them according to the education and Law of the Lord, for *"God is able to make all Grace abound toward you, that you, always having all sufficiency in all things, may have abundance for every good work."*[1204]

1. The Ceremony as the External Aspect of the Holy Mystery

The common consent of the couple is a necessary requirement so that the Holy Mystery of Marriage may take place. This involves the physical bond that is Blessed by the Creator, although, because of the invasion of sin, it did not remain as it was established and Blessed by God. Hence, as a Mystery, by means of which Divine Grace is transmitted to the newly wed, assisting them to raise their physical bond to a higher level of Holiness, it has as its external aspect their consent to receive the Blessing that only the Officiating Bishop or Priest can give.

2. The Invisible Aspect of the Holy Mystery

Few words can be characterised as the *"addition of Holiness"* with regard to the Divine Grace that is granted through the Holy Mystery. The married couple *"have Christ in their midst"* teaching them *"to be wise"* and to keep their *"marriage honourable and their bed undefiled"* as well as to keep themselves in all Holiness, so that they will *"be clean after the wedding.* Clement the Alexandrian observed that *"those who have been Sanctified, Holy is their sperm."* This is according to the Teachings of St. Paul who said: *"The*

[1202] 1 Thess. 4:4-5.
[1203] Heb. 13:4.
[1204] 2 Corinth. 9:8.

unbelieving husband is Sanctified by the wife, and the unbelieving wife is Sanctified by the husband" and that, as a result, their children "*are Holy.*"[1205] Having Christ in their midst, they become members of their members as well as "*honourable members,*" bringing "*the union of the contrary*" closer and combining both "*in flesh and in spirit*" being one body. Similarly, they become one soul, united through love and the Divine Law.[1206]

These are the secure Blessings that are granted by the Holy Mystery of Marriage, taking into consideration that the couple must approach with true and undefiled faith and repentance, having been purified through the Holy Mystery of Confession and the worthy participation in the Holy Eucharist so as to receive the Matrimonial Blessing. That Blessing, granted through the Holy Mystery, includes Prayers beseeching the Lord to grant the newly wed the fruit of the womb and the filling of their home with all the fruits of the earth and all good deeds.

CHAPTER ELEVEN
THE MYSTERY OF HOLY UNCTION

I. DEFINITION, NAMES, DIVINE INSTITUTION

The Holy Mystery of Unction is the Mystery in which, through the prayers with anointing with oil by the Presbyters of the Orthodox Church, the anointed one receives the Healing Grace of the Holy Spirit.[1207] This Divine Mystery received various names either because of the use of the oil and prayers or from the way it is celebrated. Finally, the Divine institution of this Holy Mystery is found in Holy Scripture, especially in the Epistle of St James the Adelphotheos (*"Brother of Christ"*) who urged the sick to call upon the Elders of the Church to anoint them with oil, accompanied by prayer.

[1205] 1 Corinth. 7:14.
[1206] St John Chrysostom, *To the apostolic verse: "For your sexual immortalities"*, §§ 2, 3, in Migne, *P.G.,* 51, 210 and 213. St Gregory of Nazianzus, *Homily* 40 *to the holy Baptism,* § 18, in Migne, *P.G.,* 36, 381. Clement the Alexandrian, *Stromata,* III 6, in *B*, v. 8, p. 26. St Basil the Great, *Hexaemeros,* Homily 7, in Migne, *P.G.,* 29, 324.
[1207] Cf. Plato of Moscow, *Orthodox Teaching,* pp. 159-160. Kefalas, *Catechesis,* p. 188. Frangopoulos, *Christian Faith,* pp. 218-219. Mitsopoulos, *Themata,* p. 326. Meyendorff, *Theology,* p. 199. Georgopoulos, *Anthology,* pp. 77-81.

1. Definition and Names

The Holy Mystery of Unction, according to its external aspect, is the anointing by the Presbyter with Sanctified Oil accompanied with special prayer. Its internal aspect is the granting of Divine Grace for the healing of both body and soul. *"It is the mystical ceremony with oil and prayers celebrated by the Church for the ill. The ill, being anointed with this oil with faith and good hope in God, receive His aid."*[1208]

The illnesses of the soul, which are the fruits of sin, are forgiven in the Holy Mystery of Confession. However, under no circumstances can the Holy Mystery of Unction be considered as a necessary supplement of the Holy Mystery of Confession. Neither it is necessary for one's Salvation, such as the Holy Sacraments of Baptism, Chrismation, Holy Communion and Confession. Our Salvation does not depend upon this Holy Mystery. Nevertheless, it is recommended for the healing of the illnesses of the body and soul. For, if the ill person has faith, he will recover from his illness whereas, on the other, he receives the forgiveness of his sins. It must be clearly understood that under no circumstances does this Divine and Sacred Mystery replace the other God-instituted Mystery of Confession. Through this Holy Mystery the sins, which one cannot remember, are forgiven, since the Holy Mystery of Confession is usually performed beforehand.

The various names given to the Holy Mystery of Unction were mainly due to the element of oil as well as the external ceremony. Through Sanctified Oil with prayer and anointing, it is called: *"Oil," "Holy Oil," "Unction," "Sanctified Oil," "Chrism" and "Anointing of Oil."* The Latin terms are: *"Oleum," "Unctio," "Oleum Unctionis," "Unctio Olei Sacrati," "Extrema Unctio," "Sacramentum Exeuntium," "Sacramentum Moribandorum," "Unctio Egredientium," "Unctio Emeritorum," "Unctio Infirmorum."* As a Mystery it is particularly for the ill and those who going through the process of departing this life.

[1208] Kritopoulos, *ch. 13,* in Karmeris, *The dogmatics,* v. II, p. 543.

2. The Divine Institution

The Divine Institution of the Holy Mystery of Unction is testified to by St James the Adelphotheos who said: *"Is anyone among you suffering? Let him pray. Is anyone cheerful? Let him sing psalms. Is anyone among you sick? Let him call for the elders of the church, and let them pray over him, anointing him with oil in the Name of the Lord. And the prayer of faith will save the sick, and the Lord will raise him up. And if he has committed sins, he will be forgiven. Confess your trespasses to one another, and pray for one another, that you may be healed. The effective, fervent prayer of a righteous man avails much."*[1209] Through this instruction the divine James commanded the sick to invite the Presbyters of the Church, who are no less than the Priests who have been appointed by the Church for the ecclesiastic *Diakonia*.

The anointing with Oil does not have the nature of a healing medicine such as in the case of the anointing of a wound. It must be accompanied by prayer, which is exalted as a prayer of Faith that Saves the sick. The promise of the healing of the body through the anointing with blessed Oil is combined with the promise of forgiveness of sins that the ill person might have committed and which no physical medicine can forgive.

The anointing of Oil with prayer in the Holy Mystery of Unction differs from that mentioned in the Gospel of St Mark according to which the Holy Apostles *"cast out many demons, and anointed with oil many who were sick, and healed them."*[1210] There we clearly have a Supernatural Charisma of healing. The anointing with Oil is aimed towards the awakening of faith. This verse implies that the use of Oil by the Holy Apostles was familiar to the Lord Who did not disregard it. This was characterised as a preparation of the Divine Mystery of Holy Unction. However, this anointing of Oil has nothing common to that which St James instructed.

Only the words of St James support the Divine Institution of the Holy Mystery of Holy Unction.

[1209] James 5:13-16. Cf. Mitsopoulos, *Themata,* pp. 326-327. Georgopoulos, *Anthology,* p. 77.
[1210] Mark 6:13.

3. The Testimony of Holy Tradition

The practice of the Orthodox Church and the Teachings of the Holy Fathers concerning the nature of the Holy Mystery of Unction are not so clear, nor do we have as many as for the other Holy Sacraments. Among the oldest testimonies is the *Egyptian Order,* which is identical to the *Apostolic Tradition* of St Hippolytus (2nd century) as well as the *Apostolic Orders* and the *Covenant of our Lord Jesus Christ.* Information concerning the Holy Mystery is also to be found in the *Eucholigion ("Prayer Book")* of St. Serapion.

In the *Egyptian Order* we find a brief prayer for the Sanctification of the Oil, through which the officiator beseeches God to grant to everyone who partakes of its strength and health.

In the *Apostolic Orders* we find the following: "*Let the Bishop bless the water or the oil. If he is not present let the Presbyter bless with the presence of the Deacon.*" A brief prayer followed addressed to "*the Lord, Sabaoth, the God of powers, the merciful and philanthropic Creator of the waters and giver of the oil.*" Through the prayer the officiator beseeches the Lord to Sanctify "*this water and oil in the name of the one who presented them*" (the sick) and grant him "*through Christ strength of health, deportation of sicknesses, fleeing of demons, dismissal of all threats.*"[1211]

According to the *Covenant of our Lord Jesus Christ* the Sanctified Oil is placed in a jar "*before the altar*" and the prayer is addressed to the Lord Christ Who is "*the physician of all kinds of sicknesses and all kinds of diseases, Who gives freely to be healed.*" It is requested to send upon this oil "*the Salvation of His Love to Save those who suffer and to heal the sick and to Sanctify those who return, when they approach with faith.*"[1212]

It is worthy to note that the testimonies which refer to Unction as a Holy Mystery or inform us of this, belong to the ecclesiastic writers and Holy Fathers of the Orthodox Church Egypt, from which the above orders of Sanctification originate.[1213] The first clear testimony, which characterised it as a Mystery, is found in the epistle of Pope Innocent I (+417) addressed to Decentium (*ad Decentium* 8, 12).

[1211] *Apostolic Orders,* VIII, 29, in **B**, v. 2, p. 163.
[1212] Fuller, *The anointing,* p. 113.
[1213] Bartmann, *Theologie Dogmatique,* v. II, p. 459. Origen, *In Leviticus,* Homily II, 4, in Migne, *P.G.,* 12, 418. St John Chrysostom, *About priesthood,* III, 6, in Migne, *P.G.,* 48, 644. Ibid, *To Matthew,* Homily 32, 6, in Migne, *P.G.,* 57, 384.

Pope Innocent, referring to the words of St James concerning the anointing with oil, stressed that it must be understood as referring to the sick faithful who can be anointed with the Oil of Chrismation. This special Oil was prepared by the Bishop and used not only by the Priests but also by all the Christians. Finally, Pope Innocent I forbade the anointing of unrepentant sinners with this Sanctified Oil because it is a Mystery (*"quia genus est sacramenti"*) and since it is forbidden to offer the other Holy Sacraments (Holy Baptism, Chrismation, Eucharist and Confession) to them, how can it be possible for them to receive this?[1214]

The Orthodox Church urges the faithful that when ill we should never consult diviners, witchdoctors, mediums, psychics, magicians, astrologists, tarot card and coffee cup readers or sorcerers but instead to seek healing by receiving the Body and Blood of Christ and being anointed with the blessed Oil. As faithful disciples of Christ this is the only way to receive restoration of health as well as the forgiveness of our sins. Parents are strongly advised by the Church to anoint their children with the Sanctified Oil.

II. OFFICIATORS, EXTERNAL AND INTERNAL ASPECT OF THE HOLY MYSTERY

1. The Officiators of the Holy Mystery

The officiators of the Holy Mystery of Unction are the Bishops and Presbyters of the Church who are vested with the Authority given by the Church. The Bishops authorise the Presbyters to celebrate the Mystery.[1215] The Presbyters, according to the words of St James, were not only the givers of the Divine Mystery but the officiators as well who Sanctified the oil through their prayers.

In the Orthodox Church the Holy Mystery of Unction is officiated by seven Presbyters and only in necessity by one. The presence of more than one Presbyter is according to the words of our Lord that *"if two of you agree on earth concerning anything that they ask, it will be done for them by My Father in Heaven. For where two or three are gathered together in My Name, I Am there in the midst of*

[1214] Innocent I, in Trempelas, *Dogmatique,* v. III, p. 353-354.
[1215] Innocent I, *Ad Decentium,* c. VIII, § 1, in Trempelas, *Dogmatique,* v. III, p. 355, note 22. Georgopoulos, *Anthology,* p. 78.

them."[1216]   Nevertheless, the Holy Mystery should be officiated by seven Presbyters. Each one addresses one of the seven prayers. This practice was formed during the 10th century at the time of Arsenius, Patriarch of Constantinople (1255-1260).[1217]

The anointing could also be done by the faithful who received the Sanctified Oil. This testimony is witnessed to in the *Euchologion* of St. Serapion and in the Epistle of Pope Innocent I to Decentium. It was in general use during the Middle Ages in the West.[1218]

The Holy Mystery of Unction is mainly given to the sick but not necessarily only to those who are very ill. Anyone is able to call upon the Presbyters to pray for their restoration of health. This Holy Mystery cannot be given to those who are not Baptised or who have been excommunicated as heretics or schismatics, or even to those who have mortally sinned and have not repented.

2. The External or Visible Aspect of the Holy Mystery

The Sanctification of the Oil is combined inseparably with the offering of the Holy Mystery. It is officiated by the Presbyter. In the service of the Holy Unction, we have a special prayer that is characterised by St Symeon of Thessalonica the New Theologian as a *"Prayer of Sanctification."*[1219]   This prayer is read upon the Oil by each Presbyter who partakes in the celebration of the Holy Mystery. Another prayer is repeated by each Presbyter during the anointing in a cross-shaped sign upon the forehead, the two cheeks, the chin and on both sides of each hand.

3. The Internal or Invisible Aspect of the Holy Mystery

The invisible Divine Grace, which is granted through the Holy Mystery of Unction, comprises its internal or invisible aspect. It initially relieves the sick from their bodily illness and leads them to complete recovery. Secondly, it grants them the forgiveness of sins. The objective of the Holy Mystery of Unction is primarily the healing of the illnesses of the body and not the forgiveness of sins. This is

---

[1216] Matth. 18:19-20.
[1217] Migne, *P.G.*, 140, 806.
[1218] Ott, «Precis», p. 618. Bartmann, *Theologie Dogmatique,* v. II, p. 462.
[1219] St Symeon, *About the holy ceremony of the holy oil or unction,* ch. 288-290, in Migne, *P.G.,* 155, 525-529.

clearly understood when one bears in mind that the forgiveness of sins is the objective of the Holy Mystery of Confession. In addition to the above, St James determined at first that the anointing by oil with prayer is for the healing of bodily sicknesses and secondly for the forgiveness of sins.

It is true that the ill person is not always cured of his affliction although it is certain that Divine Grace is granted through the Holy Mystery, strengthening him with patience, hope and peace. We are not always restored to good health due to the fact that the Divine Grace aims at restoring our spiritual health and leads us to Salvation. Restoration of health is granted to the ill when it will cause them to progress in virtue and for their Salvation.

The Holy Mystery of Unction is necessary to secure the restoration of our health. It must be clearly stated that this Holy Mystery does not become the medicine for Immortality and Eternal Life in this life of vanity. Otherwise, this would be contradictory to the plan of our Salvation and Regeneration through Christ Jesus. St. Paul emphasised that we should put aside our mortal bodies in order to achieve the Regeneration of the new man in Christ. He proclaimed that *"we know that if our earthly house, this tent, is destroyed, we have a building from God, a house not made with hands, eternal in the Heavens. For in this we groan, earnestly desiring to be clothed with our habitation which is from Heaven, if indeed, having been clothed, we shall not be found naked. For we who are in this tent groan, being burdened, not because we want to be unclothed, but further clothed, that mortality may be swallowed up by life."*[1220] Again *"because the creation itself also will be delivered from the bondage of corruption into the glorious liberty of the children of God. For we know that the whole creation groans and labours with birth pangs together until now. Not only that, but we also who have the firstfruits of the Spirit, even we ourselves groan within ourselves, eagerly waiting for the adoption, the redemption of our body."*[1221] One must never forget the example of St. Paul who in his illness requested three times to be healed by Christ but the Lord answered him: *"My Grace is sufficient for you, for My strength is made perfect in weakness."*[1222]

[1220] 2 Corinth. 5:1-4.
[1221] Rom. 8:21-23.
[1222] 2 Corinth. 12:9.

224

We must always bear in mind that the forgiveness of sins, under no circumstances, can be replaced by this Divine and Holy Mystery of Unction, nor can it replace the Mystery of Holy Confession. It can grant forgiveness of sins to those who truly have previously and sincerely confessed their sins in the Holy Mystery of Confession but in their weakness of mind, could not remember in detail all their sins. Consequently, the Holy Mystery of Unction is additional to that of Holy Confession.

CHAPTER TWELVE
THE SACRAMENT OF DEATH (PASSING IN THE LORD)

What are the Punishments?

Answer: The Punishments that will be bestowed by the Judge on the condemned,[1223] can be categorized as either negative and positive, or internal and external. The Eternal Punishment are:

1. First, being deprived of all God's Grace.
2. Secondly, the positive and internal Punishment, whereby the guilt of the conscience and awareness of guilt will be like an "*unsleeping worm*" that will eat at hearts, distressing them forever.
3. Thirdly, the external Punishment, according to which the soul will suffer Eternal pain of the Fire, sadness, external Darkness and communion with the evil spirits.[1224]

If one just considers the Divine Wrath resulting in the alienation of those who will be condemned by God Who is the only True Source of all Peace and Blessedness, and who will be deprived of the Vision of the Divine Glory of the Holy Trinity, this alone should be considered as an unbearable Punishment!

The negative aspect of the future Condemnation is inseparably united to the positive aspect. Primarily, there will be the disgrace that will overcome sinners due to having "*before their eyes their sins for all Eternity..*" for which they will be condemned to "*hard punishment*" "*the pain and the disgrace of which are really Eternal.*"[1225]

Undoubtedly, the descriptions of the Punishments by the Holy Fathers as mentioned above, do not differ from those revealed by our Lord and Saviour Jesus Christ, the Son of God, when He spoke of the Punishments that await the ungodly after the Final Judgement. Expressions such as "*outer darkness,*" the "*weeping and gnashing of teeth,*" the "*Everlasting Punishment,*" "*Hell,*" "*the Fire that shall never be*

[1223] Cf. Plato of Moscow, *Orthodox Teaching,* pp. 165-166. Evdokimov, *Orthodoxia,* pp. 443-447. Frangopoulos, *Christian Faith,* pp. 235-236. Mitsopoulos, *Themata,* pp. 397-403.

[1224] Mesoloras, *Symbolique,* v. II, p. 129.

[1225] St Basil the Great, *To Psalm 33(34),* §§ 4 and 8, in Migne, *P.G.,* 29, 364 and 372.

quenched," the "Worm which does not die" and "torment of Flame,"[1226] are a few of those that our Lord Himself used to describe the Eternal Punishments.

The exact nature of these Punishments is unknown since they occur in the After Life, which is beyond human senses and invisible.[1227] It may vaguely be perceived by means of the Parable of the Rich Man and Poor Lazarus,[1228] according to which the Rich Man found himself in Hell, "*being in torments*"[1229] and completely deprived from all the good things that he had enjoyed in this present life. His heart was enslaved by earthly things and the vanity of the pleasures of the flesh, which he could no longer satisfy. He was in the midst of a fiery Furnace that caused him terrible thirst and great anxiety. Also in this Parable, our Lord referred to a "*place of torment*"[1230] that is separated by "*a great gulf*"from the place of the Righteous.[1231] In addition to all this, our Lord spoke of "*the Everlasting Fire prepared for the devil and his angels.*"[1232]

"Hell," "Everlasting Fire" or "*the Outer Darkness*"[1233] is a spiritual condition that God created not for man, but because of Satan and his angels being stubbornly unrepentant. This condition is real, unchangeable and eternal, since the Will of God is Eternal and Unchangeable. No one can adequately describe this condition that is beyond any human understanding, not even St Paul who was "*caught up in Paradise and heard inexpressible words, which it is not lawful for a man to utter.*"[1234] Similarly, should anyone enter into Hell, he would be completely unable to express the terrifying things he might see, hear or feel.

What is the condition of the Righteous?

Answer: The Blessedness that awaits the Righteous, filling hearts with an inexpressible Joy and Happiness, will be due to the assurance that they have been Saved forever.[1235] The positive aspect of the future inheritance of the Righteous is expressed as "*Paradise of God,*" where "*the Tree of Life is in the midSt..*"[1236] and in which "*inexpressible words*" are heard, "*which it is not lawful for a man to utter.*"[1237] This Eternal Life is also described as the "*City of God,*" "*the Holy City, New Jerusalem, coming down out of Heaven from God, prepared as a bride adorned for her husband,*"[1238] or as "*the Tabernacle of God*" that is with men and where He "*will dwell with*

[1226] Matth. 8:12; 25:46. Mark 9:45-48. Luke 16:24.

[1227] 1 Corinth. 13:12.

[1228] Luke 16:19-31.

[1229] Luke 16:23.

[1230] Luke 16:28.

[1231] Luke 16:26.

[1232] Matth. 25:41.

[1233] Kefalas, *Catechesis,* pp. 242-243.

[1234] 2 Corinth. 12:4.

[1235] Cf. Plato of Moscow, *Orthodox Teaching,* pp. 164-165. Evdokimov, *Orthodoxia,* pp. 441-443. Mitsopoulos, *Themata,* pp. 393-397.

[1236] Rev. 2:7.

[1237] 2 Corinth. 12:4.

[1238] Rev. 20:2.

them"[1239] Furthermore it is described as the *"Father's house"* which has *"many mansions"*[1240] as well as being proclaimed as *"the Bride, the Lamb's wife"*[1241] that has *"the Glory of God."*[1242] Other descriptions of Eternal Life are: as the future City that has *"no temple in it, for the Lord God Almighty and the Lamb are its Temple;"*[1243] *"Assembly and Church of the Firstborn who are Regenerated in Heaven;"*[1244] *"an Inheritance incorruptible and undefiled;"* that *"does not fade away, reserved in Heaven;"*[1245] *"Kingdom of Heaven;"*[1246] *"Kingdom of God;"*[1247] *"Kingdom of the Father of the Lord"*[1248] or *"Kingdom prepared for the Blessed"*[1249] wherein the Lord will not only drink from the new Cup with His Disciples,[1250] but they *"shall also reign with Him."*[1251] No words can describe the perfect beauty of the Heavenly Things that await the Righteous who will partake in the Divine Nature of our Lord, watching and enjoying the Glory of the Holy Trinity, our True and Only God.

In God's Kingdom there is no fear, hunger or illness. No one is in pain, angry or flamed by desire because all these passions have been wiped away. No one will age because all will be vested with Immortality and Everlasting Joy, living together with the Angels, Archangels and all the higher Heavenly Powers. There will be no war or rebellion. There will only be the agreement of and harmony with the Saints and the oneness of mind.[1252]

The factor and cause of this Blessedness that the Saints experience, is referred to as *"Deification"* or *"Theosis"* that begins in this world. The final Purpose of the Lord's Incarnation is to lead fallen mankind towards the inheritance of the Kingdom of Heaven so that we may enjoy Divine Blessedness and be Deified. The term *"Deification"* or *"Theosis"* of our human nature and Deification of the Just, is understood as men becoming through this Deification *"partakers of the Divine Nature."*[1253] While human nature is not abolished, being absorbed by the infinite Divine Nature, it partakes according to its limitations in the Life and Glory of God. Each of the Righteous, preserving his own personality and being, is raised up to approach the Divine but remaining always limited.

In the Divine Incarnation of the Word and Son of God, the second Person of the Holy Trinity took up the whole human nature, without sin,

---

[1239] Rev. 20:3.
[1240] John 14:2.
[1241] Rev. 21:9.
[1242] Rev. 21:11.
[1243] Rev. 21:22.
[1244] Heb. 12:23.
[1245] 1 Peter 1:4.
[1246] Matth. 4:17; 5:3, 10, 20; 13:24, 31, 44, 47; 16:19; 18:23; 19:12; 20:1; 22:2; 23:13; 25:1, 14
[1247] Luke 14:15. Matth. 19:24; 21:31
[1248] Matth. 26:29
[1249] Matth. 25:34.
[1250] Matth. 26:29.
[1251] 2 Tim. 2:12.
[1252] St John Chrysostom, *To the fallen Theodorus*, I, § 11, in Migne, *P.G.*, 47, 291.
[1253] 1 Peter 1:4.

and was united with her in one Person and in one Hypostasy, His two Natures remaining "*unmixed and their Attributes unchangeable; and the Flesh was Deified, but it did not change its own Nature.*"[1254] Incomparably and to a greater degree the Deification of the Righteous, in which each one preserves his own personality, is clearly distinguished from the three Persons of the Holy Trinity because human nature is not in essence united to the Divine Nature. Human nature continues to remain human and within its own limits. However, by Grace and not by nature, it unites with the Divine Nature, participating in the Divine Life and Glory. The Word as the Infinite God "*alone has Immortality, dwelling in Unapproachable Light, Whom no man has seen or can see*"[1255] but the Deified nature of man is united with Him, thereby comprising His Divine and Mystic "*Body*" which is "*the fullness of Him Who fills all in all.*"[1256]

This union, in which the Divine and Infinite Nature of God the Word, although Hypostatically united with the human nature of the God-Man to which we are also united, remains unapproachable to us. We cannot be united in essence to it. This remains a "*Great Mystery.*"[1257] Nevertheless, our Union as members of the Church with Christ begins in this life, from the moment of our Baptism into Christ Consequently, it is perfected in that Blessed condition, becoming the Source of the new Holy and Divine Life that gives Life to the whole Body. The reason for the exaltation of the body into the "*Glory and Majesty*"[1258] of God is its Union and Communion with Christ, Who is "*the Peace of God, which surpasses all understanding*" and which " *will guard*" "*hearts and minds through Christ Jesus.*"[1259]

According to St John the Apostle, Evangelist and Theologian, "*it has not yet been revealed what we shall be, but we know that when He is revealed, we shall be like Him, for we shall see Him as He is.*"[1260] Furthermore, only by seeing Him as He is will create a great Joy, just as at the time of the Lord's Transfiguration when the two Prophets Moses and Elijah appeared before the Lord on Mount Tabor and St Peter said to our Lord Jesus: "*Lord, it is good for us to be here.*"[1261] The Vision of the Divine Glory makes all those who see participators, as St Paul taught us by saying that "*we all, with unveiled face, beholding as in a mirror the Glory of the Lord, are being transformed into the same image from glory to Glory, just as by the Spirit of the Lord,*"[1262] and the Lord said: " *the Righteous will shine forth as the sun in the Kingdom of their Father.*"[1263]

Our Lord and Saviour Jesus Christ, in His prayer addressed to His Father shortly before His Sufferings, asked Him "*that they all may be one, as Thou, Father, are in Me, and I in Thee; that they also may be one in*

[1254] St John of Damascus, *Catechesis,* III, 17, in Migne, *P.G.,* 94, 1069.

[1255] 1 Tim. 6:16.

[1256] Ephes. 1:23.

[1257] Ephes. 5:32.

[1258] Psalm 44(45):3.

[1259] Phil. 4:7.

[1260] 1 John 3:2.

[1261] Matth. 17:4.

[1262] 2 Corinth. 3:18.

[1263] Matth. 13:43. Zigabinos, *To Matthew,* in Migne, *P.G.,* 129, 416.

Us."[1264] He asked the Father to grant that all who belong to Him become "*one to another in the sameness of soul and the unity of the spirit, not disagreeing, but all having the same mind.*" As the Son "*is by nature and truly one with His Father*" likewise also we "*become the same generation to another through the intension having the unity of the Son to the Father.*" In the blessed condition all the righteous will be united in one and will copy the unity of the Holy Trinity, as far as possible to their human capability, "*for it is impossible to become equal to it*" and they shall live according to the blessed life of the Holy Trinity.

The falling asleep or passing away in the Lord is considered as the last Sacrament for the Orthodox Christians.

In man's last moments, he finds himself in a frightening condition where his soul is separated from his body. What follows is revealed to us by our Lord and Saviour Jesus Christ, the Son and Word of God the Father not only in the Parable of the Rich and Poor Lazarus, in many Biblical verses had taught us concerning the afterlife.

But, let us examine what that Parable teaches us.

The souls of each person found themselves in two different spiritual conditions:

1) Lazarus soul was received by the Angels of God and was in the bosom of Abraham, whereas,

2) The rich man's soul was in Hell, suffering tormentedly.

From the Parable, we learn that:

1) Man's soul, according to his life and works on earth, is received either by the good Angles, if he had done good, or by the Devils, if he has done evil and was heartless to those in need.

2) These two conditions are real and not imagined.

3) The suffering in Hell is unbearable and without any comfort or hope.

4) The resting of the just is indescribable beautiful and full of love and comfort.

5) None of those in both conditions can visit the others, for the gap is great between them.

6) In Hell there is no chance for repentance, for repentance is realized only as long as man is in this life. For, after death occurs, Judgement follows.

7) The petitions of those in Hell cannot be heard by God, no can their condition be changed into that of Paradise.

[1264] John 17:21.

8) The Rich man's request to Abraham to send Lazarus back in life was refused, for here on earth we have the Prophets and the Law (The Church and its Bishops and Priests), one must listen to them. For even if one is raised from the dead, those in sin will not believe ad will say that the resurrected was not really dead.

We must have in mind that after the soul's separation form its body, it passes through the *"customs"*. In other words, the evil Demons of the various passions will attempt to steal the soul from the good Angels' hands. If they find any rational reason of guilty conscience, then they will violently swatch the sinful and unrepentant soul.

Therefore, one must prepare himself for this terrifying day of departure. If we prepare ourselves to take a long trip for our vacation by issuing our passport, preparing our luggage, assuring that we have enough of currency; how much more we should prepare ourselves for the great departure into the afterlife?

Thus, we should be baptized in the Canonical Body of Christ, which is His Orthodox Church and not in any heretical groups.

Have regular Confession to our Priest in order to receive forgiveness of our sins.

To forgive those who have done evil against us, so we may be forgiven.

To love our neighbour as we love ourselves.

Receive regularly Holy Communion, for Christ assured us saying, that if we do not eat His Body and drink His Blood, we won't have eternal life.

To bless our Marriage within the Church and not by civil marriage or just living together.

To do good deeds throughout our life.

To avoid any sinful passions.

To live and manifest the Life of Christ through our own life.

By these and many more, we have our hope in the salvation which is offered by Christ to all those who believe in His Name.

BIBLIOGRAPHY

Achelis, *Die ältesten Quellen* = H. Achelis, *Die ältesten Quellen des oriental Kirchen rechts,* v. I, *Die Canones Hippoliti,* Λειψία, 1891.

Androutsos, *Dogmatique* = Χρήστου Ανδρούτσου, *Δογματική της Ορθοδόξου Ανατολικής Εκκλησίας,* εν Αθήναις, 1907. (in Greek).
(Chrestos Androutsos, *Dogmatique of the Orthodox Eastren Church,* Athens, 1907).

Androutsos, *Symbolique* = Χρήστου Ανδρούτσου, *Συμβολική εξ επόψεως Ορθοδόξου,* Έκδοσις Τρίτη, εν Θεσσαλονίκη, 1963. (in Greek).
(Chrestos Androutsos, *Symbolique from an Orthodox view,* 3rd Ed., Thessalonica, 1963).

Arseniev, *Mysticism* = Nicholas Arseniev, *Mysticism & the Eastern Church,* New York, 1979.

B = Βιβλιοθήκη Ελλήνων Πατέρων, έκδοσης Αποστολικής Διακονίας. (in Greek).
(Liberary of the Greek Fathers, ed. Apostoliki Diakonia).

Balanos, *Crisis* = Δ. Μπαλάνος, *Κρίσις της Δογματικής του Χρήστου Ανδρούτσου,* Ανάτυπον, Εν Ιεροσολύμοις, 1907. (in Greek).
(D. Balanos, *Crisis of the Dogmatique of Chrestos Androutsos,* Anatypon, In Jerusalem, 1907).

Bartmann, *Theologie Dogmatique* = Bartmann Bernard, *Precis de Theologie Dogmatique traduit par M. Gautier,* v. I and II, Mulhouse, 1951.

Bonnet, *Acta* = M. Bonnet, *Acta apostolorum apocrypha,* v. III, Leipzig, 1903.

Bryennios, *Paralipomena* = Ιωσήφ του Βρυεννίου, *Παραλειπόμενα,* τ. III, 2ᵃ εκδ., Θεσσαλονίκη, 1991. (in Greek).
(Bryennios, *Paralipomena* = Joseph Bryennios, *Paralipomena,* v. III, 2nd Ed., Thessalonica, 1991).

Damalas, *Catechesis* = Ν. Μ. Δαμαλά, *Ορθόδοξος Κατήχησις,* Αθήνησι, 1877. (in Greek).
(N. M. Damalas, *Orthodox Catechesis,* Athens, 1877).

Dositheus, *Confession* = Δοσιθέου, Πατριάρχου Ιεροσολύμων, *Ομολογία της Ορθοδόξου Πίστεως,* έκδοση Ρηγοπούλου, Θεσσαλονίκη, 1983. (in Greek).
(Dositheus, Patriarch of Jerusalem, *Confession of the Orthodox Fath,* ed. Regopoulos, Thessalonica, 1983).

Dyobouniotes, *The Sacraments* = Κ. Δυοβουνιώτου, *Τα μυστήρια της Ανατολικής Ορθοδόξου Εκκλησίας εξ επόψεως δογματικής*. (in Greek).
(K. Dyobouniotes, *The Sacraments of the Eastern Orthodox Church from dogmatic view*).

Dyobouniotes, *Dogmatique of Chr. Androutsos* = Κ. Δυοβουνιώτου, *Η Δογματική του Χ. Ανδρούτσου κρινομένη*. (in Greek).
(K. Dyobouniotes, *Criticism of the Dogmatique of Chr. Androutsos*).

Euchologion, ed. Salberos.

Evdokimov, *Orthodoxia* = Παύλου Ευδοκίμοοφ, *Η Ορθοδοξία*, Θεσσαλονίκη, 1972. (in Greek).
(Paul Endokimov, *Orthodoxia*, Thessalonica, 1972).

Evdokimov, *Icon* = Παύλου Ευδοκίμοοφ, *Η Τέχνη της Εικόνος. Θεολογία της Ωραιότητος*, Θεσσαλονίκη, 1980. (In Greek).
(Paul Endokimov, *The technic of the Icon. Theology of the Beauty*, Thessalonica, 1972).

Frangopoulos, *Christian Faith* = Αθανασίου Φραγκοπούλου, *Η Ορθόδοξος Χριστιανική Πίστις μας. (Τι Πιστεύομεν) – Λαϊκή Δογματική-*, 12η έκδ., Αθήνα, 1999. (in Greek).
(Athanasius Frangopoulos, Our *Christian Faith. (What we believe) – Public Dogmatique*, 12th ed., Athens, 1999).

Fuller, *The anointing* = F. W. Fuller, *The anointing of the Sick in Scripture and Tradition*, London, 1904.

Funk, *Didaskalia et Constitutions apostolorum*, ed. 27, v2.

Georgopoulos, *Anthology* = Δανιήλ Γεωργοπούλου, *Ανθολογία των Επτά Μυστηρίων*, Θεσσαλονίκη, 1996. (In Greek).
(Georgopoulos, *Anthology of the Seven Sacraments*, Thessalonica, 1996).

Hauler, *Didascaliae Apostolorum* = Ed Hauler, *Didascaliae Apostolorum fragmenta veronensia latina*.

Jugie, *Theologia*= M. Jugie, *Theologia Dogmatica Christianorum Orientalium*, v. I-V, Parisiis, 1926-1935.

Karabidopoulos, *Apocrypha* = Ιωάννης Καραβιδόπουλος, *Απόκρυφα Χριστιανικά Κείμενα Β΄ Απόκρυφες Πράξεις Επιστολές Αποκαλύψεις*, Θεσσαλονίκη, 2004. (in Greek).
(Ioannis Karabidopoulos, *Apocrypha Christian Texts B. Apocrypha Acts-Epistoles-Revelations*, Thessalonica, 2004).

Karmeris, *Synopsis* = I. Καρμίρη, *Σύνοψις της Δογματικής διδασκαλίας της Ορθοδόξου Καθολικής Εκκλησίας.* (in Greek).
(I. Karmeris, *Synopsis of the Dogmatique teaching of the Orthodox Catholic Church).*

Karmeris, *The dogmatics* = I. Καρμίρη, *Τα Δογματικά και Συμβολικά μνημεία της Ορθοδόξου Καθολικής Εκκλησίας,* τόμοι I & II, Αθήναις 1952, 1953. (in Greek).
(I. Karmeris, *The Dogmatic and Symbolic books of the Orthodox Catholic Church,* volumes I & II, Athens, 1952, 1953).

Kefalas, *Immortality* = Αγίου Νεκταρίου Κεφαλά, Μητροπολίτου Πενταπόλεως, *Περί Αθανασίας Ψυχής και Ιερών Μνημοσύνων,* Αθήναι. (In Greek).
(St Nektarios Kefalas, Metropolitan of Pentapolis, *The Immortality of the soul and Holy Commemorations,* Athens).

Kefalas, *Catechesis* = Αγίου Νεκταρίου Κεφαλά, Μητροπολίτου Πενταπόλεως, *Ορθόδοξος Ιερά Κατήχησις,* 4η έκδ., Θεσσαλονίκη, 2001. (In Greek).
(St Nektarios Kefalas, Metropolitan of Pentapolis, *Orthodox Holy Catechesis,* 4th Ed., Thessalonica, 2001).

Katsonis, *The canonical* = Ιερονύμου Κοτσώνη, *Η κανονική άποψις περί της επικοινωνίας μετά των ετεροδόξων.* (in Greek).
(Hieronymus Kotsonis, *The canonical view about the communication with the heterodox*).

Labadarios, *Explanation* = Panteleimon Labadarios, Archimandrite (today Archbishop of Pelusium), *The Explanation of the Holy Sacraments of Holy Baptism and Holy Chrismation according to the Eastern Orthodox Church,* Johannesburg, 1989.

Labadarios, *Marriage* = Panteleimon Labadarios, Archimandrite (today Archbishop of Pelusium), *The Explanation of the Holy Sacrament of Marriage,* Johannesburg, 1990.

Labadarios, *Sermons* = Panteleimon Labadarios, Archimandrite (today Archbishop of Pelusium), *Hellenic South African Orthodox Sunday Sermons,* v. 1, Johannesburg, 1989.

Labadarios, *Sermons* = Panteleimon Labadarios, Archimandrite (today Archbishop of Pelusium), *Hellenic South African Orthodox Sunday Sermons,* vs. 2-3, Johannesburg, 1992.

Leeming, *Principals* = Bernard Leeming, *Principals of Sacramental Theology,* London, 1955.

Lightfoot, *Apostolic Fathers* = J. B. Lightfoot and J. R. Harmer, *The Apostolic Fathers,* edited and revised by M. W. Holmes, 2nd Edition, U.S.A., 2000.

Lightfoot, *AF* = J. B. Lightfoot, *The Apostolic Fathers, Part I: S. Clemetn of Rome.* 2d. ed., 2 vols.; *Part II: S. Ignatius. S. Polycarp.* 2d ed., 3 vols., London: Macmillan, 1890, 1889; reprinted Grand Rapids: Baker, 1981.

Mansi = Mansi, Sacrorum Conciliorum nova et ampilissima Collection, vs. 1-53, Paris, 1901-1927.

Mesoloras, *Symbolique* = Ι. Ε. Μεσολοράς, *Συμβολική της Ορθοδόξου Καθολικής Εκκλησίας,* Αθήναι, 1911. (in Greek).
(I. E. Mesoloras, *Symbolique of the Orthodox Catholic Church,* Athens, 1911).

Meyendorff, *Theology* = John Meyendorff, *Byzantine Theology. Historical trends and doctrinal themes,* New York, 1987.

Miclosich, *Acta* = F. Miclosich and I. Müller, *Acta et diplomata Graeca Medii Aevi,* v. I.

Migne, *P.G.* = Accurante J.- P. Migne, *Patrologie Cursus Completus seu bibliotheca universalis, integra, uniformis, commoda, oeconomica, omnium SS. Patrum, Doctorum Scriptorumque Ecclesiasticorum, sive Latinorum, sive Graecorum, Patrologiae Graece,* Parisiis, 1857-1894.

Mitsopoulos, *Themata* = Νικολάου Μητσοπούλου, *Θέματα Ορθοδόξου Δογματικής Θεολογίας,* Αθήναι, 1983. (in Greek).
(Nicholaos Mitsopoulos, *Themata of Orthodox Dogmatique Theology,* Athens, 1983).

Ott, «Precis» = L. Ott, «Precis de Theologie Dogmatique», traduit par M. Grandclaudon, Paris, 1955.

Owen, *Theology* = Robert Owen, *Atreatise of Dogmatic Theology,* London, 2nd edition, 1887.

Papadopoulos, *History* = Χρυσοστόμου Παπαδοπούλου, Αρχιεπισκόπου Αθηνών, *Ιστορία της Εκκλησίας Αλεξανδρείας (60-1934),* Αλεξάνδρεια, 1935. (In Greek).
(Chrysostom Papadopoulos, Archbishop of Athens, *History of the Church of Alexandria (60-1934),* Alexandria, 1935).

Pedalion = The Rudder (Pedalion) of the Metaphorical ship of the one Holy Catholic and Apostolic Church of the Orthodox Christians or all the Sacred and Divine Canons of the Holy Councils, Ecumenical as well as Regional, and of individual Divine Fathers, as Embodied in the original Greek text, for the sake of authenticity, and explained in the vernacular by way of rendering them more intelligible to the less educated, By Agapius, a Hieromonach and Nicodemus, a Monk, Published by the Orthodox Christian Educational Society, Illinois, USA, 1957

Plato, *Orthodox Teaching* = Πλάτωνος, Μητροπολίτου Μόσχας, *Ορθόδοξος Διδασκαλία,* μετάφρασις υπό Αδαμαντίου Κοραή κατά την 4ην έκδοσιν του έτους 1851. Έκδοσις Βασ. Ρηγοπούλου, Θεσσαλονίκη, 1995. (In Greek).
(Plato, Metropolitan of Moscow, *Orthodox Teaching,* translated by Adamantios Koraes according to the 4th edition of the year 1851. Published by Bas. Regopoulos, Thessalonica, 1995).

Rauschen, *Fiorilegium* = G. Rauschen, *Fiorilegium Patristicum Fasc.,* VII editio altera Bonnae, 1914.

Scheeben, *Les Mystères* = Scheeben I. M., *Les Mystères du Christianisme,* translated by A Kerkvorde. J. Tixeront, *Histoire des Dogmes,* vol. I-III, Paris, 1924, 1928.

Schmemann, *Eucharist* = π. Α. Σμέμαν, *Ευχαριστία. Το Μυστήριο της Βασιλείας,* μετάφραση από τα Αγγλικά υπό Ιωσήφ Ροηλίδη, Αθήνα, 2000. (In Greek)
(Fr. A. Schmemann, *Eucharist The Mystery of the Kingdom,* translated by Joseph Roelides, Athens, 2000).

Schmemann, *The Church Praying* = π. Α. Σμέμαν, *Η Εκκλησία Προσευχομένη,* μετάφραση-επιμέλεια: Πρωτ. Δημ. Τζέρμπο, Β΄ έκδ., Αθήνα, 2003. (In Greek).
(Fr. A. Schmemann, *The Church Praying,* Translated by Protopresbyter Demetrios Tzermpos, 2nd Ed., Athens, 2003).

Sophrony, *His Life* = Archimandrite Sophrony, *His Life is Mine,* St Vladamir's Seminary Press, New York, 1977.

St. Irenaeus, *Heresies* = Αγίου Ειρηναίου Επισκόπου Λουγδούνου, *Έλεγχος και Ανατροπή της Ψευδονύμου Γνώσεως.* Εισαγωγή-Μετάφρασι-Σχόλια, υπό Ειρηναίου Χατζηεφραιμίδη, Δ.Θ., Αρχιμανδρίτου, Θεσσαλονίκη, 1991. (In Greek).
(St. Irenaeus Bishop of Lyon, *Heresies,* Translated by Irenaeus Hadjephraimides, Archimandrite, Introduction – Translation-Notes, Thessalonica, 1991).

St. John Chrysostom, *Priesthood* = Αγίου Ιωάννου Χρυσοστόμου, *Περί Ιερωσύνης Λόγοι. Εισαγωγή-Κείμενον-Μετάφρασις-Σχόλια,* υπό Παναγιώτου Χρήστου, Θεσσαλονίκη, 1960. (In Greek).
(St. John Chrysostom, *Homilies about Priesthood. Introduction-Text-Translation-Comments,* by Panagiotes Chrestou, Thessalonica, 1960).

St Symeon, *Euriskomena* = Του Οσίου και Θεοφόρου πατρός ημών Συμεών του Νέου Θεολόγου, *Τα Ευρισκόμενα,* Θεσσαλονίκη, 1997. (In Greek).

(St Symeon the New Theologian, *Euriskomena,* Thessalonica, 1977).

Trempelas, *Small Euchologion* = Παναγιώτου Ν. Τρεμπέλα, *Μικρόν Ευχολόγιον,* τόμοι Α' και Β', Αθήναι, 1998. (In Greek).
(Trempelas, *Small Euchologion,* vs. I and II, Athens, 1998).

INDEX

THE HOLY SACRAMENTS AS WAYS OF THE DIVINE GRACE, WHICH INCORPORATE US IN GOD'S KINGDOM

CHAPTER ONE
THE HOLY SACRAMENTS AS WAYS OF THE DIVINE GRACE

CHAPTER TWO
THE MEANING AND NATURE OF THE SACRAMENTS

CHAPTER THREE
THE PERFECTION OF THE HOLY SACRAMENTS

CHAPTER FOUR
THE NUMBER OF THE HOLY SACRAMENTS

CHAPTER FIVE
THE HOLY MYSTERY OF BAPTISM.

I. MEANING, NAME AND DIVINE ESTABLISHMENT

II. THE PERCEPTIBLE SIGNS OF BAPTISM.

III. THE SUPERNATURAL RESULTS OF BAPTISM AND ITS NECESSITY

IV. THE OFFICIATORS OF BAPTISM

CHAPTER SIX
THE MYSTERY OF HOLY CHRISMATION

I. DEFINITION, NAMES AND DIVINE INSTITUTION

II. EXTERNAL ASPECT, OFFICIATORS AND TIME OF RECEIVING THE HOLY CHRISMATION

III. THE RESULTS AND NECESSITY OF THE HOLY MYSTERY OF CHRISMATION

CHAPTER SEVEN
THE MYSTERY OF HOLY EUCHARIST

II. DEFINITION, IMPORTANCCE, PREFIGURES AND DIVINE ESTABLISHMENT

II. THE VISIBLE SIDE OF THE HOLY MYSTERY, TERMS OF ITS PERFECTION AND PARTICIPATION

III INVISIBLE SIDE OF THE DIVINE EUCHARIST

I. REAL PRESENCE OF CHRIST

IV. THE DIVINE EUCHARIST AS A SACRIFICE AND ITS FRUITS

CHAPTER EIGHT
THE HOLY MYSTERY OF REPENTANCE

I. DEFINITION, IMPORTANCE AND NAMES

II. THE DIVINE INSTITUTION OF THE HOLY MYSTERY & ITS POWER

III. COMPONENTS OF REPENTANCE

IV. THE ABSOLUTION AS AN ACT OF JUDGEMENT AND THE NATURE OF THE PENANCES

CHAPTER NINE
THE HOLY MYSTERY OF PRIESTHOOD

I. DEFINITION, NAMES, LEVELS AND DIVINE

INSTITUTION

II.OFFICIATORS, EXTERNAL AND INTERNAL ASPECTS OF THE HOLY MYSTERY